Garland Studies in Historical Demography

Stuart Bruchey

Allan Nevins Professor Emeritus
American Economic History
Columbia University

GENERAL EDITOR

A Garland Series

Old and Obsolete

Age Discrimination and the American Worker, 1860–1920

Judith C. Hushbeck

GARLAND PUBLISHING, INC.
New York   London
1989

Library of Congress Cataloging-in-Publication Data

Hushbeck, Judith C. (Judith Clare), 1944–
Old and obsolete : age discrimination and the american worker,
1860–1920 / Judith C. Hushbeck.
p. cm. — (Garland studies in historical demography)
Includes bibliographical references.
ISBN 0-8240-3399-X (alk. paper)
1. Age discrimination in employment—United States—History. 2. Age
and employment—United States—History.. 3. Aged—Employment—
United States—History.
I. Title. II. Series.
REF HD6280.H87 1989
331.3'.98—dc20   89-37796

Printed on acid-free, 250-year-life paper

Manufactured in the United States of America

TABLE OF CONTENTS

CHAPTER 1

INTRODUCTION

An aged man is but a paltry thing,
A tattered coat upon a stick, unless
Soul clap its hands and sing, and louder sing
For every tatter in its mortal dress.

William Butler Yeats,
"Sailing to Byzantium"

Old men are easily provoked, stingy and avaricious, sullen and quarrelsome, quick to talk, slow to hear, but not slow in wrath, praising former times, despising the moderns, censuring the present, commending the past.

- Pope Innocent III, cited by G.R. Coffman,
"Old Age from Horace to Chaucer,"
Speculum 9 (1934):249-77.

Economic discrimination against the old and the near-old in the United States has received considerable recent attention in the scholarly and policy-making communities. However, in contrast with issues of economic discrimination against other groups, age discrimination's history has been little documented. The economic history of blacks and women, in particular, as well as various ethnic groups at different times, has been explored far more thoroughly.

This is no doubt at least in part because these groups' unequal access to economic opportunity and advancement in the twentieth century is so demonstrably the result of a long tradition of quite explicit and powerful sanctions against their participation, on anything approaching an equal footing with white males, in economic, political, and social life. Research into discrimination against these other groups has long had an historical bent. The origins of economic discrimination against the aged are not as well understood.

The thesis explored here is that ageist attitudes permeate late twentieth century America in our tendency to categorize and hence value human beings according to their stage in the life cycle; and that these attitudes are a consequence of the particular manner in which industrial capitalism unfolded in this country. It will be argued that the ageist bias in American society can be traced to the revolution in the nation's industrial structure in the period between 1860 and 1920. It was within these years that the economy's occupational structure was transformed in ways that were to be particularly detrimental to older members of the working class.

In these decades, the U.S. moved decisively away from agriculture and toward industry as its engine of development, its entree into a position of world leadership, and its route toward rising real standards of living. This massive and rapid shift in the economy's under-lying base brought with it tremendous personal and social dislocations for many individuals and groups, but older workers were among those particularly affected by the system's emergence from petty capitalism into industrial capitalism.

The study focuses specifically on the declining labor force participation of white males who made up the great majority of the paid labor force between 1860 and 1920. The historical situation of older blacks is not included, and in only a few instances are older women mentioned. This inattention is not meant to suggest that blacks' and women's labor market status was unaffected by their growing older, but rather, their situations were atypical in the American economy of the time. In the period covered, blacks overwhelmingly remained tied to rural agriculture in the South, mostly as tenant farmers; and females were a very small proportion of the labor force, typically young and confined to a very narrow range of occupational choice. The focus here is on the "typical" or majority experience.

Until the second half of the nineteenth century, the American economy had been primarily agrarian, rural, and oriented toward the family to provide a social safety net for those who were unproductive for reasons of health or age. The old were a small minority of the population (less than three percent of Americans in midcentury) but they possessed great economic and political influence relative to their numbers. They dictated the behavior of members of the family unit by virtue of their years and experience, and through their dis-proportionate control of the assets most relevant to pre-industrial production: the land, and the knowledge, authority and wisdom to put it to best use.

Institutional barriers to the continued economic usefulness of older workers began to surface in the United States at the time of the Civil War, when the economy entered its industrial phase. The year 1860 has been chosen as a beginning point because the Civil War was so powerful an impetus to U.S. development, demanding a new scale of enterprise capable of quickly organizing and moving masses of people and supplies to where they were needed.

Once the war had ended, and construction of the transcontinental railroad and canal networks resumed, lessons learned during the conflict were refined and put to peacetime use. Wartime exigencies had amply demonstrated the value of an integrated, reliable, and rapid means of transporting people and commodities. Thus, after the war the railroads proved to be a highly significant force for integrating disparate regions into a national market and imposing fairly uniform characteristics on labor, capital, goods, and services. Market relationships became more extensive as the relevant marketplace in which various economic actors participated was expanded beyond the nearest town, village, or county.

With industrialization, both older and younger workers were displaced from their accustomed pursuits, but older people in particular discovered that the skills and attributes they had spent years accumulating were being devalued. They found their labor power becoming increasingly redundant in an economic system that was coming to be dominated by large-scale, bureaucratically-administered and hierarchically-structured manufacturing and commercial enterprises.

An important feature of the 1860-1920 period is that although this was the era of the growth of huge monopolies, the dominance of the "robber barons," and the beginnings of the assembly line, it was also an era of the most intense and cutthroat competition. Throughout this period, there is an apparent contradiction between the increasing degree

2

of monopoly power and wage-workers' consequent loss of autonomy in the performance of their work, on the one hand; and on the other, the intensification of competition between and among economic actors that compelled these actors to weed out the less fit, including the older players. The playing out of ineluctable economic forces greatly enriched a few, vastly improved the average American's standard of living, and yet diminished the status of the aged.

The closing year 1920 was chosen because by that time the employment difficulties of older Americans had begun to be widely perceived, if not yet adequately treated. The earliest state commissions on old age dependency and unemployment, as well as pensions, were established in the first two decades of the twentieth century; the first full-length monograph on the subject of old age dependency appeared in 1912; special bureaus to help age-handicapped workers were created during World War I; and the print media by 1920 were giving increased attention to the "old at 40" phenomenon. The 1920s, in fact, witnessed a worsening of the plight of older workers and the elderly, but the situation of older Americans in this decade has already been extensively covered, largely as background for analyses of the Social Security Act of 1935. In addition, by 1920 the bulk of the industrial and institutional transformations had already occurred which most profoundly affected Americans' working lives.

Overview of the Transformation

Several major institutional changes in the American economy between 1860 and 1920 had implications for the situation of older workers. The most important were:
- Agriculture and small, family-controlled firms (which were congenial to older people's continuing employment) were substantially replaced by manufacturing and finance as the source of economic growth.
- Regional economic relationships were supplemented and supplanted by a national economy made possible by westward migration and the establishment of transcontinental travel and communication.
- Urban centers grew to dominate towns and rural areas as the locus of employment, production, and accepted cultural norms, resulting in a corresponding weaken-ing of family ties and older people's parental authority.
- Wage work in the service of impersonal employers, increasingly in centralized facilities, became the norm, with a commensurate decline in opportunities for self-employment and productive autonomy.
- Very rapid technological advances rendered many skills obsolete, encouraged task specialization in production, and generated substantial increases in firm size to spread capital costs over a large volume of output.
- Growing macroeconomic instability accompanied increasing economic centralization and the homogenization of labor and product markets, and thus intensified workers' vulnerability to sporadic bouts of unemployment.

3

The appearance of new management techniques, designed to maximize the usefulness of costly and short-lived capital, led to deskilling[1] and to workers' loss of autonomy and individuality in the workplace.

Changing Industrial Structure and
the Redefinition of Work

All of these transformations encouraged and reinforced the economy's tendencies toward increasing concentration of production and capital in fewer hands. This concentration, it will be argued, had both a technological and an organizational or managerial imperative.

The nation's low population density, and hence its labor scarcity, from the beginning had generated interest in and growing reliance on the use of machines to do the needed work wherever possible. Although Great Britain and Europe continued to be the source of most scientific breakthroughs, Americans quickly became world leaders in putting new discoveries to practical use. Capital became a more substantial contributor to output, while its lifespan was dramatically shortened by the ongoing invention of bigger and better machines. Consequently, firms had to be of a certain minimum size to make profitable use of these technological marvels; for at the very least, capitalists had to recover the cost of their equipment before it became obsolete.

In contrast to Britain's earlier industrial revolution, which had given workers new implements and cheaper energy sources to perform essentially the same tasks they had been doing previously, innovations in the United States in the latter part of the nineteenth century engendered a revolution in the very nature of work itself. American industrialization, according to Robert Reich, required not only "large-scale systems of factories, specialized equipment, reliable sources of materials and channels of distribution," but also an altogether "new organization of work."[2]

To a considerable extent, the technological breakthroughs that came about in various efforts to conserve scarce and costly labor did indeed require a centralization of physical

---

1 "Deskilling" is used here in the sense popularized by the late Harry Braverman, in his Labor and Monopoly Capital: The Degradation of Work in the Twentieth Century (New York: Monthly Review Press, 1974). In Braverman's analysis, workers in the service of others, particularly in large, impersonal enterprises, were separated from their skills for reasons of both efficiency and control. Narrowing the skill content of jobs was more efficient because it reduced the number of decisions a worker might have to make as well as the amount of time spent moving between tasks or laying down a tool or implement to pick up another.

Deskilling was also important for purposes of employer or managerial control because it restricted the workers' knowledge of the production process, thus lessening their potential threat as competitors. It also reduced the costs of labor turnover when workers quit or were fired. These issues are more fully explored in Chapter 6.

2 Robert B. Reich, The Next American Frontier (New York: Time Books, 1983), p. 27.

capital, either because a unique power source such as water was necessary or because the machinery itself was of a scale that precluded its use in small independent shops. Yet much of the economic centralization that occurred between 1860 and 1920 had no direct technological imperative but was geared explicitly to gaining monopoly control of the nation's economic base. As the capitalist and managerial classes consolidated their control over physical assets and attained ever-greater market power, they increasingly sought to capture the sources of supply requisite to industrial enterprise.

They sought, in particular, increased control over workers, control that was grounded in the minute partitioning of production tasks well beyond the degree of specialization dictated by the state of technology. The labor scarcity that initally biased American techniques toward capital intensity was partly corrected by a policy of open immigration, which was primarily an undertaking of young and increasingly unskilled workers by the turn of the twentieth century. U.S. businesses could most readily make use of large numbers of culturally diverse workers by minimizing skill requirements and regularizing production processes in ways that de-emphasized the significance of what the individual worker could contribute. Even highly "skilled" work became ever more finely divided so that workers knew very little about the overall processes of which their work was a part.

Such changes in both the nature of jobs and the job environment were rapid and profound, and they caught many people in midlife and beyond with skills and trades that could no longer be counted upon for self-sufficiency or economic security. Whereas in the agrarian economy of the early nineteenth century, work life had been largely controlled by biological considerations, in the industrial economy of late century, labor force participation was coming to be determined institutionally and socially. As a group, workers' accommodation to industrialization was to accept a rising standard of living at the price of a loss of autonomy and security. The greatest losses in this tradeoff were to the older skilled workers who lost income and prestige as the economic value of their skills declined; while at the same time they found it difficult to obtain employment in impersonal corporate concerns geared to speed, drudgery, and a rapid wearing-out of labor.

A further important feature of American economic life relevant to an examination of the downward socioeconomic mobility of the elderly is less tangible than the events just described, but no less vital to the economic history of old age. This relates to the question of why the American economy, in contrast with other industrializing nations, developed market institutions of unprecedented size and power, yet failed to generate adequate countervailing social welfare mechanisms. The answer lies significantly in the nation's individualistic philosophy.

One of the consequences of the unique American experience was the generation and perpetuation of an ideology of individualism. The United States was peopled by risk-takers, individualists, mavericks, and no small number of misfits. It was a nation of leavers, people who chose to abandon all that was familiar to take their chances on the unknown. This uniquely American trait has dominated the national political and social value system. Enterprise, independence, competition, and self-reliance came to be stressed over community, sharing, cooperation, and mutual support.

When the nation's manpower scarcity was largely overcome owing to labor-saving technology and the supply of workers from abroad, older Americans became redundant as producers, yet there was no safety net to cushion their unemployment and dependency. The enormous power of the individualist philosophy--best reflected in the Social Darwinism of the late nineteenth century--prevented the establishment of a formal income support system until well into the twentieth century, long after less prosperous countries had addressed the problem of aged poverty. A nation of individualists saw only individual problems, not social or institutional ones, and tended to blame those in distress for their plight.

Furthermore, labor organization on a broad scale, which was late in developing in the United States, also reflected this individualistic attitude. American unions were trade- or industry-specific, largely uninterested in sociopolitical life beyond the resolution of bread-and-butter issues, and lacking any overarching sense of working class solidarity.

Finally, the historic mainstay for those in need, the family, was itself undergoing fundamental changes in the period under study, as sons chose different occupations from fathers and mobility separated the generations. When younger generations were able to free themselves from parental control, they often cut the ties of responsibility for looking after aging parents.

Ageism

Age discrimination in the U.S. has very different origins, and has followed a different path, than either racial or sex discrimination. Both blacks and women can trace their economic status to a prior condition of formal or de facto servitude; their historic economic function in capitalist societies has been to facilitate the participation of white males in the economic order. Older people's economic disenfranchisement, on the other hand, arose only with increases in impersonal market activity and the rate of change of technology. Prior to industrialization, their economic circumstances and social status had been relatively secure. As will be seen, there was apparently considerable tension between the old and the young in preindustrial America, but it was primarily because of the disproportionate control that older people maintained over economic resources and approved routes to upward mobility.

Thus, although negative conceptions about old age did not suddenly appear in the late nineteenth century, before that time such conceptions had little power to diminish older people's economic security, owing to their great influence and authority in economic, social and political life. They may have been resented for the privileges they monopolized, in much the same way that any dominant group or nation is the target of resentment from the less fortunate or less powerful. But discrimination against them was not an issue before the Civil War, if discrimination is defined as a widespread tendency to exclude some groups from labor force participation and its fruits, or from other meaningful social roles, based on external characteristics.

Economic discrimination against the elderly could not exist until their hold on valued resources had been loosened. Such control began to disappear as a consequence of American capitalism's evolution in a manner that made elders' unique skills, special know-how, and long experience irrelevant to emerging industrial conditions. But their lost edge did not merely place older people back on a more equal footing with the rest of the working population. Rather, under conditions of industrial capitalism, age became an impediment, and even a barrier, to employment.

6

The growth in size of corporations and the proliferation of rigid work rules to take the place of workers' discretion served as a wedge between employer and employee. So, too, did the separation of ownership from control within corporations. Increasingly, hired managers were responsible for staffing decisions made according to carefully-prescribed rules, among them age hiring limits. Tailoring jobs to individual abilities and circumstances, which had been possible when workers and employers labored side by side in a system of petty capitalism, was no longer practicable. Furthermore, as large enterprises sought ever greater precision in and control over the work process, the training of workers became an internal firm function and an item of cost subject to minimization.

Hence, those already at work were increasingly measured by rigid standards of output, with the pace of work determined by the faster--and generally younger--workers. Those applying for work were increasingly judged by superficial characteristics of race, ethnicity, and with growing frequency, age. Individual traits became less important as determinants of success.

For example, Germans were believed to be more hard-working than Poles, who were preferred to the Irish, and so forth. And younger applicants were automatically preferred over middle-aged and older applicants for the growing proportion of jobs in which the requisite skills could be quickly learned. The older person was more likely to want higher wages to support dependents, was thought to be more prone to sickness and accidents, was widely perceived as rigidly set in his ways and resistant to new methods, and at any rate constituted a less wise investment of a firm's training funds because of his shorter anticipated worklife expectancy.

The rapid pace of work in mechanized industry, frequently paired with the need for great stamina, created a strong bias toward hiring younger, healthier applicants from the widening pool of available labor. Massive immigration combined with labor deskilling to drive down the cost of labor in production and further encourage the substitution of unskilled and semi-skilled work for labor power requiring skills with a long gestation period. Older workers were physically disadvantaged by the new employment standards and were unable to compensate for it because theirs were the costly skills which technology was explicitly geared toward making unnecessary.

Why Study Yesterday's Problem?

A historical study of economic discrimination against the elderly is vital to an understanding of the ageist bias which continues to permeate American society generally, and labor markets in particular. The bias is itself fundamentally economic, as opposed to social or political, for the reason that ours is a uniquely instrumental, activist society. Americans are judged, and judge themselves, according to one predominant criterion: what they "do" in the world of remunerative employment. Those who "do" little or nothing--the underemployed, unemployed, part-time employed, retired, and so forth--are implicitly devalued and often suffer feelings of inadequacy, along with society's disesteem.

The Protestant work ethic is so much a core characteristic of American economic life, and is so closely linked with financial rewards and economic security, that we have perhaps lost sight of a time prior to the advent of rapid economic change when role-modeling and leadership by longevity gave meaning and value to the lives of older people.

7

Rapid economic change under conditions of free-market capitalism has resulted in the establishment of "roleless roles" for the elderly, who often are excluded from participating in a system that equates success with employment. They have been moved out of established, recognized, productive positions into roles that are generally poorly defined, marginal and without prestige.

Those historical studies focusing or touching on the problems of the elderly in the U.S. have been primarily idealist (that is, grounded in attitudinal changes irrespective of what was happening to the country's material/economic base)[3]; predominantly sociological (examining family/community structures and the sharing of amorphous group roles, without regard to how these roles affected and were affected by economic institutions); or essentially anthropological, concerned with contrasting individual/group security in advanced capitalist economies with the economics of primitive accumulation.[4]

In addition, there are many works in labor history that document losses for particular groups of individuals with advancing industrialism, especially losses from unemployment. These typically divide the participants in economic life into capitalist and worker classes, and among workers the focus is usually on groups categorized by industry, degree of unionization,

---

3 In particular, two wide-ranging histories of the aged as a distinct demographic group in the U.S. are David H. Fischer's Growing Old in America (New York: Oxford University Press, 1977); and W. Andrew Achenbaum's Old Age in the New Land: The American Experience Since 1790 (Baltimore: Johns Hopkins University Press, 1978). These are primarily histories of ideas, attitudes and intergenerational politics, and they shed considerable light on evolving views of the aged in America's past, but contemporaneous economic phenomena are not assigned a causal role.

4 See, for example, Ethel Shanas and Marvin B. Sussman, Family, Bureaucracy, and the Elderly (Durham, N.C.: Duke University Press, 1977); John C. McKinney and Frank T. DeVyver, eds., Aging and Social Policy (New York: Appleton-Century-Crofts, 1966); Donald O. Cowgill and Lowell D. Holmes, eds., Aging and Modernization (New York: Appleton-Century-Crofts, 1972); Zena Blau, Old Age in a Changing Society (New York: New Viewpoints, 1973); Barbara Anderson and Margaret Clark, Culture and Aging (Springfield, Ill.: Charles C. Thomas, 1967); Minna Field, The Aged, the Family, and the Community (New York: Columbia University Press, 1972); Tamara K. Hareven, Family and Population in the Nineteenth Century (Princeton, N.J.: Princeton University Press, 1978); Clark Tibbits, ed., Handbook of Social Gerontology (Chicago: University of Chicago Press, 1960); Ernest W. Burgess, Aging in Western Societies (Chicago: University of Chicago Press, 1960); Irving Rosow, Social Integration of the Aged (New York: The Free Press, 1967); Robert H. Binstock and Ethel Shanas, eds., Handbook of Aging and the Social Sciences (New York: Van Nostrand Reinhold, 1977); Milton Barron, The Aging American: An Introduction to Social Gerontology and Geriatrics (New York: Thomas Y. Crowell Co., 1962); James D. Manney, Jr., Aging in American Society. An Examination of Concepts and Issues (Ann Arbor: University of Michigan, 1975); Jon Hendricks and C. Davis Hendricks, Aging in Mass Society (Cambridge, Mass.: Winthrop Publishing, 1977); Beth B. Hess, ed., Growing Old in America (New Brunswick, N.J.: Transactions Press, 1976).

race, sex, region or ethnicity; age is, if anything, of only secondary importance.[5] Still other studies have emphasized the changing nature of work, and the importance in people's lives of the dynamics of control over the production process as capitalism matured.[6]

The American history of aging has thus received less scrutiny from economists than it has from sociologists, anthropologists, historians and psychologists.[7] Yet all the social

5 Among such histories or historical works are Elizabeth F. Baker, Displacement of Men by Machines: Effects of Technological Change in Commercial Printing (New York: Columbia University Press, 1933); George L. Bolen, Getting a Living: The Problem of Wealth and Poverty--Of Profits, Wages and Trade Unionism (New York: Macmillan, 1903); Elizabeth B. Butler, Women and the Trades: Pittsburgh, 1907-1908 (New York: Russell Sage Foundation, 1911); William L. Chenery, Industry and Human Welfare (New York: Macmillan, 1922); John R. Commons, David L. Saposs, Helen L. Sumner, E.B. Mittelman, H.E. Hoagland, John B. Andrews, and Selig Perlman, History of Labor in the United States, 1896-1932, 4 vols. (New York: Macmillan, 1935); John R. Commons, Race and Immigrants in America (New York: Macmillan, 1907); John R. Commons, Trade Unionism and Labor Problems (New York: Ginn and Co, 1905); Edward T. Devine, Misery and Its Causes (New York: Macmillan, 1909); Paul Douglas and Aaron Director, The Problem of Unemployment (New York: Macmillan, 1931); Charlotte Erickson, American Industry and the European Immigrant, 1860-1880 (Cambridge: Harvard University Press, 1957); Henry George, The Condition of Labor (New York: United States Book Co., 1891); Robert F. Hoxie, Scientific Management and Labor (New York: D. Appleton and Co., 1915); John Mitchell, The Wage Earner and His Problems (Washington, D.C.: P.S. Ridsdale, 1913); Robert Ozanne, A Century of Labor-Management Relations at McCormick and International Harvester (Madison: University of Wisconsin Press, 1967); Irwin Yellowitz, Industrialization and the American Labor Movement, 1850-1900 (Port Washington, N.Y.: Kennikat Press, 1976); Irwin Yellowitz, The Position of the Worker in American Society, 1865-1896 (Englewood Cliffs, N.J.: Prentice-Hall, 1969).

6 See, in particular, Richard C. Edwards, Contested Terrain: The Transformation of the Workplace in the Twentieth Century (New York: Basic Books, 1979); Harry Braverman, Labor and Monopoly Capital: The Degradation of Work in the Twentieth Century (New York: Monthly Review Press, 1974); Stephen A. Marglin, "What Do Bosses Do? The Origins and Functions of Hierarchy in Capitalist Production," Review of Radical Political Economics 6, 2 (Summer 1974), pp. 60-112; Katherine Stone, "The Origins of Job Structures in the Steel Industry," Review of Radical Political Economics 6, 2 (Summer 1974), pp. 113-73; Daniel Nelson, Managers and Workers: Origins of the New Factory System in the United States, 1880-1920 (Madison: University of Wisconsin Press, 1975); David Gordon, Richard Edwards, and Michael Reich, Segmented Work, Divided Workers (Cambridge: Cambridge University Press, 1982).

7 For general reference works on the economics of aging in the twentieth century, see Michael J. Brennan, Philip Taft, and Mark P. Schupak, The Economics of Age (New York: W.W. Norton and Co., 1967); James H. Schulz, The Economics of Aging, 4th ed. (Dover,

sciences have tended to focus more upon symptoms than upon the roots of changes in the elderly's situation, and in particular the focus has been demographic.[8] This may have been mainly for pragmatic reasons. Social gerontology developed after World War II and had its greatest growth in the 1950s, when in the U.S. and other developed countries there began to be practical concerns with the rapid growth in the numbers of the elderly, and the problems associated with an increase in the proportion of nonproductive and dependent persons in the population.

In essence, the view has been that the elderly are of economic and social concern now, where they were not in the past, because falling birth rates and increasing longevity have combined vastly to swell their numbers. The institutionalization of retirement as a distinct period in the life cycle has itself been a consequence of economic development, and has reinforced a practical interest in the economics of old age. Both declining fertility and longer life-spans are by-products of economic development, and it is thus not very surprising that only somewhat recently has attention been paid to the implications of growing numbers of the elderly in the population.

What is surprising is that latter-day studies have stopped short of examining the origins of the demographic and hence economic problem in the early industrial era.[9] No

---

Mass.: Auburn House Publishing Company, 1988); John J. Corson and John W. McConnell, Economic Needs of Older People (New York: Twentieth Century Fund, 1956); Juanita M. Kreps, ed., Employment, Income, and Retirement Problems of the Aged (Durham, N.C.: Duke University Press, 1963).

8 See, for example, Juanita M. Kreps et al., Economics of a Stationary Population: Implications for Older Americans (Washington, D.C.: Government Printing Office, 1977); Henry D. Sheldon, The Older Population of the United States (New York: John Wiley and Sons, Inc., 1958); Neal E. Cutler and R.A. Harootyan, "Demography of the Aged," in Aging: Scientific Perspectives and Social Issues, ed. by Diana S. Woodruff and James E. Birren (New York: Van Nostrand Reinhold, 1975); Paul Paillat, "Bureaucratization of Old Age: Determinants of the Process, Possible Safeguards, and Reorientation," in Family, Bureaucracy, and the Elderly, ed. by Ethel Shanas and Marvin B. Sussman (Durham, N.C.: Duke University Press, 1977), pp. 60-74; Steve L. Barsby and Dennis R. Cox, Interstate Migration of the Elderly: An Economic Analysis (Lexington, Mass.: Heath/ Lexington Books, 1975); Shmuel N. Eisenstadt, From Generation to Generation: Age Groups and Social Structure (Glencoe, Ill.: The Free Press, 1956); George E. Rejda and Richard J. Shepler, "The Impact of Zero Population Growth on the OASDHI Program," The Journal of Risk and Insurance 40 (September 1973):313-25; Ralph Thomlinson, Population Dynamics (New York: Random House, 1965); E.A. Wrigley, Population and History (New York: McGraw-Hill Book Co., 1969); David Hobman, ed., The Social Challenge of Aging (New York: St. Martin's Press, 1978).

9 It should be pointed out that there has been considerable research into the family and social relationships of the elderly. Such relationships were in many ways inextricably bound up with people's lrelationship to the productive process prior to and during the early stages

study in economics has taken as its focus the analysis of the roots of age discrimination in employment, or the elderly's rate of technological unemployment under conditions of industrialization and increasing economic concentration. Even economic analysis that takes a historical perspective on distributional phenomena has largely ignored the old, whereas considerable attention has been paid to the history of the labor force participation rates of blacks, females and regional/ethnic minorities.

Several reasons might account for this lack of an historical perspective on economic discrimination against older Americans. In the first place, awareness of ageism has been primarily a post-World War II phenomenon which even today is confined to a rather small sub-specialty of social science inquiry. Indeed, the term "ageism" has entered the language only rather recently.[10] Ageism has a considerably broader meaning than purely economic discrimination on the basis of chronological age, although such discrimination constitutes perhaps its most damaging manifestation. Ageism also has reference to the cultural stereotyping of older people, and to the dread of aging and the aversion to the old which this dread generates. In other words, ageism is reflected both in oppressive behaviors toward the elderly, as well as in oppressive attitudes toward age.

Second, labor force discrimination on the basis of age is not the sort of discrimination people are usually aware of until they or those close to them actually experience it. At that point, it is likely to lead to feelings of inadequacy and shame, and to withdrawal.[11] It is commonly experienced by the individual, and even frequently seen by others, as a problem of personal failure, and not as a problem endemic to our particular socioeconomic institutions and cultural value system. Awareness of discrimination against older workers is increasing as a natural accompaniment of population aging, yet it remains a relatively unexplored area of economic inquiry.

Third, there is a very real dearth of the hard data which can rigorously support the origins of discrimination against the elderly in the United States. Until within the last half-century, data collection relating to employment and income issues was primitive and inexact. The profoundly individualistic ethos which had motivated settlement, the fervor for independence which prompted the American Revolution, the opportunities for individual betterment which the country's natural resource endowment made possible--all these factors doubtless underlay a reluctance to place great importance on what were probably temporary vicissitudes.

---

of industrialization. Thus, studies of the impact of urbanization, industrialization, and so forth on the nuclear family are indirectly "about" the economic history of aging.

10 Robert H. Butler, first director of the National Institute on Aging of the National Institutes of Health, is credited with coining the word in the 1960s. See his Why Survive? Being Old in America (New York: Harper and Row, 1975), p. 11.

11 Who has not experienced the letdown of realizing, upon leaving a job, that they will be and quite readily can be replaced, that they are not indispensable? For older Americans, this is more than the realization of a moment, it is rather a stage of life in an action-oriented society.

Also important from the standpoint of the economic fortunes of the nation's elderly, until the past two decades they have not had well-organized and politically effective associations to raise people's consciousness and promote needed change. The influence of the "gray lobby" has helped to make information about the economics of age much more readily available and utilized than previously.

Lastly (and somewhat parenthetically), the elderly may lack appeal as a subject of scholarly examination because a progress-oriented culture such as ours has preferred to look forward rather than backward. We have historically devoted our collective attention to issues bearing on the prospects for the nation's young and those in their most productive years. As an example of how this has manifested itself, one might cite the slowness of the medical and allied professions in developing specialties in gerontology and in the diseases and disabilities of later life.[12]

All such manifestations of prejudice enrich the focus of this work--the world of work, where, it is argued, older Americans first began to experience significant isolation from mainstream culture and popular norms. Late in the twentieth century, it is again in the domain of work where this process is being reversed, for two fundamental reasons. First, the United States is facing waning international competitiveness and pronounced shifts in industrial structure, arising from technological change, capital mobility, and fiscal imbalance. At the same time, while older Americans constitute the fastest growing popu- lation group, the dwindling supply of youthful employees is beginning to cause employers to reassess their negative view of older workers. It appears that, at least for a time, Americans of middle age and beyond who wish to work will have greater control over this decision than at any time for the past century or more. In this context, an understanding of the economic history of old age can help us to clarify our policy options both now and for the future.

---

12 Such relative inattention to the physical and emotional problems of older people is only now disappearing as the sheer numbers of this group put pressures upon the health care and social welfare systems. (But simultaneously and somewhat ironically, huge federal budget deficits are rendering the elderly's most important targeted programs, Social Security and Medicare, tools of partisan politics subject to ideological swings. Older Americans are thus getting more of the public's attention, but much of it is negative.) Innumerable other examples of an anti-age bias might be drawn from our literature and popular culture, in which old people are depicted as cute and conniving, or mindless and bathetic. Popular culture of course tends to treat all age groups unrealistically, but there exist few older role models, realistic or not, in novels, films and television fare.

CHAPTER 2

THE STATUS OF THE ELDERLY IN THE ECONOMIC CLIMATE OF ANTEBELLUM AMERICA

Introduction

The relative status of any population group is fundamentally affected by society's value system, which in the U.S. today is in one major respect little changed from a century or more ago. The dominant values in American society have always related to how people get their livelihood--to their ability to occupy and maintain an essential economic role. Historically, the economic security of the elderly was guaranteed to the extent that they were able to own property and exercise control over the opportunities of younger generations. Such status rested on the ownership of productive resources and implied a command of strategic knowledge and possession of vital skills. Such command over human capital assets by the aged required, first, a relatively static, low-productivity economy characterized by a high degree of mutual dependence; and second, a system of production based upon skills that were developed over many years of worklife experience.[1]

These conditions prevailed in the economic climate of the United States until the middle of the nineteenth century, when an industrial revolution brought tremendous social and personal dislocations that entailed distinct losses and gains for various groups in the population. By far the greatest impact of the adverse effects of industrialization (and its concomitant, urbanization), was on the elderly. The greatest blow dealt them was the loss of their economic independence.

To be sure, this loss was experienced by all who found themselves permanently located in the wage-earning classes. People as workers were demoted in status from employers (or potential, prospective employers) to lifetime employees, and their workplace became the factory or the office instead of the home or its adjoining shop. The relative size of the group which had independent businesses, professions, trades, and land ownership diminished; as the number grew who were employed by industrial, commercial, and governmental organizations where individual discretion over location and hours of work was sharply limited.

A striking consequence of the decline in self-employment was that wage workers began to lose their jobs as they grew older; they were forced to "retire" during economic downturns or at the behest of an employer, rather than of their free will.[2] Even where workers organized in trade unions to protect their interests as wage workers, increasingly they found they had to trade employment rights for pension rights or other welfare plans

---

1 Irving Rosow, Social Integration of the Aged (New York: The Free Press, 1967).

2 The concept of retirement as we understand it today was practically unknown a century ago; people "retired" at various stages of life for study, contemplation, rest. They did not retire permanently until physically ill or disabled.

provided by employers (if any), so that only modest economic security was gained for the loss of an active economic role.[3]

An associated role loss for older persons was their former favored position in the extended family. A fragmented, urban way of life developed, bringing with it greater economic and social differentiation and population mobility of all sorts. Among these were: distinctions along residential lines, as population density increased rapidly; occupational differences arising from the division of labor and technological change; and cultural cleavages accompanying the new commercial values that competed with traditional mores and folkways.

The older concept of mobility was disappearing with the onslaught of large-scale production and concentrated wealth and power. This concept held that any skilled worker, with meager capital and sufficient ambition, could move into self-employment or the employing classes. The "new mobility" placed the aging worker in jeopardy not only through the dilution of authority within the family, but in diminished opportunities for making a living even as an employee.

Thus, waning physical powers combined with a short employment horizon and a strong attachment to "the old way of doing things" to render the older individual a marginal participant in the market for employment. While simultaneously, in the home (to a lesser extent in rural areas):

> No longer were the grandfather and the grandmother [who might be in their early forties or younger] the center of the absorbing social life of their descendants but often became unwanted hangers-on, taking part by sufferance in the activities of their children and grandchildren...deprived of the society of their family and having lost associates on the job and other friends by death or departure to other communities, they found themselves cursed instead of blessed by leisure time in abundance and little or nothing to do with it.[4]

Family Life and Work Life of Older People
Before the Civil War

The dominant structure of production in the U.S. economy remained virtually unchanged throughout the nation's colonial period and for 70-odd years after independence. The older generation had control of the land, which was the vital determinant of economic well-being when roughly 90 percent of the population lived on farms and earned their livelihoods primarily from the soil.

The typical enterprise, whether a farm or a firm, was small enough to be operated by the owner with the help of family members and perhaps a few hired hands. The capital requirements of such enterprises were not large, and production was almost exclusively for local markets. Although the hours of work were typically long, even grueling, such "self-exploitation" was dictated by the internal imperatives of the family enterprise's survival and

---

3 Robert J. Havighurst, "Life Beyond Family and Work," in Aging in Western Societies, ed. by Ernest W. Burgess (Chicago: University of Chicago Press, 1960), p. 303.

4 Ernest W. Burgess, "Aging in Western Culture," in ibid., p. 20.

hopes for success, and hence was a direct expression of the pursuit of self interest and upward mobility shared by all Americans.[5]

For the older family member who might be in failing health or not up-to-date on the newest ways of doing business, there was the opportunity gradually to reduce the hours of work in accordance with individual circumstances, progressively allowing younger members to assume control under personal supervision. Such relative autonomy enabled gradual retirement from the world of work, which was in any event not a distinct sphere readily separable from family life. This was true even for older workers as employees, who were often treated as members of the family and could continue to work at tasks commensurate with their energies.

Indeed, powerful economic forces bound families together in ways that, if they discriminated at all, did so against younger generations. Landed wealth was the basis for power, and as Fischer points out, aging parents maintained control over land and other possessions "nearly to the end of their lives. Children tended to remain economic dependents long after they had reached physical maturity."[6] Thus, the conventional view that earlier Americans lived predominantly in extended families--with adult children providing financial support to their aged parents--is not accurate, on two counts.

First, the nuclear family type has always been the norm in the United States, as it has in Anglo-Saxon culture generally; three-generation family units have been correspondingly rare.[7] Second, when three generations did live together it was more typically the aged parents who were depended upon by the young who had not yet left home, or by middle-aged offspring who had suffered financial reverses. In fact, as Fischer notes,

> Even wealthy fathers who could easily have provided for themselves and their children at the same time were slow to set those children free....land was an instrument of generational politics--a way of preserving both the power and the authority of the elderly. Sons were bound to their fathers by ties of economic dependency; youth was the hostage of age.[8]

But in the not-uncommon case of the impoverished elderly living alone, prior to the modern era older Americans could typically count on proximity to kin; and while nearness to relations was no guarantee of economic support or security, it served to enhance older people's ability to continue to make a contribution for as long as possible.

The relationship of the older individual to his/her community in primitive societies

---

5 The example today is the Asian extended family, whose members run convenience stores and ethnic restaurants for long hours at no pay, under working conditions that would violate statutes and standards of decency for "regular" employees.

6 Fischer, Growing Old, p. 52.

7 James H. Schulz, The Economics of Aging (Belmont, Cal.: Wadsworth Publishing Company, 1976), p. 81; Fischer, Growing Old, pp. 23, 146-47.

8 Fischer, Growing Old, p. 52.

provides a fascinating comparison to the situation facing nineteenth-century older Americans. In much earlier times the welfare of the aged was directly <u>determined by</u> as well as <u>a determinant of</u> how well the community fared. The elderly were valued, along with everyone else, according to the balance between what they put into the system and what they took out of it. When in primitive economies the balance shifted, and an elderly member's contribution was outweighed by what he or she consumed of the group's resources, elderly dependency threatened the group and expulsion, abandonment, and neglect were common.[9]

Such a harsh calculus was necessitated by primitive groups' slim margin of survival. Although we can conjecture that comparatively few individuals in primitive societies survived to anything approaching modern notions of "old age," those who did so appear to have constituted a significant problem, as suggested by the disproportionate attention paid to them in folklore and myth.[10] Primitive societies varied widely in the ways they handled the dilemma posed by their decrepit elderly, but their customs almost always included great respect for the healthy old. One of the leading authorities on the family life of old people in primitive societies, Leo Simmons, noted that "the most striking fact about respect for old age is its widespread occurrence. Some degree of prestige for the aged seems to have been practically universal."[11]

A major distinction between preliterate, preindustrial economic systems and those closer in time to our own rests on the slippery notion of individualism. The ancient village community was a network of people bound together by exceptionally close ties of kinship in a communal or <u>Gemeinschaft</u> type of social organization. In such a society competition was greatly restrained, and in fact in the modern sense did not exist. Prices were strictly regulated by custom, and Ely notes that "sharp practice and hard bargaining were viewed with disapprobation and often severely punished."[12]

---

9 There have been rare instances of such practices even in the late twentieth century. For example, the Masai of Africa have been known to "unceremoniously throw the old dependent outside the village <u>bwoma</u> and forget about him, while the Polar Eskimos rather sorrowfully put him out on the ice--in both cases to die." Irving Rosow, "And Then We Were Old," in <u>Growing Old in America,</u> ed. by Beth B. Hess (New Brunswick, N.J.: Transactions Press, 1976), p. 44. Other primitive civilizations have killed their old outright, or even eaten them, as their way of dealing with the old-age problem. More respectful were the ancient Issedones who gilded the heads of their elderly and offered sacrifices to them; at the other extreme, the Bactrians fed their old folk to wild dogs, while the Sardinians threw their elders from high cliffs and laughed as they landed on the rocks below. Fischer, <u>Growing Old,</u> p. 6.

10 Isaac M. Rubinow, <u>The Quest for Security</u> (New York: Henry Holt and Company, 1934), p. 219.

11 Leo Simmons, <u>The Role of the Aged in Primitive Society</u> (New Haven: Yale University Press, 1945), p. 79.

12 Richard T. Ely, <u>Evolution of Industrial Society</u> (New York: The Macmillan Company, 1903), p. 427.

Ethical obligations extended to all life relationships within the community, but once outside, in neutral territory abutting three or four other such villages, moral law was supplanted by very different customs and usages--those of the marketplace. Within the community the individual was submerged within the group which in turn provided security for weaker or dependent members. Where people did not strive for individual distinction, self-sufficiency was a group project and the threat of individual failure or insecurity was minimized.[13]

With the development of systematic agriculture there arose a radically different attitude toward the elderly, and it is this "agricultural attitude" to old age that has characterized most of Western pre-industrial civilization. In farming, experience and judgment play the most important roles and thus the carriers of these qualities command respect. Mental attributes, in addition to purely physical ones, become a crucial determinant of economic security. In addition, in agricultural endeavors physical effort is less strenuous, the hazards less pronounced, speed and agility less of a consideration than in primitive hunting-and-gathering societies.

Thus, to the extent that industrial development began to take place during the Middle Ages, it did little to alter the dominance of agricultural values. Much as the old man in the agricultural group remained in command of resources and the group's behavior to the end of his days, the aging town or village worker, too, was frequently a skilled independent artisan who owned his own tools and could compensate for reduced muscle, agility, and speed through accumulated skills and expertise that were needed by others. Even under feudalism there existed an implicit labor contract which, in Rubinow's words, "usually extended over the lifetime and included the family as a unit."[14]

The Structure of Production in the Antebellum Period

The dominant form of productive organization in the U.S. prior to the nineteenth century closely mirrored the model sketched by Adam Smith. Enterprises were run by owner-managers and their families, the owner typically working alongside any hired help. The latter were frequently temporary apprentices, who could reasonably expect to become petty capitalists themselves upon accumulating modest savings and business experience.

For the owner of even a marginal enterprise, such an arrangement afforded a maximum of economic security. Getting through bad times might require increased "self-exploitation" and longer hours by unpaid family labor, but barring catastrophes an independent means of making a living was, if not assured, at least likely. Of course, there existed a large number of exceptions to this scenario, notably slaves, Native Americans and those committed to periods of indentured servitude. But such family firm/farm establishments were ubiquitous; in the early nineteenth century some 80 percent of all white Americans were self-employed. Thus this situation may be seen as typical in this period.

---

13 Donald O. Cowgill, "A Theory of Aging in Cross-Cultural Perspective," in Aging and Modernization, ed. by Donald O. Cowgill and Lowell D. Holmes (New York: Appleton-Century-Crofts, 1972), p. 12.

14 Rubinow, Quest for Security, p. 222.

The economy in this period, up until the mid-nineteenth century, remained over-whelmingly agricultural, undercapitalized, and oriented toward local markets. Low popu-lation densities and the existence of only the most rudimentary modes of land transportation made for a stable and fairly static economic environment. This "stability" was enforced by historically unique geographical/demographic circumstances. Never before had such an immense land mass been inhabited by a people possessing so strong a future orientation and such a clear will to progress.

By the start of the nineteenth century, annual improvements in output and living standards were only just beginning to become possible and desired on a wide scale, yet the very settling of the colonies had been premised on such abstract notions as freedom, indivi-dual dignity, responsibility, and self-determination. Indeed, a thinly-veiled anarchy seems to have reigned in most early settlements, but the veil--Protestantism--was a powerful mediator of relationships. What kept the intensity of economic competition at such a relatively low level until the 1800s were the twin phen- omena of a huge land/labor ratio and the lack of any rapid, reliable mode of trans- portation. Until the canal and railway systems were substantially in place, the relevant economy from the viewpoint of most Americans was the nearest village, community, or town.

By about the 1840s, when the country entered its initial period of rapid economic growth, a somewhat modified form of economic organization had begun to be apparent in the nation's economy, the stage of capitalist development anatomized by Marx. The owner-entrepreneur began to devote more and more time to managerial and financial duties, thus separating himself from the workers. A capitalist class began to emerge, a class quite distinct in function from the working class.[15]

Initially, the working lives of older people showed little outward sign of change. Indeed, older individuals, primarily shopkeeper-merchants and craftsmen who might also be part-year farmers, were likely to be among the vanguard of those entering the new ranks. With financial requirements still quite modest, optimum scale of production still relatively small, and production methods not yet significantly altered by the machine revolution to come, the implications of this transition for most older people were benign. If anything, they stood to benefit from the new order to a far greater degree than younger persons lacking sufficient financial assets and expertise to take advantage of the new opportunities. The entrepreneur could still ply his trade while giving advice and guidance to those working for him. And these employees could continue to view their jobs not just as a way to make a living, but as preparation for one day having shops of their own. Thus were the basic handicraft skills acquired and dispersed, without being significantly transformed by tech-nological changes either within the craft or in the broader economy.

By the early 1900s, the U.S. economy was rich and growing rapidly by historical standards, yet most of its wealth was still potential, latent in its enormous resource base and its highly skilled, energetic labor force. Abundant lands still remained to be settled by those possessed of minimal capital and an adventurous and entrepreneurial spirit. For the less physically daring, urban centers along the Atlantic coast offered abundant opportunities for setting up shop and going into business for oneself or in partnership with others.

---

15 See Robert T. Averitt, The Dual Economy: The Dynamics of American Industry Structure (New York: W.W. Norton, 1968), p. 4.

Given this economic climate, there was a basis for an age-graded hierarchy that favored those of more advanced years, at least as long as they remained healthy; and so long as most Americans resided in and near far-flung towns and villages, and the means of production remained fairly static and widely diffused among the population. This is not to suggest that there were not constant refinements in production techniques and farming methods. Given the nation's vast resources, there developed in American workers a proclivity for "tinkering" to optimize and conserve scarce labor.[16]

The elderly along with all others were expected to remain economically and socially useful as long as they were physically able to do so. In fact, a popular and quintessentially Protestant prescription against deterioration in later life was more work, not a retreat from it in retirement.[17] The fact that the elderly offered a reservoir of knowledge and experience conferred upon them unique economic value as "living encyclopedias." This was especially true in agriculture, which prior to the Civil War accounted for approximately 60 percent of all paid labor and a vast majority of all workers over the age of 60. [18]

---

16 This was a feature of American life much commented upon and admired by de Tocqueville, who also noted Americans' disdain for basic science and their almost exclusive attention to science's purely practical applications:

"... hardly any one in the United States devotes himself to the essentially theoretical and abstract portions of human knowledge ... every new method which leads by a shorter road to wealth, every machine which spares labor, every instrument which diminishes the cost of production, every discovery which facilitates pleasures or augments them, seems [to the Americans] to be the grandest effort of the human intellect." (Alexis de Tocqueville, Democracy in America, vol. 2 [New York: The Century Co., 1898], pp. 40, 48, 52-53).

An American contemporary noted:

"The genius of this new country is necessarily mechanical. Our greatest thinkers are not in the library, nor the capitol, but in the machine shop. The American people is intent on studying, not the beautiful records of a past civilization, not the hiero-glyphic momuments of ancient genius, but how best to subdue and till the soil of its boundless territories; how to build roads and ships; how to apply the powers of nature to the work of manufacturing its rich materials into forms of utility and enjoy-ment. The youth of this country are learning the sciences, not as theories, but with reference to their application to the arts. Our education is no genial culture of letters, but simply learning the use of tools." (J. Milton Mackie, From Cape Cod to Dixie and the Tropics [New York, 1864], pp. 200- 201, cited by Nathan Rosenberg, Technology and American Economic Growth [New York: Harper and Row, 1972], p. 33.)

17 Charles Caldwell, Thoughts on the Effects of Age on the Human Constitution (Louisville: John C. Noble, 1846), pp. 6, 14-18, cited by Achenbaum, Old Age, p. 19.

18 Achenbaum, Old Age, p. 19.

As noted earlier, the idea of retirement as we think of it today was unknown prior to the Civil War. Although the increasing frailties and debilities of age often prevented people from continuing in their jobs, there was no definition of retirement that applied uniquely to older people. Individuals of all ages retired in different situations (for example, almanacs of the period make reference to farmers who "annually 'retired' from winter's storms to their family circles.")[19] Certainly mandatory or induced retirement because of age was unheard of in antebellum America, because the notion was not yet widespread that an aging worker was an obsolescent one.

The Aged as a Vital Economic Link

Prior to the advent of modern sanitation systems and standards of personal hygiene, all age groups were plagued by illness, injury, and untimely death. A precarious existence for all worked to enhance the status of the elderly in the predominant value system of the time, if it did not necessarily provide older people with economic security per se. It was considered a salutary achievement to have lived a long life, and indeed, writes Achenbaum, the sheer "number of elderly people in the United States had become a powerful ideological weapon to demonstrate that the New World environment was conducive to human existence and societal progress." Because "virtue was associated with longevity, Americans concluded that the elderly could teach others how to live morally and healthfully."[20]

Consequently, such age discrimination in employment as existed in the early years of the Republic was usually against people considered too young to hold positions, particularly in the political realm. Antebellum laws frequently prevented persons from voting and holding office on the basis of their not being old enough for such responsibilities, but rarely because they were considered too old. The Constitution set only minimum ages for the Presidency and Congress, and the states barred young but not old men from holding governorships or seats in the legislatures. Only in judicial appointments was a pro-aged bias ambiguous. A few states did set a maximum age for such posts, but most sought to limit only the number of years in office, without regard to chronological age.

Thus, according to one student of the American history of old age,

> ...the veneration and general respect people showed toward the old...reached its zenith in the nineteenth century....Grandparents, as well as parents, were authority figures. Older men dominated public life. The young were expected to listen and aspire until they were old enough toi command respect. Society was geared to the aging. Public care for older people was even less than it is now, but that was more than compensated for by the usually unquestioned obligation of the younger members of a family to look after the welfare of the older ones if need be.[21]

---

19 Ibid., p. 22.

20 Ibid., pp. 12, 16.

21 John Tebbel, "Aging in America: Implications for the Mass Media," Monograph No. 2 (Washington, D.C.: National Council on the Aging, Inc., 1976), p. 2.

The elderly were thus officially exalted in antebellum America, and so it is not surprising that this era of maximum economic freedom and self-sufficiency for older people should correspond to what might be termed the twilight years of favorable social attitudes toward the elderly. Scholars such as Achenbaum and Fischer agree that positive valuations of older people's worth had begun to disappear by the second half of the nineteenth century.[22] Economic relations among age groups can partially account for this: Resentment of those who possess wealth and power by those who aspire to it is a constant theme in human history.

Yet such a simplistic explanation cannot adequately account for the departure from the extraordinary esteem that was accorded the elderly in America's colonial and early nationhood period. This was a time when the older generations had a virtual monopoly on status and prestige, and maintained tight economic control via an elaborate set of inheritance rules and ritualized social customs giving pride of place to age.

For example, primogeniture, a dominant feature of feudal life in the property-holding classes, had been transplanted relatively intact to "classless" North America. Despite the historically unique degree of personal freedom granted to the first generations of North Americans, the tradition of near-total property transmission to first-born sons held sway in modified form through the eighteenth century. The practice had its rationale in European feudal society as a means of maintaining a family's economic status. So long as only first-born sons were eligible to inherit the family lands, there could be no dissipation of assets and class position over time, such as would occur if holdings were passed on democratically to all heirs. Keeping the estate together was the overriding concern; modern democratic issues such as fairness and individual rights and feelings were irrelevant.

Such a rationale for the practice of primogeniture, or its variants, cannot reasonably be said to have existed in the United States.[23] Of course, customs and traditions may be transplanted to locales where they are inappropriate or even dysfunctonal, and they may remain in place largely unquestioned for a very long time. Also, to a certain extent the American colonies were feudal: Lands were not, at first, there simply for the occupying, but were granted to individuals and groups at the pleasure of the crown and its governors.

But never were there population pressures on the available land to justify or encourage European-style inheritance customs,[24] nor was there the class-consciousness that conditioned so much of European behavior generally.[25] The problem facing the early

---

22 In fact, Fischer argues that the revolution in attitudes toward older people in the U.S., from veneration to disdain, occurred somewhat earlier, between 1770 and 1820, based primarily upon literary evidence as to the changing language of age relations in that period. Achenbaum dates the trend toward negative stereotyping from the years after the Civil War.

23 However, in densely-populated New England the practice thrived late in the nineteenth century as the farmlands became increasingly exhausted.

24 Again, with the possible exception of New England.

25 As will be shown in Chapter 7, the lack of a feudal tradition of noblesse oblige in the United States was to hasten the decline in the fortunes of older people once industrialization was fully underway.

colonists was indeed antithetical to the Europeans': How to settle a huge continent and create a civilization literally from scratch, with few people, thousands of perilous miles from all that was familiar, established, proven. The historical evidence is overwhelming that it was the elders in the early settlements who forged the vital link between the old and new worlds.

Because of abundant lands in the U.S., most families were landed, and thus land became, as Fischer has noted, "an instrument of generational politics." Its control guaranteed the power and authority of the elderly and kept the younger generations bound to the older by ties of economic dependency.[26] Even the sons who had been made, or had become on their own, economically independent, were tied to their elders through subtler forms of parental authority.[27] The passing on of land holdings to any offspring was an act of late life, or of death. Landed property was frequently conferred upon an aging farmer's offspring within a comparatively short span of time in antebellum America; the oldest child might be past 40 and the youngest barely 20 and still living at home. In this context, the concept of retirement for an older individual had a unique meaning, as described by Fischer:

> ...'retirement' by the father from the business of farming [meant] not complete disengagement, but a passing on of the major responsibility for managing the family's lands. Final retirement came with the gift or sale of the homestead....Retirement in that special sense seems to have been normal among America's farming families....It was even universal, at a certain age. But that age was very advanced--around sixty-six or sixty-seven. It was beyond the average age of death for adult males. Most men never lived to reach it, and those who did usually died only a few years afterward.[28]

For the unpropertied elderly, economic security was tenuous, as it had always been. In the absence of private pension plans and governmental programs of old-age assistance, older workers forced out of their occupations by chronic illness or disability had to rely on any accumulated savings or the sale of assets to maintain economic independence. And although the majority of older men had assets in the mid-nineteenth century, more than one-fourth of those over 60 had estates valued at under $100 at the time of the Civil War.[29] Many of those with only meager resources at their disposal faced the constant

---

26 Fischer, Growing Old, p. 52.

27 An example of this was the case of a Samuel Sewall, Jr., who in middle age was referred to by his 64-year-old father as "my Samuel" and was constantly criticized for his handling of his family life and personal conduct. (Milton Halsey Thomas, ed., Diary of Samuel Sewall, 2 vols. [New York, 1973], passim, cited by Fischer, Growing Old, pp. 57-58.)

28 Fischer, Growing Old, pp. 54-55.

29 Achenbaum, Old Age, p. 29.

threat of old-age dependency; not even individuals who had experienced some considerable economic success in their prime were immune.[30]

Yet chronological age per se was less the cause of such misfortunes than were such factors as mismanagement and poor luck. There have always been individual aged paupers, but they were primarily individual problems. In the United States they were not to become a broad social problem until the last half of the nineteenth century when a sustained period of rapid technological and organizational changes rendered obsolete the skills and knowledge of large numbers of older workers, while simultaneously stressing their irrelevance to the new industrial order.

Another of the more prominent of early American social rituals granting stature to older people, one which was independent of family relations, was the practice of "seating at the meeting," a reference to both the meetinghouses of New England communities and to seatings at church for special public occasions. Honorable seats were assigned according to one's dignity, which was based by custom on three criteria: sex, age, and wealth/power (or social status).[31] These characteristics were usually without need of definition in the precisely circumscribed world of early America; women, non-whites, and youth could aspire to no better than second-class status.

Thus, along with considerable inequality between sexes and races, there was inequality according to age. Yet, what is striking is how discrimination against the old differs historically from sexism and racism in the United States. Ageism in the first two American centuries did exist, but it was anti-youth, and only in the last century or so did it begin to turn anti-elderly. Early American veneration of older people was not merely an ingenuous credo, but was made real through such practices as those just described. Young people were put in their place and kept there by strong economic and social forces.

Age was venerated in early America, then, for the most pragmatic of reasons. Older people's knowledge and experience, which were readily transferrable to the new circumstances, were indispensable.[32] In an era in which the rising generations still were expected (and themselves expected) essentially to replicate the occupations and lifestyles of parents and grandparents, the greatest relevant knowledge was typically held by those possessing the greatest years. In matters of trade and commerce, agriculture, finances, political organization, religious training, and so on, older people were the sine qua non of economic and social life.

---

30 Even the Presidency was not an ensurer of economic well-being in later life; Jefferson and Monroe were faced with financial ruin in their final years. (Ibid.)

31 Fischer, Growing Old, p. 38.

32 The idea of what constitutes "older," "age," etc., is of course a social construct and a matter of relativity, about which there exists an enormous anthropological and sociological literature. There were few early Americans who would be considered old by the standards of today, although to the extent that they did exist, they can be assumed to have been hardy individuals. What is important for the present argument is that roles and status were ascribed in America's past according to an age-graded hierarchy which granted greatest esteem to older as opposed to younger people.

Yet it is undoubtedly true that much of the veneration with which the elderly were regarded was disingenuous, or perhaps wishful thinking. It would be a mistake to suppose that the elderly were always loved or universally admired. Possessing the power they did, they naturally would have been occasional targets of considerable envy, resentment, and abuse. The linguistic evidence gathered by Fischer provides a fascinating picture of Americans' love-hate relationship with their elders, who were simultaneously esteemed and resented for their predominant influence in the political economy. A large vocabulary of abuse had been invented for them as early as the 1820s [33] when they remained firmly in control of economic relations and political power. Ironically, by the turn of the century, when old people were disproportionately in economic distress, the disparaging epithets seem largely to have disappeared.

The glorification of age could also be partly attributable to the stringently religious orientation of some of the earliest settlers, to biblical injunctions to "honor thy father and thy mother." But religious piety cannot begin to account for the long reign of the aristocracy of the elderly in the United States. Aged members of the population fulfilled a vital economic function, quite beyond all the other social, religious and familial norms which gave them their position in American society. And it was this ineluctable economic role which exalted them and relegated youth to second-class citizenship.

On the eve of the Civil War the privileged position of older people in the American economy, grounded in their ability to serve as transmitters of vital knowledge, was at its apogee. They provided the requisite know-how to accomplish essential tasks of economic and political life and served as both exemplars and arbiters of appropriate behavior. Their position was reinforced by the strong sanction of tradition.

Yet some observers noted myriad small ways in which the established intergenerational economic order was beginning to break down. Ralph Waldo Emerson, in his celebration of "Old Age" in an 1862 Atlantic Monthly, gave lie to the myth when he wrote, "Youth is everywhere in place...We do not count a man's years, until he has nothing else to count....In short, the creed of the street is, Old Age is not disgraceful, but immensely disadvantageous."[34] Emerson was not alone in noting that, quite apart from the civil disorder occurring at the time, change was clearly in the air. Family relations, regional characteristics, occupations, production processes, transportation modes and routes--all were beginning to be altered in subtle and as-yet undetected ways; and all would play a role in making age a "disadvantageous" attribute.

---

33 For example: "old cornstalk" for an ineffectual old man, "old goat" for a lecherous old man, "fuddy-duddy" for a pompous old man; "granny" for a weak old man, "mummy" for an ugly old man, "geezer" for an eccentric old man, "goose" for a silly old man, "galoot" for an uncouth old man, and "backnumber" for an anachronistic old man. Old women were disparaged with less vigor and frequency, but at any rate abusive language toward older women had been in existence for centuries. Fischer, Growing Old, pp. 90-93.

34 Cited by Achenbaum, Old Age, p. 36, fn 30.

Technological Change in the
Antebellum Period

It is important to examine in some detail the nature of the developing tensions between social mores and actual economic conditions as they related to the prospects for older workers to perform remunerative work. For most of the nineteenth century the United States' industrial revolution was characterized by the transition to new ways of doing old things. In agriculture, grains were grown according to evolving scientific principles; in manufacturing, iron, textiles, clothing and the like were increasingly fashioned in plants whose average size and extent of capitalization were increasing, and whose work forces were ever more finely divided according to function.

Most important, as early as the beginning of the nineteenth century the United States was leading the world in standardization and relatively large-scale production of interchangeable parts, which were later to become the basis of the assembly line. The change in technique occurred first in the production of staple items of household consumption, such as guns and clocks. Only somewhat later would it be used in manu- facturing generally, particularly in metal-using products such as sewing machines, locks and hardware, agricultural implements, locomotives, typewriters and bicycles (and automobiles early in the twentieth century). As precision in tool operations improved and cheaper, more reliable measurement devices became available, the degree of interchangeability possible through the use of machinery continued to increase, and the amount of required hand labor was correspondingly reduced.

The factor-proportions problem, the extreme relative scarcity of labor and its inelastic supply, served to encourage the rapid adoption, from Britain and through domestic invention, of new techniques which were to give rise to capital-intensive production processes. (Capital, too, was initially scarce, but its mobility enabled the U.S. to attract foreign investment to overcome the shortage of domestic savings.) This imbalance in factor supply conditions not only predisposed production toward the use of capital, but also had the interesting consequence of biasing the time horizon of American producers. Machines were built with an eye to their early scrapping; they were deliberately made to be non-durable so that their owners could at minimal cost replace them with newer machines embodying the most up-to-date knowledge. Maximizing the productivity of labor required that workers have available machines incorporating the latest technology, all the more so because repairing and maintaining old machines was itself a costly use of labor.[35]

---

35 See H.J. Habbakuk, American and British Technology in the Nineteenth Century (Cambridge: Cambridge University Press, 1967); Peter Temin, "Labor Scarcity and the Problem of American Industrial Efficiency in the 1850s," Journal of Economic History 26, (September 1966):277-98; Temin, "Labor Scarcity in America," Journal of Interdisciplinary History 1 (Winter 1971):251-64.

Temin argues that the very dearness of capital in the U.S. (especially extremely high short-term interest rates in the decades of the 1830s through 1850s) encouraged flimsily constructed machines; Habbakuk attributes their rapid obsolescence to the fact that American entrepreneurs wore out their equipment by running it for long hours at a rapid pace. For purposes of this discussion what matters is less the why of obsolescence than the widespread agreement on its existence. (A parallel can be drawn for the labor input. By

Thus, constant refinements in the application of new technologies and processes were characteristic of American economic life before 1860, but these ongoing adjustments were made at the margin of production. They were evolutionary and gradual, and did not constitute radical departures from the past either in terms of industrial structure or in regard to the operation of labor markets, which remained localized, idiosyncratic, and not highly specialized. After 1860, however, the industrial revolution would take a turn that was to have profound implications both for the relations among economic classes and for the employment prospects of older workers. In particular, after 1875 the revolution embraced the production of altogether new commodities, as opposed to the familiar commodities merely turned out by new methods as in the early decades of the century.

The wealthy in 1860 probably possessed nothing that their counterparts of a century earlier had not also been able to obtain. They might have things in greater quantity, or larger or better made, than people of lesser means, but their riches were more likely to be displayed in the dimensions of their homes and the numbers of servants they employed than in their personal use of commodities. As the scale of production increased and the great fortunes were earned nearing the turn of the century, wealth increasingly was displayed in ownership of luxury goods unavailable to the average American.[36] Conspicuous consumption began to take on its modern Veblenian form.[37]

This transition of course had implications for the relationships among economic classes as the distribution of wealth became both more unequal and more obvious. But even more fundamentally, what would be required in order for the average American of the late 1800s to possess goods that had once been considered the province of the rich was the widespread use of new production technologies and the organization of production processes upon an unprecedented scale. American prosperity came to be based upon large-batch, single-product, inflexible methods of production which narrowed the range of appropriate individual worker skills and contributed to the practice of hiring according to superficial characteristics--along color, ethnic, sex, and age lines. At the same time as choice in consumption was dramatically extended, most Americans in their roles as workers faced constricted opportunities for self-directed, experience-conditioned, and skill-enhancing employment.

In the pre-Civil War era, the pragmatic character of American production techniques alluded to above was clearly illustrated in the application of machine tools to produce goods for which the demand was both large and reasonably certain. Firearms provide a convenient example because their manufacture (or perhaps more correctly, machinofacture) was extensively studied by a visiting parliamentary committee from Great Britain in the 1850s. The committee's somewhat overawed report lends credence to Harry Braverman's thesis

---

century's end, older workers in particular were to become obsolete and be "scrapped" for not embodying the most recent advances in knowledge or ways of doing things.)

36 W. Arthur Lewis, Growth and Fluctuations, 1870-1913 (London: George Allen and Unwin, 1978), p. 29.

37 Conspicuous consumption is the term coined by Thorstein Veblen in 1899 to describe striving for status through the consumption of non-essential goods and services. See his Theory of the Leisure Classs (New York: Penguin, 1979).

that the rise and success of U.S. industrial capitalism relied in considerable measure on the progressive de-emphasis of the skill, judgment, and experience of trained craftsmen:[38]

> The workman whose business it is to "assemble" or set up the arms, takes the different parts promiscuously from a row of boxes, and uses nothing but the turn-screw to put the musket together, excepting on the slott, which contains the band-springs, which have to be squared at one end with a small chisel. He receives four cents per musket, and has put together as many as 100 in a day and 530 in a week, but his usual day's work is from 50 to 60. [39]

The difference between "assembling" and the customary method of "fitting" of parts is compelling. It could take a matter of weeks at most to train a worker to proficiency at the task described above. The enormous cost of the older handicraft system relying on exacting fitting activities was only just beginning to be appreciated, and the parliamentary committee saw with fresh eyes the extent to which "'assembling' a firearm was a technical innovation of major proportions."[40]

Firearms were the first mass-consumption goods to be produced. This came about because in 1788 Eli Whitney had obtained a contract for 4000 muskets for the U.S. Army, whose time constraints impelled the inventor to feats of daring-do. Although failing to meet his quota (only 500 were ready on time), Whitney arranged a demonstration for President John Adams in which he disassembled guns, scrambled their parts and reassembled them with no loss of quality. This was the first and clearest prototype for the new technique. Not only was there economy to be had in manufacture, but also in repairs and replacements.[41] The great profit potential of mass production had been dramatically demonstrated.

The textile industry had led the way as the first significant mass-production industry, but weaving was not amenable to interchangeability of parts, and at any rate the textile industry's accomplishments could at first be replicated only where a power source, water-power at the time, could be monopolized by an entrepreneur. Where this was possible, concentration of production was the rule, and variations of automatic machinery were

---

38 Harry Braverman, Labor and Monopoly Capital: The Degradation of Work in the Twentieth Century (New York: Monthly Review Press, 1974).

39 "Report of the Committee on the Machinery of the U.S.A.," cited by Nathan Rosenberg, ed., The American System of Manufactures (Edinburgh: University of Edinburgh Press, 1969), pp. 142-43. Emphasis added; seasoned judgment on the part of the worker obviously was superfluous in such circumstances.

40 Rosenberg, Technology and American Economic Growth, p. 95. The lesson was not lost on Henry Ford, who was to carry such processes to unprecedented levels. "In mass production there are no fitters," he wrote in his contribution, "Mass Production," to the 22nd edition of the Encyclopaedia Britannica. Cited in ibid.

41 John M. Peterson and Ralph Gray, Economic Development of the United States (Homewood, Ill.: Richard D. Irwin, 1969), pp. 209-10.

everywhere in use in textile manufacturing after 1815. But applications of standardization and interchangeable parts did not require particular locational advantages, at least not at first, nor did they require excessive quantities of capital. What was needed was the maintenance of free markets (a laissez-faire philosophy of governance) and the presence of entrepreneurship. While a discussion of entrepreneurship is beyond the scope of this study, there can be no doubt that this elusive quality[42] was crucial to the inventiveness of American business and to the rapid rate of economic growth in the nineteenth and early twentieth centuries.

Entrepreneurship, coupled with the use of standardized and interchangeable parts, enabled such early American success stories as Chauncey Jerome, who applied the new techniques to clock manufacture in the 1820s and 1830s, at which time he boasted of having "ten thousand...in the works at one time." For less than 50 cents he was able to manufacture a product that would have cost at least $5 if turned out by craftsmen. On the eve of the Civil War his five Connecticut factories were producing 500,000 well-made, inexpensive clocks per year because every aspect of their manufacture was "systematized in the most perfect manner."[43]

Coincidentally, Jerome's experiences are particularly relevant to an examination into the origins of an ageist bias in the American economy. After a long and remarkably successful career, he grew poor as he grew old. In his memoirs, which he wrote to make money, he vividly expressed an ambivalence toward the system which had first rewarded and then downgraded him:

> One of the most trying things to me now, is to see how I am looked down upon by the community since I lost my property. I never was any better when I owned it than I am now, and never behaved any better. But how different is the feeling towards you, when your neighbors can make nothing more out of you, politically and pecuniarily. It makes no difference what, or how much you have done for them heretofore, you are passed by without notice now. It is all money and business, business and money which make the man now-a-days; success is everything.[44]

Leaving aside the obvious self-pity and possibly self-serving nature of Jerome's remarks, they reveal that even the pluckiest, the most accomplished and fortunate of Americans, could be victims of an age prejudice which discouraged their continuing participation in economic life.

---

42 Brilliantly analyzed by Joseph Schumpeter in The Theory of Economic Development: An Inquiry into Profits, Capital, Credit, Interest, and the Business Cycle (Cambridge: Harvard University Press, 1934).

43 Chauncey Jerome, History of the American Clock Business for the Past Sixty Years, and Life of Chauncey Jerome (New Haven: F.C. Dayton, Jr., 1860), pp. 90, 92, 105, cited by Richard D. Brown, Modernization, The Transformation of American Life (New York: Hill and Wang, 1976), p. 129.

44 Jerome, History of the American Clock Business, p. 75, cited by Brown, Modernization, p. 151.

The Role of Government in Promoting Economic Growth

An analysis of the background forces which influenced the revolution in the national economy and in older Americans' economic status would not be complete without an assessment of the government's role in attempting to foster growth and development. The dominant governmental philosophy/policy in the years leading up to the Civil War was an emphasis on stability, on the security of property rights, and on the need to avoid so far as possible the levying of taxes on enterprises and entrepreneurs. Such infrastructure and publicly provided goods as existed were financed by an assortment of tariff duties and excises whose incidence fell mostly on wage-workers and farmers.[45]

Some of the nation's first industrial capitalists were the beneficiaries of a government policy which vacillated between laissez-faire and largesse. Government's major contributions to the growth of industrial capitalism, and indirectly to the proletarianization of the workforce, were threefold:

(1) Government's heavy financing of the nation's turnpike, river, canal, and railroad networks pried open remote regions; linked together settlements, towns, and regions; and promoted more-or-less universal demand and supply characteristics for the country.

(2) Government's reliance on very high import duties (in addition to income derived from the sale of public lands) as the major source of federal revenues provided a powerful shield for domestic manufactures against foreign competition. Such overtly protectionist policies of course raised prices for domestic consumers while conferring substantial market power upon the manufacturing concerns affected, particularly wool and woolen goods, and iron and steel products. Protective duties rose rapidly from an average on all imports of below 209 percent in the two decades prior to the Civil War to an average in 1867 of 47 percent. This was done on the grounds that revenues were needed to finance the war effort, but tariffs were to remain high on dutiable imports until World War I. [46]

(3) Government actively promoted immigration to expand the size of the available pool of labor. Between 1820 and 1860, 5.5 million immigrants arrived.[47] By the close of the century nearly a million Europeans were being added to the population each year, a phenomenon without parallel in modern history and one having profound ramifications for the economic security of the existing labor force. Between 1860 and 1900, the population

---

45 Theodore Saloutos, "The Agricultural Problem and Nineteenth-Century Industrialism," in The Changing Economic Order: Readings in American Business and Economic History, ed. by Alfred D. Chandler, Jr., Stuart Bruchey, and Louis Galambos (New York: Harcourt, Brace and World, 1968), p. 337.

46 Peterson and Gray, Economic Development of the United States, pp. 298-99.

47 In 1860 total population was about 32 million. Herman E. Krooss, American Economic Development: The Progress of a Business Civilization, 3rd ed. (Englewood Cliffs, N.J.: Prentice-Hall, 1974), pp. 74-78.

of the United States would rise by 140 percent owing largely to immigration, and the civilian labor force would grow by 170 percent.[48]

To these factors might be added a fourth way in which government encouraged large-scale capitalist enterprise, albeit indirectly, owing to the exigencies of the Civil War. The need to provision and transport large numbers of soldiers mandated new forms of production. For example, the Union Army's requirements of large and regularly supplied quantities of shoes, food, blankets, clothing, etc., forced a kind of rationalization on certain producers of these commodities. Government contracts financed a few key groups of entrepreneurs in these lines of business, and virtually overnight merchant capitalists were converted into industrialists who continued to hold a decided advantage over their competitors when the war ended.[49]

There were, to be sure, public policies which favored Americans generally. Most of these were involved in one way or another with transferring lands in the public domain into private hands as rapidly as possible. The motives were arguably egalitarian but the results were not.

In the first place, such moves served the republic both in terms of increasing the productivity of the expanding transportation systems and in terms of making the nation more secure against aggression. Furthermore, land grants such as those contained in the Homestead Act of 1862 served as a safety valve for workers who were beginning to be overtaken by the industrialization process. The nearly-free access to western lands defused some of the tensions generated by rapid socioeconomic change. By providing those who were willing to relocate with greater protection against the rising unemployment and economic insecurity accompanying their loss of independence as workers, homesteading served a vital and dual function.

Unfortunately, the idealism that gave rise to such federal acts was obliterated by their sorry record of deception, chicanery, and outright fraud. The greatest beneficiaries of federal and state land grants were special interests. For the railroads they were a giveaway. And the distribution plans allowed for large estates and high-quality lands to be bought up (fraudulently as well as legally) by speculators who held it for appreciation. Of the unproductive land that was acquired,[50] most was by those hoping to make a living from the land and much of it was subsequently abandoned. According to one scholar, only

48 Louis M. Hacker, The Course of American Economic Growth and Development (New York: John Wiley and Sons, 1970), p. 188. Immigration reached an all-time high early in the twentieth century with an annual flow of nearly one million individuals between 1905 and 1914. Albert W. Niemi, Jr., U.S. Economic History: A Survey of the Major Issues (Chicago: Rand McNally College Publishing Co., 1975), p. 211.

49 Hacker, Course of American Economic Growth, p. 144. True assembly-line techniques were used for the first time in the U.S. in slaughtering and packing meat for the Union war effort. Ibid.

50 The government continued to own the majority of the least productive land.

about 400,000 families (a total of about 2 million people) were able to acquire free land holdings and retain them.[51]

This was in part because as early as 1862 the frontier had reached the edge of the arid part of the country, where the standard of 160 acres was too small to allow a settler family to make a decent living.[52] In addition, farm failure rates were extremely high (see Chapter 3). Commercial agriculture required a degree of skill as well as access to capital and to long-term agricultural credit to make it viable, and these were frequently lacking for transplanted urban industrial laborers. The Homestead Act's greatest accomplishment was the lure it provided to tenant farmers from northern Europe, where an oversupply of agricultural labor was generating an outward push on populations.

Whatever was the impact of the homesteading provisions on the nation's rate of economic growth in the nineteenth century--and there is considerable debate on this question--it seems clear that they brought about little change in the distribution of land holdings, and even less in the distribution of productive wealth.

Governments at all levels were decidedly laissez-faire or pro-business, providing a favorable climate for risk-taking and innovation. After mid-century, manufacturing production was large enough and growing fast enough to provide a significant stimulus to national economic growth and the transformation of the American economy to industrial capitalism. Industrial growth was spurred by regressive taxes, falling on workers' wages and farmers' incomes but not on the profits of companies and individuals.[53] There existed no regulations or controls in the public interest, no health and safety legislation, no broad commitment to public education; and, beyond the subsidies to transcontinental transportation, little building of infrastructure. Most of the country's hospitals, libraries, universities, community centers, and so forth were financed by the private sector as part of the spreading practice of corporate philanthropy.

The Spread of the Market Economy
and Labor's Initial Response

The reason for the great spurt in growth that occurred between 1840 and 1860 was the greatest American railroad building boom of all time, giving much of the eastern United States a connected rail system. By the 1890s, the nation's continental limits would be reached, and the U.S. would be bound together economically and politically to make possible the nation's emergence as a truly unified industrial economy.

Among the most important outgrowths of railroad construction was the emergence of an altogether new scale of economic organization. For the first time Americans would

---

51 Fred A. Shannon, The Farmer's Last Frontier: Agriculture, 1860-1897 (New York: Farrar and Rinehart, 1945), p. 55.

52 Gary M. Walton and Ross M. Robertson, History of the American Economy, 5th ed. (New York: Harcourt Brace Jovanovich, 1983), p. 193.

53 Farmers and workers also bore the brunt of the free markets' extreme business cycle swings; farm prices were tied to world production, and rates of unemployment rose very high during periods of recession and depression.

be able (owing to the harsh necessity during the Civil War of recruiting, transporting and deploying masses of people and supplies) to create, organize, and sustain a mammouth commercial enterprise. When the war's lessons were turned to profitable peacetime use, an organization revolution occurred.

Whereas before the Civil War the corporate structure was a significant part of manufacturing in only one industry--cotton textiles--by 1900 nearly two-thirds of manufacturing output was to be produced by corporations.[54] The trend toward concentration and centralization would be accelerated by the introduction and rapid dispersion of many totally new commodities--telephones, sewing machines, typewriters, gramophones, cameras, and horseless carriages--and by the ascendancy of assembly-line techniques for their manufacture.[55]

But one of the key elements in the transformation in the working lives of older Americans was already beginning to catch on before the revolution in transportation expanded markets and increased the mobility of goods, services, and people. The transformation was predicated, as noted above, on the feasibility of using interchangeable components, eliminating dependence on handicraft skills in many aspects of production, and doing away with the detailed fitting operations of small-batch manufacturing. Interchangeable product parts not only permitted assembly without fitting, but they also allowed for a much greater degree of specialization than would otherwise have been possible.

Although minute specialization of tasks does not necessarily imply a shift in the location of production from the home or the small shop to the factory, such a shift did tend to be the consequence. This was because of internal economies to be gained from the centralization of machine tools, which lowered inventory costs of intermediate goods in transit,[56] and because the growing reliance on capital was destroying the traditional basis for the kind of entrepreneurship that could be exercised in the independent shop.[57]

Furthermore, the abolition of the fitting tasks which relied on experience and seasoned judgment on the part of the producer meant that once cheaper labor became more abundant with mass immigration, new workers could be quickly trained and older, costlier

---

54 Averitt, The Dual Economy, pp. 8-9.

55 Lewis, Growth and Fluctuations, p. 29.

56 Stephen Marglin's analysis of the social, as opposed to technological, determinants of factory production deserves mention. He concluded that hierarchical work environments developed not for reasons of efficiency per se, but to ensure a role for capitalists, who stood to profit by imposing themselves between producers and the market. The subject of the motivations underlying large-scale organizations is complex and somewhat beyond the scope of the present study. But hierarchicalization and bureaucratization are important aspects of the decline in employment opportunities for older individuals, particularly in this century as retirement according to chronological age has come to be the norm. See Stephen A. Marglin, "What Do Bosses Do? The Origins and Functions of Hierarchy in Capitalist Production," Review of Radical Political Economics 6 (Summer 1974): 60-112.

57 Irwin Yellowitz, Industrialization and the American Labor Movement, 1850-1900 (Port Washington, N.Y.: Kennikat Press, 1977), p. 37.

ones easily replaced. This resulted in downward pressure on wages,[58] as well as a revolution in the economy's structure of occupations. As the number of job categories grew with specialization, their average skill requirements progressively declined. Further, the increasing division of labor that minimized the role of skill and experience in carrying out production also served to discourage entry into the entrepreneurial ranks.[59]

Thus, with interchangeability as its basis, technological change in the nineteenth century would evolve and become institutionalized in a unique way. A relatively small group of specialized firms developed in the manufacturing sector, oriented to solving a wide range of technical problems. Within these capital-goods-producing firms was amassed an impressive array of problem-solving techniques which trickled down to the rest of the economy. As machine tools and equipment, and the processes of production more broadly, became ever more sophisticated and complex, the labor component in production was streamlined, routinized, and simplified. The revolution that occurred in the transportation of goods and services led to an expansion of markets which lowered costs and accelerated the adoption of skill-leveling innovations. From the point of view of the national economy, interchangeable parts were the precursor of interchangeable labor.

Labor's Initial Response to Technological Change

A dominant characteristic of American labor in this period (with the notable exception of slaves) was its extraordinary mobility. Because the U.S. lacked a feudal heritage or tradition, and because it was populated by a self-selected citizenry, the notion of economic and geographical mobility had from colonial times been deeply embedded in the American psyche. Recognition of this concept is vital for an appreciation of the unprecedented degree of personal freedom--in particular, freedom from rigid locational and employment ties--that characterized the American economy at midcentury.

What, then, was the response of American labor to the growing threats to its economic security? Although craft unions spread rapidly in the 1840s and 1850s (there was as yet no attempt to organize unskilled labor), and these pushed for practical concerns such as higher wages, shorter hours, and public education, they accounted for only a small segment of the labor force on the eve of the Civil War. American workers as a whole appear to have remained quite complacent about the structure of the work process itself, perhaps in part because it took some time for the message to sink in that traditional routes to successful self-employment were rapidly disappearing. That distinctly American

---

58 There has been much debate on whether real wages improved during our period. The most recent consensus seems to be that average real wages rose, although not steadily, for most of the period between 1860 and 1920, because of the explosion in economic activity and improvements in productivity unequalled in the world. Industrialization was so rapid that bottlenecks were a continuing problem, for want of labor as well as capital and entrepreneurship. Without the tides of immigrants to fill low-skill jobs, wages would probably have skyrocketed. Recessions and their attendant high rates of unemployment of course were a substantial brake on many workers' income growth. See footnote [66] of this chapter.

59 Yellowitz, Industrialization, p. 37.

pragmatism was also perhaps partly responsible for workers' implicit acquiescence in the process of skill-leveling. Certainly the United States had no experiences comparable to the machine-smashing tactics of the eighteenth-century British Luddites, who saw technology as the enemy of their skills and security.

Quite the contrary, workers in the U.S. typically saw the machine as their friend. By the 1840s British and French observers were commenting on how intrigued Americans were by practical gadgets. They noted that the workers were proud of the sheer quantity of their output, in contrast with their British counterparts who, no doubt in keeping with their guild heritage, took greater pride in quality and craftsmanship.[60]

Later fears of overproduction had yet to be aroused in the American workforce. Not only does there appear to have been little suspicion on the part of workers in this period that machines could put people out of accustomed jobs, but machines actually were considered employment-enhancing. The U.S. economy was import-substituting throughout the first half of the nineteenth century, and imports could be reduced through the lowering of costs made possible by new inventions. Reductions in imports translated into greater domestic employment opportunities and a rising standard of living.[61]

There were, to be sure, several discomfiting signs, at least when assessed with the benefit of hindsight. The American pace of work in factories was fast, far faster than in Europe, with the work more tightly organized to maximize economies of repetition. Factory discipline was strict, if not grueling, the consequence of an impersonal, systematized approach to manufacturing. This was particularly the case in the New England textile mills from the 1830s onward; and in the 1840s and 1850s in factories producing such staples as clocks and watches, sewing machines, plows and reapers, shoes and ready-made clothing, guns and pistols.[62]

Employers' constant attempts to circumvent the problem of a scarcity of skilled labor led to organizations that tended to homogenize labor in the production process. And although job openings were growing more rapidly than the domestic labor force, the line of immigrants was beginning to form. From 8,385 immigrants in 1820, by 1850 the annual rate had reached nearly 370,000 additions to the nation's population, the majority of working age.[63]

---

60 Lewis, Growth and Fluctuations, p. 126.

61 Ibid.

62 Alfred D. Chandler, Jr., "The Coming of Big Business," in The Comparative Approach to American History, ed. by C. Vann Woodward (New York: Basic Books, 1968), p. 223.

63 U.S. Bureau of the Census, Historical Statistics of the United States, Colonial Times to 1957, Series C88-114 (Washington, D.C.: Government Printing Office, 1960); U.S. Department of Commerce, Statistical Abstract (Washington, D.C.: Government Printing Office, 1972), p. 93, cited by Niemi, U.S. Economic History, p. 13.

Furthermore, by 1860 many crafts had already experienced skill-leveling through division of labor, while increasing mechanization served to intensify the substitution of semi-skilled and unskilled workers for craftsmen. Yellowitz, Industrialization, p. 5.

Ironically, the general push toward greater routinization of work tasks, and toward increased reliance on factory-wide rules rather than individual discretion, coincided with the drive toward universal primary education. By 1840, 80 percent of American adults were able to write, a rate second only to Germany's 82 per cent.[64] While some threshold of literacy is certainly necessary to launch an industrial revolution, Americans at midcentury were perhaps being over-educated for the nature of many of the jobs that would be available. By late in the nineteenth century, the upward trend in average educational levels was to work to the disadvantage of older workers' employment opportunities; ceteris paribus, employers preferred to recruit those with lengthier, more recent schooling, who were typically the young.[65]

As altogether new consumer goods became widely available--many of which were themselves saving of skilled labor, such as the sewing machine and the typewriter--average skill and training requirements for factory work continued to fall. Considerable technical and managerial genius, and some good fortune, obviously attached to these new inventions, and skill was required for the most efficient use of plant and equipment. But opportunities for the pursuit of the much-vaunted "success ethic" were being eroded for workers possessing specific established skills. The older craftsmen might continue to be employed in preference to unskilled and unschooled labor for some positions, but they were to be increasingly overqualified or misqualified. They could not, at any rate, expect to be paid commensurate with the skill and training in which they had invested, once these attributes began to lose their relevance to emerging production methods.

When the economic landscape began to be transformed by industrialization, specialization, and finally automation, labor's freedom and mobility would assert their darker sides. The lack of a feudal tradition meant that no ties of reciprocity existed to sustain those workers left behind, for whatever reason, by progress; and the opportunity to leave one place readily for another meant, all too often, the severing of the relational ties on which older family members, in particular, depended for both economic and emotional security. In the late nineteenth century, older workers were to discover that they had the freedom to be downwardly mobile in a society that placed great value on the opposite. The nation's personal, political, and juridical freedoms conveyed also a freedom from the obligational ties which could serve to cushion individual failures in less open societies.

---

64 Carlo M. Cipolla, Literacy and Development in the West (Baltimore: Penguin Books, 1969), cited by Lewis, Growth and Fluctuations, p. 138.

65 It was about this time that standardized tests began to be used. If progress meant greater efficiency, efficiency implied the use of "objective" criteria in order to apportion opportunities in an equitable manner. Testing also constituted a search for order amid the societal chaos that accompanied the industrialization process. It was felt that order could be restored by setting standards to govern people in much the same manner as standards set the width of railroad tracks. Initially developed to weed out the "feeble-minded" for sterilization and to aid in establishing which immigrant groups were most desirable, such tests could also be used for hiring purposes, and individuals most recently exposed to classroom examinations were likely to fare better than those more removed from them. See Mike Sager, "Testing Anxiety," Washington Post Magazine, 16 January 1983, pp. 6-7.

By any standard of wealth, productivity, or technological progress, the great leap into industrialization was testimony to the American spirit of invention and enterprise. Despite the fact that workers' wages rose during much of the 1860-1920 period,[66] such gains must be weighed against the significance of workers' economic, social, and psychic costs. According to one historian of the movement for social insurance, the industrial age "not only changed the occupational structure,...it transformed the status of the industrial laborer, the conditions under which he labored, and in a sense the very meaning of work."[67]

Conclusion

The great transformation of the U.S. economy from petty- and merchant-capitalism to industrial capitalism, begun in the early decades of the nineteenth century, took off into self-sustaining, steady growth with the cessation of Civil War hostilities. Only limited industrialization had been possible until there existed a truly national economy, that is, a national transportation system and national markets for capital, goods and services, and

---

66 The data are somewhat sketchy and inconsistent on this point. Average real wages increased until the 1890s but the record is mixed after 1895. Additionally, improvements in wage rates were in many years more than outweighed by income losses from protracted unemployment, while a progressively shorter workweek caused hourly wages to increase. See Alvin H. Hansen, "Factors Affecting the Trend of Real Wages," American Economic Review 15 (March 1925):39; Don D. Lescohier, Working Conditions, vol. III of History of Labor in the United States, 1896-1932, ed. by John R. Commons et al. (New York: Macmillan Co., 1935), pp. 52-61 passim.

The question of whether or not workers were becoming better off at the turn of the century was for many years answered in the negative based upon a study undertaken by Paul Douglas showing no rise in real wages for the 1890-1914 period. See Paul H. Douglas, Real Wages in the United States, 1890-1926 (Boston: Houghton Mifflin, 1930). Yet constant real wages did not jibe with the enormous expansion of output during the period, so until rather recently economic historians appear to have accepted the conclusion that monopoly power must have deprived workers of a share of the increased production. This impression was contradicted by a 1961 study by Albert Rees which made use of a revised cost of living index to demonstrate that hourly earnings rose significantly between 1890 and 1914. See Albert Rees, Real Wages in Manufacturing, 1890-1914 (Princeton: Princeton University Press, 1961), p. 4. Although recent research casts doubt on the contention that monopoly prevented the growth of real wages, it does not refute the social historians' long-standing position on the very serious social and personal costs of the spread of crowded slums, tenements, and ghettos which became a hallmark of urban industrialization during this period. See Douglass C. North, Growth and Welfare in the American Past, 2nd ed. (Englewood Cliffs, N.J.: Prentice-Hall, Inc., 1974), p. 153.

67 Hace Sorel Tishler, Self-Reliance and Social Security, 1870-1917 (Port Washington, N.Y.: Kennikat Press, 1971), p. 14.

labor. Once these were essentially in place, the decline of home production, cottage industry, and "bespoke"[68] trades was rapid and nearly total.

The completion of the East-West railroad linkages in the late 1860s signalled the beginning of the end of the dominance of regional markets in the American economy. Although expansion beyond the Mississippi River had been substantial by as early as 1815, the West still had little influence on methods and patterns of production in the rest of the economy. The vast majority of the labor force was either outside the market nexus or only peripheral to it. In 1815, almost half the population was concentrated in the Northeast, where urbanization and market arrangements were most highly developed, and slightly more than one-third lived in the South.[69] Canal and railroad construction in the period leading up to the Civil War made possible a regional division of labor among the West, South, and Northeast, which fundamentally altered the nature of internal trade and enhanced the mobility which was to be so crucial to the nation's economic growth.[70]

The markets which grew up for various products paved the way for labor specialization in areas where it had previously been virtually unknown, and fostered an historically unique degree of mutual dependence among regions.[71] Indeed, according to Victor S. Clark, as early as "the decade of the 1830s...the tendency toward specialization and localization was clearly evident."[72]

The settling of the frontier, now accessible via waterways, rail, and toll roads, increased the demand for capital and labor in the West, and it was this new demand for labor in particular (largely supplied by migration from the East and to a lesser extent from the South) which was to have important ramifications for the nature of employment in the United States. It "redirected the labor force from consumer goods agricultural production into investment goods," notes North, and "expanded the market labor force by pulling labor

---

68 These were similar to cottage production but took place in urban shops, where household goods were turned out to order, made by hand by free artisans who were not wage-laborers and who might or might not own their tools and equipment.

69 Douglass C. North, The Economic Growth of the United States, 1790-1860 (New York: W.W. Norton and Co., 1966), p. 63.

70 A few data for the railroads indicate the magnitude of this transportation revolution. From just under 10,000 miles of trackage constructed in the 1850s, the network expanded to 52,000 miles in 1870, and to over 166,000 miles in 1890. (North, Economic Growth, p. 142; Irwin Yellowitz, The Position of the Worker in American Society, 1865-1896 [Englewood Cliffs, N.J.: Prentice-Hall, 1969], p. 8.)

71 Louis B. Schmidt, "Internal Commerce and the Development of National Economy Before 1860," Journal of Political Economy 47 (December 1939):798-822.

72 Victor S. Clark, History of Manufactures in the United States, 3 vols. (New York: McGraw-Hill, 1929), 1:452.

[primarily farmers] out of a self-sufficient existence into a money economy."[73] Everywhere, except perhaps temporarily in the South, the implications for individual economic security were to be profound.

Despite this homogenizing trend, it should be kept in mind that the U.S. remained a predominantly agricultural economy throughout the nineteenth century, having only 20 percent of its population living in urban centers on the eve of the Civil War, and 40 percent so classified in 1900.[74] But in rural life, too, though to a lesser extent and more slowly than in urban areas, markets increasingly came to link the once self-sufficient family farm to the broader economy. As markets increased in importance, farms as well as firms became increasingly specialized, further enhancing market relations.

U.S. economic history in the nineteenth century was a classic example of Adam Smith's contention that productivity growth is fundamentally a function of the division of labor. In the early part of the century, localized industry, primarily in the Northeast, made possible a large number of specialized firms which became increasingly specialized in function as the relevant markets expanded. Whereas initially a firm would have to carry out all ancillary activities involved in production and marketing, it became able, through market growth and task specialization, to let other firms take over various aspects of production with greater efficiency. A similar process was at work to a lesser degree in non-urban areas with the growth of transportation facilities and retail trades.

By 1850 craftsmen had already begun to face division of their work, and artisans were frequently to be found working for others making parts of a product assembled by fellow workers. As early as the 1860s, although mechanization was not yet extensive, labor leaders referred with nostalgia to the era of the independent master craftsman. While machinery had not yet begun to displace large numbers of workers, trends were becoming evident in the division of tasks, the increasing scale of productive enterprises, and the increasing concentration of production in factories.[75]

Such developments clearly threatened the economic security and the status of the theretofore independent artisans, who promised to become permanent members of a wage-earning class. Although small entrepreneurs and merchant capitalists did not suddenly or completely disappear from the American landscape, the diminution of their role was increasingly evident as they accommodated change by taking on jobs as middlemen and retailers in the expanding national economy.[76]

Under industrial capitalism, relying as it did on increasing concentrations of productive capital, on the extensive use of credit, and on a wage-labor force, it became necessary for growing numbers of laborers to leave their homes and assemble in factories to make use of the expensive machinery which no individual worker could any longer afford to own for himself. To an increasing extent those who supplied the factors of production

---

73 North Economic Growth, p. 197 (emphasis in the original). See Chapter 3.

74 Bureau of the Census, Historical Statistics of the United States, Colonial Times to 1957, p. 14. "Urban" is defined here as communities of 2,500 or more inhabitants.

75 Yellowitz, Industrialization, p. 4.

76 Ibid., p. 9.

became separated into quite distinct socioeconomic classes. One set of persons might supply an enterprise with capital, another with land, and a third with labor power. Under these circumstances the organizer/entrepreneur/promoter achieved a new importance, and a fourth factor supplier, the captain of industry, came into existence.

The shift to industrial capitalism made possible by a unified national economy relied upon several phenomena to be explored in the following chapters, all of which to some extent operated to the detriment of older workers. First, the emphasis on capital investment in plant and equipment by the industrial capitalist meant that achievement came to be measured in terms of accumulations of wealth and success in the pecuniary arts, rather than according to the older values of craftsmanship and self-sufficiency. Second, rationalization of production in factories--product standardization, factory discipline, regulated hours, division of labor by function, close supervision, steady work pace, and remuneration by hourly wages or piece-rates--meant a rather total separation of the individual worker both from ownership in the means of production and from any say in how long or how hard to work at any given time. In addition, as employees became a factor of production, the link between worker and employer was broken in large establishments, so that individual circumstances and characteristics were no longer accommodated in hiring and placement decisions.

Finally, the consequent increases in productivity made possible even greater concentrations of wealth and decision-making authority, which in turn were applied to technological innovations that further reduced the skill component of work and hence the market-clearing price of labor. The more skilled workers, typically older individuals, were those who suffered the greatest reverses from skill-leveling. With the erosion of the economic value of their skills, they found themselves at a competitive disadvantage when seeking employment in organizations that were increasingly being structured along hierarchical and bureaucratic lines.

CHAPTER 3

THE IMPACT OF STRUCTURAL TRANSFORMATIONS ON OLDER WORKERS: WIDENING MARKETS, AGRICULTURAL DECLINE, URBANIZATION, AND IMMIGRATION

Introduction

The role of older Americans has been examined in the context of American economic life prior to the sweeping changes brought by the Industrial Revolution. Now it is necessary to assess the impact of several key phenomena that determined or hastened the transformation of the nation's industrial structure after 1860 insofar as the circumstances of older Americans were affected. To this end, this chapter will explore the interrelations of the following forces and institutions:

1. The unification of the national economy--primarily via the establishment of railroad linkages among previously semi-autonomous regions--which facilitated improved communi-cations and greater standardization of goods, services, and workers;

2. The spread of market activities to supplement and largely replace the at-home production and informal barter arrangements which had predominated when regions and districts were commercially remote from one another, with the result that the nature of work began to be fundamentally altered for the vast majority of Americans;

3. The relative decline of agricultural production, as measured both by the percentage of the population so employed and by agriculture's share in the gross national product;

4. The growth of towns and cities at the expense of the countryside as the locus of production, market activity, and employment;

5. The alteration of family relationships as members were distanced from one another both geographically and in terms of their employment experiences and prospects; and

6. The role of massive immigration in meeting the economy's labor scarcity and speeding the advent of mass production, labor specialization, and depersonalized working relationships.

As will be shown, each of these influences on American economic development was also a force for reshaping the socioeconomic position of older Americans by limiting their employment prospects and hence reducing their once-vaunted role in economic life.

Forging the Links to Increased Market Activity: The Role of the Railroads

It would be impossible to assess the impact of industrialization on older Americans without examining in detail the role of the railroads as a force in the development of the U.S. economy.[1] Not only was the establishment of a national rail system the primary

---

1 An enormous literature has grown up within the field of American economic history to assess the impact of the railroads on the pace, timing, and direction of American development. At one extreme, Rostow argues that it was primarily the railroad that set in

determinant of the rapidity with which markets came to mediate between economic actors, thus proletarianizing the work force; but also, by enhancing the external economies that firms could capture from large-scale operations (as geographically-dispersed production units were able to become vertically integrated), the railroads gave direct impetus to industrial concentration.

A natural concomitant was the increased concentration of population in urban areas and in localities possessing access to trunk lines. For the railroads, there were increasing returns from growing population density. And once established, urban centers generated conditions that encouraged their growth into metropolises,[2] particularly as cities became the home of immigrants whose place of residence was the major influence on the choice of destination for family members and friends who came later.

In addition, the development of the American railroad provides us with an unparalleled example of the sort of diffusion of new technology that almost instantaneously revolutionizes many other industries and markets and hence the occupational structure and the nature of work. This diffusion of technology involved both durable capital goods--rails, rolling stock, engines, and so forth, the requirements for which gave rise to or vastly enlarged a host of businesses--as well as innovations in the techniques and institutions of finance and management. (As an example, it was in the railroads that the professional hired manager first replaced the owner-manager.[3]) Thus the expansion of the railroads had stimulating effects on the national economy partly owing to the services they themselves provided and partly owing to the opportunities they opened up for other enterprises.

According to Schumpeter's theory of innovations, the economic transformation of capitalist society is begun by innovation in some production function, that is, by new

---

motion the nation's take-off into self-sustaining growth (1843-1860). (W. W. Rostow, The Stages of Economic Growth: A Non-Communist Manifesto [Cambridge: Cambridge University Press, 1960]). Others such as Fishlow and Fogel have disputed this conclusion and pointed out that railroads lagged behind fundamental developments in the economy, and at least in the early years, largely duplicated the routes of already-existing forms of transportation. According to the Fishlow/Fogel analysis, although the railroad was a very important development in nineteenth-century transportation, alternative forms of transportation could have accommodated the distribution of commodities without substantially affecting the economy's rate of growth. (Albert Fishlow, American Railroads and the Transformation of the Ante-Bellum Economy [Cambridge: Harvard University Press, 1965]; Robert W. Fogel, Railroads and American Economic Growth: Essays in Econometric History [Baltimore: Johns Hopkins University Press, 1964].) The consensus of historians seems, however, to be that the railroad was the most strategic investment and important growth force in the late nineteenth century. See Niemi, U.S. Economic History, pp. 73-91.

2 Urbanization's impact on older Americans, and the changing character of cities by the turn of the century, will be examined later in this chapter.

3 Krooss, American Economic Development, p. 372.

41

combinations of inputs in the production process.[4] Any innovation of such major proportions as the railroad was a potent economic force, for once such a large-scale project was conceived and plans were carried out for its execution, it was possible for other innovative ideas to be explored and implemented. Overcoming obstacles (such as hostility to the new project, or aversion to risk) in the first enterprise allowed for social and psychological barriers to be lowered for other industries.

Fundamentally, what was involved for industrialization to get solidly underway was the need to remake labor both in terms of new skills and habits and in terms of redistribution of the population.[5] In the case of the railroads, the very nature of the prospective future was altered: It took on a character more favorable to individuals and firms with new ideas, and less favorable to individuals and firms whose position was well- entrenched.[6] The criteria for status and success were being gradually but radically altered. No longer would the traditional underpinnings of economic security, ownership of land and leadership through experience, suffice to enable the majority of older Americans to maintain their accustomed control of their economic fate.

As the obstacles to new projects and methods were gradually reduced by the establishment of new railway networks, there followed a wavelike proliferation of many sorts of new enterprises. Region after region was affected by new construction, as national development--spurred by the earlier rail beds and the canal networks and plank roads before them--vastly expanded the horizons of enterprise. The process of railway growth, begun in the 1830s, was continuous to the second decade of the twentieth century, averaging about 10 percent per year for the period.[7]

The ending of the Civil War had established transportation and communication as the nation's preeminent economic and political priorities. Public subsidies to the railway companies between 1865 and 1900, conservatively estimated, exceeded $100 million and 100 million acres of land.[8] The social savings resulting from these allocations were enormous.

---

4 Joseph A. Schumpeter, Business Cycles: A Theoretical, Historical, and Statistical Analysis of the Capitalist Process (New York: McGraw-Hill Book Co., 1939), vol. 1, chapters 3, 7; Schumpeter, The Theory of Economic Development (Cambridge: Harvard University Press, 1934), chapters 2, 6. Schumpeter's analysis of innovations is not, however, a general theory of economic development. Innovations--internal factors which are at work within a given economic system--are joined by external social factors and by growth in population and the level of savings, to bring about economic change (Business Cycles, p. 86).

5 See Allyn A. Young, "Increasing Returns and Economic Progress," The Economic Journal 38 (December 1928):527-542.

6 See Leland H. Jenks, "The Railroads as an Economic Force in American Development," The Journal of Economic History 4 (May 1944): 1-20.

7 Ibid., p. 5.

8 This is according to Edward C. Kirkland, A History of American Economic Life (New York: Appleton-Century-Crofts, 1969), pp. 273-76. Other estimates range considerably higher, for example that of David Ellis, who argued that the railroads used 131 million acres

For example, in 1865 it cost 83 cents to ship 100 pounds of grain from Chicago to New York, but by 1910 the cost was only 9.6 cents. Average rail freight rates dropped from 2.2 cents per ton-mile in 1870 to less than one cent in 1910. A traveler in the mid-1830s required a month to get from New York to Chicago; in the early 1850s the trip took almost two days by rail; and 50 years later, 2 days' train travel took one twice as far, from Chicago to the West Coast.[9]

As the driving force in economic development, the railroads operated as a pacesetter for the national economy by creating a new structure of demand for various factors of production. The adjustment process was one of periodic disruption of the economic structure, and of the activities of individuals and communities. The land requirements for railroad rights-of-way were largely met by the government's granting of new land which had previously had no economic value, so the costs of acquisition were low. However, the coming of the railroad did lead to considerable land speculation, and land booms occurred in communities even before any track was laid. The macroeconomic result was that labor was to a considerable extent distracted from productive to pecuniary activity as many of the nation's great fortunes were made.

As to the railroads' capital needs, the construction phase created an initial demand for durable goods comprising the system's physical stock of plant and equipment, which meant benefits for innovators in such industries as lumber, quarrying, iron milling, and carriage works. This phase of durable goods demand became in turn a demand for wage laborers to mine, quarry, and mill. As wages were spent, markets were expanded and specialization increased in widening ripples of economic activity throughout the nation. In addition, the direct demand for labor power to build the railway network triggered the first waves of immigration, and went a long way toward disciplining the domestic labor force and new arrivals to the requirements of work within large-scale, bureaucratically-managed enterprises.

A final manner in which the railroads were pacesetters for industrial capitalism in the U.S., one which will be elaborated upon in subsequent chapters, was their administrative methods. Such an enormous undertaking as linking widely separated communities and regions required an unprecedented degree of managerial sophistication and specialization.

The railroads were in many respects very different concerns than were factories or even canal systems. In manufacturing, the largest factories were in textiles, of which at

---

of federal land plus 49 million acres of state lands, worth together more than $500 million. (David M. Ellis, "Comments on 'The Railroad Land Grant Legend in American History Texts,'" Mississippi Valley Historical Review 32 (March 1946):557- 63.) Still another historian puts the total of all forms of direct assistance from the public authorities between the 1830s and 1890s at as much as $1.5 billion. (Hacker, Course of American Economic Growth, p. 185.) Different estimates hinge upon the distinction between the number of acres offered and the number actually used; and on whether the land is valued at the nominal price of government land during the era of the land grants ($1.25 per acre), the average selling price of government land at this time (less than $1.00 per acre), or the sale value of the land to the railroads. See Niemi, U.S. Economic History, pp. 84-86.

9 Krooss, American Economic Development, pp. 371-72.

midcentury fewer than 50 had a capitalized value of as much as $500,000. [10] In terms of industry structure, the largest of manufacturing concerns up to the 1860s confined their operations to one or two sites; an entrepreneur or manager could personally visit all departments of an enterprise in a matter of hours, and confer with any worker within minutes. The manager of a canal company had an obviously less localized enterprise to supervise, but duties were limited to routine maintenance and collection of tolls; actual transportation on the canals was done in boats owned by individuals.[11]

Because the railroad companies owned not only the tracks and their rights-of-way, but also owned and operated almost all vehicles using their trackage (extending perhaps many hundreds of miles), no single individual could make an inspection of the enterprise in fewer than several days, and thus close supervision of subalterns was highly impractical. The managerial role was further complicated by the need for a precision of operation as fine as that found in a mass-production factory turning out complex products made of interchangeable parts. Thus, far more than any other capitalist enterprise up to their time, the railroads had to ensure that their workforces were strictly disciplined and subject to rigid regulations in order to minimize costly and potentially fatal mistakes.

This, however, was just the tip of the iceberg. Freight cars had to be kept track of, to make sure they were in the right place at the right time and not contributing to traffic jams or lying idle on a siding; revenues were collected by scores of ticket agents, freight agents and conductors, producing an accounting nightmare which even banks of that time did not face; stockholders demanded profits, yet what would or would not be a profitable service was frequently nearly impossible to ascertain in advance; capital expenditures grew with increased traffic, requiring more equipment, bigger rail yards and terminals, and extended trackage; statistics had to be assembled, maintenance and operating costs estimated, freight and passenger loads predicted, and rates determined.[12]

In many significant ways, then, the impetus to national economic growth provided by the railroads altered the fabric of society, both directly and indirectly. It did so directly by making possible an extended market which was the prerequisite to extensive division of labor in the workforce; and indirectly by influencing factor markets, population settlements, and business combinations, and by demonstrating to others the feasibility of running an enterprise that was diversified and geographically dispersed.

The multiplier effects of the railroad effort, economic and social, are incalculable. But it is probably not an overstatement to suggest that the rail system of the United States was the major influence on what occurred in the economy in the period being examined, and in particular between 1860 and the late 1890s. American (and worldwide) capitalism entered into the long and deep depressions of the 1870s through the 1890s as an essentially

10 Evelyn H. Knowlton, Pepperell's Progress, History of a Cotton Textile Company, 1844-1945 (Cambridge: Harvard University Press, 1948), p. 132.

11 Alfred D. Chandler, Jr., and Stephen Salsbury, "The Railroads: Innovators in Modern Business Administration," in Changing Economic Order, ed. Chandler, Bruchey and Galambos, p. 233.

12 See ibid., pp. 230-57.

competitive, free-market economy and emerged by the years 1902-1905 in the form of consolidated monopoly capitalism.[13]

What resulted was a new emphasis on efficiency, on productivity, and on hierarchical work governed by stringent procedural rules, as well as a significant reduction in viable opportunities for self-employment. There were a fortunate few older workers whose trades had not been substantially altered by the new mix of jobs and skills demanded by this new economic structure, but most were at a severe disadvantage as they confronted the job-supplying bureaucracies late in the nineteenth century. This subject will be taken up again in Chapter 4.

Agriculture: The Older Worker's Last Frontier

The waning fortunes of American farming are an important aspect of older people's diminished opportunities for employment in the period under investigation. Farming was both a means of subsistence and a way of life, whereas industrial work was almost exclusively only the former. Beyond providing for greater individual/family autonomy, farming was typically carried out in a social and community environment which encouraged the networks of mutual aid and emotional support that were particularly vital to older people's well-being. Although the relative decline in agricultural occupations (and therefore rural residence) did not substantially alter the rural community environment, it separated families, as industrial jobs were increasingly pursued by younger generations. Thus much of what had been the mainstay of the elderly's social safety net was removed.

While the United States has never been a labor-surplus economy in the sense meant in the underdevelopment models of W. Arthur Lewis or John Fei and Gustav Ranis,[14] periodically between 1860 and 1920 the American farming sector was oversupplied with labor relative to its requirements. The result was major occupational and geographic shifts during this period, from farming and self-employment into wage-labor status, from jobs relying on skill and experience to those relying on strength and endurance, and from rural areas into growing cities.

Yet throughout the last half of the nineteenth century, the majority of the American population continued to make its living by farming and ancillary crafts. However, a significant drop-off had already occurred since early in the century. Between 1810 and 1850

---

13 This is according to Averitt, The Dual Economy, pp. 9-14. One recent study has argued that the predominantly competitive era in American capitalism was eclipsed by the economy's tendencies toward monopoly control as early as 1895-1896. See Alfred Sohn-Rethel, Intellectual and Manual Labour: A Critique of Epistemology (Atlantic Highlands, N.J.: Humanities Press, 1978), p. 146.

14 See W. Arthur Lewis, "Economic Development with Unlimited Supplies of Labour," The Manchester School of Economic and Social Studies 22 (May 1954):139-91; John C. Fei and Gustav Ranis, Development of the Labor Surplus Economy: Theory and Practice (Homewood, Ill.: Richard D. Irwin, 1964).

the proportion of workers engaged in agricultural pursuits fell from 80 to 55 percent.[15] By 1890, 9.5 million persons (43 percent of the labor force) worked in agriculture, as against 8.5 million in manufactures, mining, transportation, and trade.[16]

This shift resulted in the development of considerable tensions as the forces unleashed by the transformation of the economy from an agricultural to an industrial base made farming more dependent on--if not actually subservient to--the rest of the economy. As subsistence farming became drawn into the market nexus, farmers attempted to accommodate themselves to the evolving methods of production and distribution, with limited success. At stake was a fundamental redefinition of what constituted wealth, status, and progress under the new rules of the game. Most of the nation's wealth in the beginning was invested in agriculture, and the agrarian tradition and way of life were strongly resistant to change, particularly so given the percentages of the population involved.

In 1880, 71.4 percent lived in rural areas (communities of less than 2,500 inhabitants), and 60 percent did so in 1900, comprising 37.5 percent of the employed labor force; by 1920 the population would be 48.6 percent rural, comprising 27 percent of the active labor force.[17] People in places smaller than 2,500 population were of course not all farmers, but all were closely connected with agricultural life and dependent upon farming's vitality for their prosperity.

The Demographics of Agriculture

The 45-and-older age groups were particulary hard-hit by the relative decline in the importance of agriculture during the post-Civil War era, as well as by the farm sector's worsening terms of trade in relation to industry up until the late 1890s. Of the 1.065 million men 65 and older in gainful occupations in the year 1900 (out of a total over-64 male population of 1.56 million), 44.5 percent were employed in agriculture. This represented 56.9 percent of native whites and 40.9 percent of foreign-born whites.[18] For the age group 45-64, 45.4 percent were farmers at the turn of the century, as compared with only 36.7 percent of the 15-44 age group.[19]

15 Stanley Lebergott, Manpower in Economic Growth: The American Record Since 1800 (New York: McGraw-Hill Book Co., 1964), p. 101.

16 Rubinow, The Quest for Security, p. 223.

17 U.S. Bureau of the Census, Historical Statistics of the United States, Colonial Times to 1957 (Washington, D.C.: Government Printing Office, 1960), p. 14. See also Milton L. Barron, The Aging American: An Introduction to Social Gerontology and Geriatrics (New York: Thomas Y. Crowell Co., 1962), p. 32.

18 Rubinow, Social Insurance, pp. 312, 408.

19 Achenbaum, Old Age, p. 67.

Such data as exist on occupational structure by age in this period would seem to indicate that most older Americans chose to stay on the land for as long as possible.[20] A farm in the family was a cushion not only for the old, but also against the random misfortunes experienced by urban relations whose employment was terminated for whatever reason. For example, the depressions of the 1870s and 1890s brought sizable back-to-the-land movements of unemployed city-dwellers, as have all depressions to some extent, although most recession-induced sojourns back to the family homestead were only temporary. But this created further financial strains and contributed to agriculture's dilemma of overproduction and falling prices.

In general, though, younger family members were more likely than their elders to strike out for the opportunities offered by city life and industrial occupations. Mechanical improvements were reducing the need for farm labor, and this phenomenon may have been coupled with a youthful impulse to escape the isolation and monotony of rural life. At any rate, demographers almost universally have noted a tendency for rural areas to become increasingly older in average age in the process of industrialization.[21]

Older farmers whose families were fragmenting in the last half of the nineteenth century had four unattractive options: (1) to lease their lands to tenants, (2) to sell off tracts of land to speculators or newcomers if they could, (3) to follow their offspring into the cities, or (4) to hire farm labor to replace family members who had left (a costly option available only to the most prosperous). But the situation became untenable for older farmers when they faced poor health or disability, for without their children and grand-children nearby to see to their needs, they faced destitution. Charitable societies and voluntary associations had existed since the earliest days of the republic, but were increasingly inadequate to cope with the extent of old age dependency engendered by the forces of industrialization destroying the system of family economy.[22]

The geographic and occupational shifts inherent in the relative decline of farming's importance thus had the greatest impact on the nation's older population. Agriculture was to be effectively the last refuge of older workers seeking to retain some semblance of independence, yet for the first several decades of the period under examination, from 1860 to the mid-1890s, farming in the U.S. was a highly unstable occupation.

---

20 This will be discussed in subsequent chapters.

21 See for example, Ethel Shanas and Marvin B. Sussman, eds., Family, Bureaucracy, and the Elderly (Durham, N.C.: Duke University Press, 1977); Philip M. Hauser and Raul Vargas, "Population Structure and Trends," in Aging in Western Societies, ed. by Ernest W. Burgess (Chicago: University of Chicago Press, 1960), pp. 29-53.

22 See Rubinow, Social Insurance, p. 304; Robert J. Havighurst, "Life Beyond Family and Work," in Aging in Western Societies, ed. by Burgess, p. 303. Chapter 7 will explore some the the political/philosophical issues involved in the national debate over the need for social welfare policies targeted toward the dependent aged.

Overexpansion of Agriculture

The beginnings of the problem of agriculture resided, first, in the nation's land policies. Although ostensibly intended to benefit agriculture and spread the ownership of real property, the record indicates that in the final analysis land distribution was geared to the interests of the railroads, speculators, and the politicians, and worked irreparable harm to farming as a self-employed occupation.[23] Rapid territorial expansion between 1850 and the 1890s encouraged immigration and the westward movement of the indigenous population, but what these new farmers could not appreciate at the time was the degree to which such shifts into farming would increase agricultural output considerably beyond the likely demands of the market.

To a considerable extent foreign markets for commodities had relieved downward pressure on prices early in the nineteenth century, but this outlet had become less effective by late in the century when competition among farmers was virtually worldwide. In Europe, especially in France and Germany, the response to global competition in foodstuffs was a raising of agricultural tariffs, particularly in the 1870s and 1880s. But in the U.S., a net exporter, no such tariff protection was possible.[24] For the typical small-scale farming enterprise, the dilemma was that it was highly productive but barely profitable.

Yet on the prime farming land of the north central states, the average farm size did not shrink as it did for farms generally, but rather grew steadily, from 123.7 acres in 1880 to 171.4 acres in 1920.[25] On these lands, very high land costs (as opposed to large capital requirements) determined tenancy,[26] and the homesteading movement had little impact. Where valuable lands were acquired by homesteaders, tax assessments rose rapidly.[27]

---

23 See Benjamin Horace Hibbard, A History of the Public Land Policies (New York: Macmillan Co., 1924), esp. pp. 539-46 on "Effects of the Land Policies on Agriculture"; Paul W. Gates, "Land Policy and Tenancy in the Prairie States," Journal of Economic History 1 (May 1941):60-82.

24 Some farmers, particularly in the South, were wedded to protective tariffs, receiving direct protection on such output as wool, sugar, hemp, and flax; and others were convinced that the system of tariff protection in general enhanced their prospects in the domestic market. Farmers were thus divided on this issue as on many others. But the majority suffered for the benefit of the few. See Edward Atkinson, "Common Sense Applied to the Tariff Question," Popular Science Monthly 37 (September 1890):593-96.

25 Kirkland History of American Economic Life, p. 490.

26 Ibid., pp. 490-41.

27 C.F. Emerick, "An Analysis of Agricultural Discontent in the United States. I.," Political Science Quarterly 11 (September 1896):433- 63; Emerick, "An Analysis of Agricultural Discontent in the United States. II.," Political Science Quarterly 11 (December 1896):601-39; Theodore Saloutos, "The Agricultural Problem and Nineteenth-Century Industrialism," in Changing Economic Order, ed. Chandler, Bruchey, and Galambos, p. 337;

Up until the end of World War I, farmland prices in general rose even when farm commodity prices were falling, because the agricultural population continued to increase absolutely (although declining relative to urban population) on a fixed quantity of arable land.[28] Furthermore, land speculation in connection with the railroad building boom prevented prices from moderating through the 1890s.[29] Those homesteaders who occupied inferior or remote soil tended to be only marginally engaged in market activity,[30] and their efforts to be economically self-sufficient frequently ended in failure, when they either became tenant farmers and agricultural laborers or moved to the cities.[31]

The opening of new territories to cultivation exacerbated what would at any rate have caused agriculture's fortunes to decline relative to industry. Through the operation of Engel's law, throughout history and in all nations economic development has entailed a declining share of agriculture in total productive enterprise. Because of the low income elasticity of demand for agricultural products, gains in farm productivity created a problem not shared in other sectors: surplus production owing to a slowing rise in demand. In the mid-1870s, city workers on average spent about 58 percent of their incomes on food, but by the close of World War I, the figure had fallen to 41 percent. Compounding this was the agricultural sector's low price elasticity of demand, whereby periodic bouts of overproduction merely drove down prices and reduced farm incomes.

The dilemma confronting those who made their living from the land in the second half of the nineteenth century had both an extensive and intensive dimension. Both the settling of new land and the application of more and better capital to existing farmlands

---

Charles J. Bullock, Selected Readings in Public Finance (Boston: Ginn and Company, 1906), pp. 208-12.

28 Krooss, American Economic Development, p. 139.

29 Kirkland, History of American Economic Life, pp. 376-81; Paul W. Gates, "Frontier Estate Builders and Farm Laborers," in Views of American Economic Growth, 2 vols. (New York: McGraw Hill Book Co., 1966), vol. 2: The Industrial Era, ed. by Thomas C. Cochran and Thomas B. Brewer, pp. 136-40.

30 In fact, as late as the 1850s, when commercial farming was already widespread, it was far from universal even in well established parts of the northeast. One anonymous commentator estimated that the typical Connecticut River Valley farmer in 1853 spent $100 a year in cash (compared with $10 in 1820) and was still producing on his own farm most of what he needed. Cited by Krooss, American Economic Development, p. 119.

31 See Gates, "Frontier Estate Builders," pp. 136-47; Saloutos, "The Agricultural Problem," pp. 335-55. At the other end of the scale from modest family farms were the "bonanza farms" of the 1870s and 1880s. These were farms of several thousand acres (some in the millions of acres in the southwest) that were owned by members of the Eastern elite who were enchanted by the spirit of bigness everywhere evident in industry and who sought to emulate the new methods on the land. Most of these huge farms died out by the depression of the 1890s, but in the interim any commonality of these land monopolists with the typical farm family was mere happenstance.

increased the food supply much more rapidly than the growth of domestic demand. Although nearly 3.5 million workers left the agricultural sector betwen 1870 and 1900, the attractions of homesteading caused the number of farms to double in that period, from nearly 2.66 million to over 5.73 million.[32] At the same time the number of acres making up the average farm fell sharply with westward expansion, from 199.2 acres in 1860 to 146.2 acres in 1900. [33] On all but the best lands, a farm of the latter size was a marginal enterprise. Improvements in farming technology served to widen the gap between the most successful enterprises and the agricultural majority.

Mechanization in Agriculture

In the 1860-1920 period, the number of persons fed per American farmer nearly doubled.[34] Agriculture in the U.S. mirrored a distinctive feature of American innovation, which was directed toward making possible the exploitation of large quantities of natural resources with relatively little labor; or toward substituting units of the abundant factor for units of the scarce factor (labor, and to a lesser extent capital). To this end, a major thrust of farming innovation after the Civil War was toward increasing the acreage that could be cultivated per farmer.

To a significant extent this was accomplished by substituting animal power for human power, but it also necessitated an increase in capital-intensiveness. In cereal production (corn, wheat and oats), output more than trebled between 1840 and 1910. According to one careful study, some 60 percent of this increase could be attributed to mechanization which raised the acreage-to-labor ratio, and virtually all of the productivity growth in the period was owing to the combination of mechanization and westward territorial expansion.[35]

----

32 Hadley W. Quaintance, "The Influence of Machinery on the Economic and Social Conditions of the Agricultural People," in Cyclopedia of American Agriculture, ed. by L.H. Bailey (New York: Macmillan Co., 1907-1909), 4:109.

33 U.S. Bureau of the Census, Statistical Abstract of the United States (Washington, D.C.: Government Printing Office, 1904), p. 509.

34 Walton and Robertson, History of the American Economy, p. 361.

35 William N. Parker and J.L.V. Klein, "Productivity Growth in Grain Production in the U.S., 1840-60 and 1900-10," in Output, Employment and Productivity in the U.S. After 1800, ed. by Dorothy S. Brady (New York: National Bureau of Economic Research, 1966), pp. 523-82. Of course this process rested fundamentally upon earlier developments and improvements in transportation; in addition to the railroads, the iron steamship and refrigeration had by the close of the nineteenth century taken routine commerce well beyond national borders, producing a high degree of regional agricultural specialization worldwide. See A.J. Youngson, "The Opening of New Territories," in The Cambridge Economic History of Europe (Cambridge: Cambridge University Press, 1965), vol. 6: The Industrial Revolutions and After: Incomes, Population and Technological Change, pp. 139-211. Cited by Rosenberg, Technology and American Economic Growth, p. 26.

To the extent that overproduction of farm commodities was the proximate cause of farm distress, mechanization would appear to be the most significant determinant of the large increase in farm output. Thus, at the same time as the conditions for success or even just survival in farming were being altered by market activity, farmers were being forced to attempt to expand and mechanize in order to lower their unit costs to compete with the expanded volume of commodities produced on newly-settled lands as well as with farm output from other nations. But individual farmers could not effectively capture the economies afforded industry by mass production and distribution. Farmers' attempts at expansion and mechanization increased their debt and financing difficulties, as well as resulting in the recurrent commodity gluts which kept the returns to agriculture precariously low on all but the largest and best-managed farms.[36]

Mechanization and improved methods led to rising productivity and superior crops, particularly grains. But the gains from mechanization were primarily labor-saving rather than increases in yields per acre. For example, the wheat yield per acre averaged 15 bushels in 1900 compared to 13.9 in 1840, but the person-hours per 100 bushels fell in that period from 233 to 108. [37] Corn yields showed only somewhat smaller improvements from mechanization; the introduction of the cultivator in the 1860s, replacing the hoe, and of the corn picker in the 1890s, were responsible for major reductions in needed labor inputs.[38] Even cotton, which did not benefit as greatly from mechanization, posted improved yields as a result of its extensive cultivation in newly opened areas of the southwest, combined with the increased use of fertilizers.[39]

Thus, the major impact of technological change in farming was a substantial reduction in the number of hands necessary to produce any given volume of output. The most striking improvements were made in what previously had been the most labor-intensive operations, harvesting and post-harvesting work: 70 percent of the total gains from mechanization were due to only two innovations, the thresher and the reaper.[40]

John Kendrick has estimated that as a result of the spread of farming technology, output per unit combined inputs increased by about 50 percent between 1860 and 1899.[41] The majority of this increased productivity was attributable to the movement of surplus workers toward urban centers, as machines took over many time-consuming tasks. In the first two decades of the twentieth century, agricultural productivity growth virtually ceased,

36 Saloutos, "The Agricultural Problem," p. 342; Paul W. Gates, "Discussion of Theodore Saloutos' paper, 'Land Policy and its Relation to Agricultural Production, 1862-1933,'" Journal of Economic History 22 (December 1962):473-76.

37 Peterson and Gray, Economic Development of the United States, p. 287.

38 Parker and Klein, "Productivity Growth," p. 544.

39 Peterson and Gray, Economic Development of the United States, p. 287.

40 Parker and Klein, "Productivity Growth," p. 544.

41 John W. Kendrick, Productivity Trends in the United States (Princeton: Princeton University Press, 1961), pp. 362-67.

as innovations were almost exclusively focused on the industrial sector.[42] Partly as a result, the period 1900-1920 was one in which American agriculture's downward fortunes were temporarily reversed.

Agriculture and Industry

As a result of the interplay of technology and westward expansion, the terms of trade between agriculture and industry were changing in industry's favor for the three decades after the close of the Civil War. Up to the late 1890s agricultural prices were falling relative to industrial prices. Farmers in general suffered a double burden in the last half of the nineteenth century. The fall in farm prices would have hurt them as debtors even if industrial prices had fallen proportionately, but the widening gap between industry and agriculture merely made things worse. The typical farmer in this period not only sold cheap but bought dear because the products of agriculture simply did not command the premiums that finished goods did.[43]

So American farmers mounted a broad attack on the "monopoly power" which kept prices high against them--in particular the railroads, the banks, and the industrial mergers and trusts. Farmers became ardent free traders (reasoning that if the rules of the game that applied to them were broadly in effect, their situation would necessarily improve), and were the leading opponents of industrial tariffs.[44] Their associations, far-flung and lacking even regional cohesiveness, were the underpinnings of the Populist political movement that thrived in the U.S. in the last quarter of the nineteenth century.

Of course, not all farmers were equally harmed by the changing terms of trade in this period. Midwestern farmers may have gained as much from falling freight rates between 1870 and 1890 as they lost in lower wheat prices. Furthermore, the farm sector comprising the largest and most scientifically-run farms was benefitting from the productivity gains from mechanization. But enough of the agricultural labor force was negatively affected to generate a substantial protest movement.[45]

Industry benefitted from the farmers' situation. Inexpensive raw materials were almost as vital to minimizing production costs as was the supply of immigrant labor. The farmers' low profits translated into higher profits for industry. Falling agricultural prices

---

42 Ibid.

43 Although farm (money) wages rose slowly and steadily after 1850, their rate of growth was far below that of industrial wages: 30 percent between 1850 and 1900, compared to 70 percent off the farm. Krooss, American Economic Development, p. 138.

44 Emerick, "Analysis of Agricultural Discontent. II.", p. 639.

45 Lewis, Growth and Fluctuations, p. 27. In this political domain, too, the U.S. differed from Europe. In industrializing England, Germany and France, radicalism and political activism were urban, working-class phenomena, whereas in the U.S. it was the large farming population (still 43 percent of the labor force in 1890) which provided the impetus to mass democratic politics. The urban workforce would take up the cause in the first 15 years of the twentieth century, when the rate of growth of real wages in industry slowed sharply.

meant a lowering of food prices paid by industrial workers, so that wages paid by industry were lower than they otherwise would have been; alternatively, more remained of workers' wages after buying necessities, so they could purchase manufactured goods. Manufacturers' receipts were enhanced either way.

While proclaiming the farmer the backbone of the nation, the industrialists, as part of a smaller and more cohesive group, methodically went about getting their way in the halls of Congress and in state legislatures. The result was public policies amenable to manufacturing interests and harmful to agriculture: open immigration, high protective tariffs on finished goods, and a tax system which placed most of the burden on farmers and industrial laborers.[46] The final straw for farmers was that they were at the mercy of whatever freight rates the railroads chose to set; yet paradoxically, even low freight rates could be undesirable because they served to draw more acres into cultivation and intensify the competition.[47]

When the farmers got around to organizing, it was too little, too late. The interests of agriculture were simply too diverse and conflicting, and its practitioners too widely separated in geography, crop specialization, and economic circumstances. Finally, most farms were too small to make organizing appear practicable. Many of the failures in agriculture were doubtless inevitable. Some farms were not located with an eye to proximity to major distribution and purchasing points; others were underfunded by migrants lacking sufficient savings, credit-worthiness, or access to capital markets; many were simply badly managed or operated without a basic familiarity with farming principles.[48] But the failures were not all self-inflicted; an undetermined number were merely the result of an

---

46 A uniform tax on property had been put in place at a time when real property comprised the great majority of the national wealth, and when personal property consisted of items which were readily visible to the tax assessor, such as domestic livestock, implements, structures, etc. By the second half of the nineteenth century, however, this index of ability to pay was outmoded (yet it was not until 1913 that the tax code caught up with material circumstances and greater equity was restored to the system).

The increasing complexity of business enterprise, as the number of banks, manufacturing, and commercial establishments mushroomed, made possible sizable increases in personal property values which escaped taxation. Most such property was located in cities, where its owners were more readily able to avoid the assessors. See Edwin R.A. Seligman, Essays in Taxation, 9th ed. (London, Macmillan and Co., 1913), p. 15.

47 Saloutos, "The Agricultural Problem," pp. 344-45.

48 There was, as well, the motive of greed which drove many Americans to acquire low-priced land following the passage of the Homestead Act. Farming was not the primary interest or intention, according to Paul Gates, of a large but unknown proportion of homesteaders. These migrants sought out cheap land with an eye to future sale at attractive prices, but because land values rose more slowly than expected, they became farmers largely by default. They were almost by definition not good farmers. See Paul W. Gates, "Discussion of Theodore Saloutos' paper, 'Land Policy and its Relation to Agricultural Production,'" Journal of Economic History (December 1962):473.

implicit governmental policy of neglect of the farm sector, coupled with the inexorable decline in the importance of agriculture in a nation undergoing industrialization.

Eventually, after the mid-1890s, the farm sector's fortunes reversed temporarily, as the gains from mechanization slowed and farm output lagged behind population growth. This situation lasted only until the deep farm depression of 1920, and was an aberration in the long secular decline in American agricultural prosperity. One of the last havens for older workers had begun to provide only an erratic and tenuous livelihood, a pattern that continues to this day.

The Growth of Cities

Throughout the 1860-1920 period, as the factory rather than the farm increasingly determined in which direction the nation moved, there occurred a significant shift of population toward urban centers. In 1860 fewer than 20 percent of Americans lived in cities or towns of 2,500 or more, but by 1900 this figure was 40 percent. By 1920, the Census reported that for the first time more than half of the population (51.4 percent) were urban dwellers. This demographic shift coupled with population growth increased the number of urban dwellers from 6.2 million in 1860 to 54.2 million in 1920. [49]

Demographics of Urbanization

The migration of rural inhabitants into towns and cities, the centers first of commerce and then of manufacturing, had long been a characteristic of New England and the Middle Atlantic states. Indeed, the decade of 1810-1820 was the only one in American history in which the urban population did not grow faster than the rural population.[50] The industrial population was still quite small as of 1860, yet by 1870 its rate of growth had leaped ahead; in that decade the farm labor force grew only 15.3 percent compared to a 61.4 percent growth in the manufacturing labor force. In 1860 famers outnumbered manufacturing workers three to one; by 1920 there were nearly the same number of each.[51]

The Midwest, traditional heartland of American agriculture, was most rapidly transformed. In the 1880-1890 decade, Chicago's population doubled, at the expense of rural regions from Iowa to Ohio, from half a million to a million, making it the second largest city in the nation. This was the decade of most rapid growth in both the number of cities (population 2,500 or greater) and in urban population.[52]

In the South, the regroupings of industrialization bore a resemblance to New England's experience a century earlier, as prejudice among whites against factory work was broken down. By 1900 cotton mills began to have difficulty attracting marginal farmers into

---

49 U.S. Department of Commerce, Historical Statistics of the United States (Washington, D.C.: Government Printing Office, 1960), p. 14.

50 Krooss, American Economic Development, p. 108.

51 Walton and Robertson, History of the American Economy, p. 435.

52 Peterson and Gray, Economic Development of the United States, p. 309.

54

mill villages as either permanent or seasonal operatives, so advertisements began to be circulated in rural areas farther afield, painting an attractive picture of industrial life. Agents, sometimes accompanied by satisfied workers, were sent out to enlist workers from among the mountain farmers and the poor farmers of the coastal plains.[53]

Such overt bidding for factory labor was probably relatively rare. At any rate, outside the South the move to the cities was a natural response to changing economic opportunities. Like everything else about this period, urbanization was also part of the westward movement. Three of the nation's ten largest cities in 1890 (St. Louis, San Francisco, and Cincinnati) had scarcely existed in 1850. The proportion of the population living in cities larger than 100,000 increased from five percent of the population in 1850, when there were six cities, to almost 19 percent in 1900, when there were 38. [54]

Urbanization and Industrial Structure

The urban transformation as it related to the processes of production and the nature of work will be examined in the chapters that follow. But first it will be shown how urbanization per se contributed to the forces revolutionizing the economy and its impact on the status of older Americans. It did this in two ways.

First, there emerged in the markets spawned by cities a new type of consumer-goods industry producing both altogether new products and traditional ones turned out by new methods. The firms in these consumer industries formed themselves into large combinations of vertically-integrated enterprises to achieve production and marketing economies. This happened in the meat, flour, and tobacco industries as well as in the newer manufacturing industries turning out guns, clocks, sewing machines, typewriters, farm implements and other appliances.

Second, an even more striking concomitant of the growth of cities occurred in heavy industry, in the growth of demand for producer goods. Prior to the Civil War there had been relatively little need for copper, steel, power machinery, and so forth, to build sewer and water systems which were for the most part provided for the wealthy by private companies.[55] Urbanization brought a steadily rising demand for such facilities, followed by other new demands for gas lighting, telephone and power lines, street railways, and the construction materials needed for steel-frame skyscrapers by the late 1880s. These new needs resulted in large, centrally-controlled, vertically-integrated firms overseeing vast operations ranging from the raw materials stage to finished products.

These enormous enterprises and the ancillary businesses they spawned were a powerful magnet drawing people (primarily but not exclusively immigrants) to cities for the jobs and higher standards of living they offered. In this sense, urbanization, together with the spread of the factory system itself, was a manifestation of a "peculiarity" in the supply and

---

53 Kirkland, History of American Economic Life, pp. 515-16.

54 Hacker, Course of American Economic Growth, p. 241.

55 Walton and Robertson, History of the American Economy, pp. 426-27.

demand for labor that was pointed out by Alfred Marshall.[56] An individual selling his services as a commodity has to present himself where those services are to be delivered, unlike the merchant selling material goods who is able to send them on. The buyer of labor services need not be present to receive them, and indeed, in the case of the corporate business form in particular, might be utterly ignorant of the conditions under which he is repeatedly making the purchase.

This asymmetry in the market for labor has everywhere created industrial cities characterized by enormous working-class enclaves or ghettos in proximity to the giant plants where employment was concentrated. Within these enclaves, labor tended to be highly immobile in a geographic sense. The owners of capital and the professional classes congregated in neighborhoods at as great a remove as possible from the manufacturing center while still allowing access to the amenities of city life.[57]

The Changing Nature of Cities

A further important development in urbanization was the changing character of cities themselves. In 1860 the "large" American cities--there were nine with populations of 100,000 or more--had been commercial, not industrial. New York, Baltimore, Boston, Pittsburgh, Chicago, and others, were all seaports, river towns, or lake towns. Not until after 1875 did these older cities also become significant industrial centers, with the undifferentiated merchant capitalist being supplanted by the specialized industrial capitalist.[58] Many of the newly emerging large cities were almost wholly industrial, their existence and fortunes tied to the railroad network and to the dominant attribute of the industrial age, specialization of labor function. Thus, Minneapolis meant flour-milling; Kansas city, meatpacking; New Haven, guns and clockmaking; Paterson, New Jersey, silk mills; and so forth.[59]

This changing character of cities had important labor market consequences. Cities oriented toward commerce (transportation, distribution, marketing) were readily compatible with a wide range of opportunities for employment in small, autonomous plants and shops geared to the needs and attributes of both customers and workers. Such conditions are major influences on the degree of employment security for workers of middle age and beyond.

---

56 Alfred Marshall, Principles of Economics, 8th ed. (London: Macmillan and Co., 1930), pp. 566-67.

57 Interestingly, surburbia, which is commonly thought to be a post-World War II phenomenon, had reached significant proportions by 1890 in response to the extremely high population density in the most congested urban areas. Commuting had occurred as early as 1850, and had become commonplace in the nineties, largely owing to a major technological breakthrough of the previous decade, the urban electric trolley. Krooss, American Economic Development, p. 108.

58 Hacker, Course of American Economic Growth, p. 240.

59 Carl Bridenbaugh, Cities in the Wilderness (New York: Alfred A. Knopf, 1938).

Industrial cities had a quite different character. They were dominated to a far greater extent by large, impersonal economic organizations seeking only to maximize profits. They did this as much by streamlining and routinizing their methods of management and administration as by making use of available technology to produce quality products to meet an established or perceived demand. Later chapters will explore in depth the sometimes subtle distinction between the technological and organizational imperatives at work during the industrial era. What is important at this point is to note that the changing character of cities went hand in hand with precisely those alterations of the economic landscape which were to put older people at a disadvantage in seeking and retaining employment and economic security.

Urbanization and the Elderly

For older Americans, the nation's industrialization was almost as consequential for economic and family life as were the changes in the structure of industry and growing dominance of hierarchical enterprises. To be sure, more older Americans at the turn of the century continued to make their living from farming than in any other occupation. But the family labor system which prevailed in agriculture was itself being altered by the magnet of the cities.

Variations on the extended family had always been more typical of rural than of urban living, but younger family members increasingly eschewed the parochialism and paternalism of rural life and sought new opportunities in urban areas. The nation's urbanization was to contribute to the economic insecurity and isolation of older people as family members. Population concentrations in urban areas separated family members from each other as dwellings shrank in size with greater density, and family members increasingly made their livings in diverging occupations.

The closing of the frontier in the 1890s significantly reduced the degree of internal migration that had characterized westward expansion, although some newly-arrived immigrants continued to head west. But the cities by that time were indisputably the locus of the preponderance of production, job openings, and economic growth. With the growth of cities, older people were faced with the "iron law" of the increase of old age dependency under a system of wage labor.

The negative social and economic consequences of aging were most striking in the industrialized areas, for in rural areas such changes occurred much more slowly and less noticeably.[60] Gerontological research indicates that, other things being equal, stability of residence and occupational structure tends to suggest a high status for the elderly, while mobility tends to undermine it.[61] The growing importance of cities, with their heightened

---

60 Indeed, the roles of older Americans in many rural communities are very little different today than they were a century ago. (Havighurst, "Life Beyond Family and Work," p. 303.)

61 Yet urban residents do not necessarily have a monopoly on mobility. For example, early hunting and gathering peoples were also highly mobile, and their mobility seems to have produced a lower status for the aged as compared with the more settled, primitive

interpersonal competitiveness, social stratification, and anonymity, placed greater emphasis and value on occupational or economic mobility. In this domain, the majority of older Americans were at a competitive disadvantage. Even had they not tended--in contrast to the young--to cling to pre-industrial attitudes and methods, they were widely viewed as being unable to conform to modern ways. They began to be ghettoized in urban areas, a phenomenon that persists to this day.

Furthermore, not only stability of residence has historically fostered a high status for the old, but also, as noted earlier, ownership of property, particularly in land. In agriculture, where people have commonly had highly developed concepts of property, the effort to save for old age usually took the form of acquiring property rights in land. Down to the present, ownership of property has been a hedge against economic dependency. As one study of the subject has noted, "To the extent that old people have been...able to retain their rights to property...[they have maintained] not only economic security but also prestige and power."[62]

The shifting economic climate and social values that accompanied the industrialization/urbanization process confronted older Americans with a paradox. To the extent that they maintained ownership of real property, their status was to some degree safeguarded. But such ownership was rooted in an agrarian value system that was increasingly irrelevant to the new order; it no longer conferred prestige or influence over the behavior of others as it once had.

Within cities, the democratization of property ownership, in the form of consumption of personal commodities and aspirations of home ownership, represented real gains for the average working person, both in living standards and in economic security (security being somewhat narrowly defined, that is, so long as they had stable employment). But it also constituted a relative devaluation of the older generations whose property claims were established in accordance with earlier norms. On the other hand, the price of greater geographic rootedness implied by property ownership was, as Engels noted,[63] a restricted freedom of movement once people were dependent for their livelihoods upon mass, impersonal economic organizations. And again, in such settings older workers were to be devalued on account of their age from the first phases of corporate capitalism.

Urbanization and Consumerism

Within cities, property ownership as a symbol of socioeconomic success took new forms. In the last quarter of the nineteenth century, with the spread of wage labor and

---

agricultural societies. Donald O. Cowgill, "A Theory of Aging in Cross-Cultural Perspective," in Aging and Modernization, ed. by Donald O. Cowgill and Lowell D. Holmes (New York: Appleton-Century-Crofts, 1972), p. 10.

62 Ibid. See also Irving Rosow, "And Then We Were Old," Transaction/Society 2 (January-February 1965):10; Erdman B. Palmore and Kenneth Manton, "Modernization and Status of the Aged: International Comparisons," Journal of Gerontology 29 (1974):205-10.

63 Friedrich Engels, The Housing Question (1872), in Marx- Engels Selected Works, Vol. 2, 5th ed. (Moscow: Foreign Language Press, 1958).

the effective disappearance of self-sufficiency for the majority of Americans, many observers became alarmed about workers' insecurity. The dependence theme, in particular workers' progressive loss of meaningful status through labor, became a major element in social philosophy.[64] As older values and aspirations were collapsing, and new roles and relationships were being defined, the stability of American society (always less than in most other cultures) appeared threatened. What was needed was a new set of arrangements that would bind the working classes to the emerging economic environment.

The solution proved to be a supplanting of the traditional goals and symbols of success--independence and social mobility--by the new hallmarks of achievement--home ownership and possessions. Business interests accordingly emphasized the fact that industrialization made possible low-cost production of items previously accessible only to the wealthy. It raised real wages as productivity increased, and granted the workers a higher standard of living than had been possible under a system of hand labor. For most Americans, progress was increasingly measured by the average citizen's ability to amass possessions only recently considered luxuries. Thus, as one labor historian has expressed it, "...the anxious consumer replaced...the independent artisan"[65] as the mainstay of the economic system.

Consumerism, then, became a dominant feature of the urban economy. In particular, more and more members of the urban working class began to pursue the goal of owning their own small house and lot. Business interests regarded the spread of home ownership as a healthy trend, because it helped tie workers to the existing system by incorporating both tangible assets and less tangible (but no less real) status. As Engels and others noted, home ownership helped keep a check upon radical sentiments, since once a worker became a member, however marginal, of the property-holding classes, he was much less likely to challenge those owning yet more property, for fear that his own holdings could be harmed. Furthermore, workers who had to make monthly mortgage payments would undoubtedly be more docile and fearful of dismissal than workers paying rent.

Most important of all, perhaps, home ownership, by greatly reducing labor's geographical mobility, made it easier for employers to secure workers at the wages they were willing to pay. In realization of this fact, many city workers whose jobs were not secure, or who did not possess vital skills, were loath to consider acquiring a home. Such a tie to real estate would strip away one of the few ways they had of dealing with unpleasant or terminated employment--their physical mobility.[66] On the other hand, from the point of view of the owners and managers of firms, home ownership by workers not only made workers more dependent but it further encouraged spending on household consumption, and thus created markets for the waves of commodities unleashed by industrialization.

The intensification of market activity which accompanied urbanization indirectly fostered a new definition of poverty, that is, relative deprivation. Although poverty has

---

64 See, for example, Tishler, Self-Reliance and Social Security; Yellowitz, The Position of the Worker in American Society; Roy Lubove, The Struggle for Social Security, 1900-1935 (Cambridge: Harvard University Press, 1968).

65 Yellowitz, Industrialization, p.42.

66 Yellowitz, Position of the Worker, p. 27.

always been defined in a social context as well as by absolutist criteria, with urbanization, poverty took new forms. The conditions of modern industry failed to provide motives for saving for the future that were sufficiently strong to take the place of those that were disappearing. In particular, the saving goal of enabling the following generations to inherit the family enterprise in ever-better financial shape--both for the sake of the heirs and to ensure that the elders would be looked after in their nonproducing years--was now weakened.

One consequence of people's living closely together in cities was an expansion of insistent demands for better food, living conditions, educational opportunities, and so forth, to keep up with others. By daily observing the habits of those better off, urban Americans experienced constant pressure to advance their standards of consumption at the expense of putting something by for the future. Thus people "confronted with the problem of supporting a family in a modern city" found the cost of living always to be "as Mark Twain has said 'a little more than you've got.'"[67]

Even middle-class Americans who could have saved a part of their income for old-age security were unlikely to do so. Voluntary savings were uncommon, and compulsory savings plans unpopular (see Chapter 7). The majority of people, according to Fischer, appear to have existed "only for the economic moment," even while the clergy stressed the gospel of saving and teachers drove home the lessons of thrift. "Americans borrowed and bought beyond the limit of their means," evidencing the "national attitude which H.G. Wells called our 'optimistic fatalism.'"[68]

With increasing urbanization, the older, outmoded measures of a worker's success, his independence and mobility, had stood in the way of the growth of large capitalist enterprises. However, the new measures, homes and material possessions, uniquely served the interests of the purveyors of merchandise, while at the same time having enough appeal, as Yellowitz has phrased it, to "win the sufficiency of approval from wage earners necessary for any status symbol to be effective."[69] The new standards for gauging success and status thus enabled the conversion of artisans into industrial wage-labor by creating social values that could bind the workers to the new economic order.

At the same time, urbanization put new pressures on the elderly via the structure of families themselves. In agricultural settings, the bad times might be gotten through with equal sacrifice by either greater exploitation of the family system of economy or by spreading receipts more thinly over the family unit to include more and less productive members. Urbanization and the phenomena that accompanied it--such as smaller dwellings, weakened intergenerational employment patterns, improved hygiene and medical knowledge and thus greater attention to family planning--placed a greater burden on families seeking to provide for their older, less employable members.

---

67 H. R. Seager, "Social Insurance," pp. 10-11, incomplete citation by Abraham Epstein, Facing Old Age: A Study of Old Age Dependency in the U.S. and Old Age Pensions (New York: Alfred A. Knopf, 1922), p. 6.

68 Fischer, Growing Old, pp. 164-65.

69 Yellowitz, Industrialization, p. 43.

The Fragmentation of the Family as an Economic Unit

The increase in the numbers and proportions of people living in cities contributed to old-age poverty by rupturing family ties that had once provided economic security. With growing specialization of labor, the spread of mechanized and rationalized industry, and the growth of firm size, an ever larger percentage of workers were being separated from their traditional skills. Wage-earners faced diminished employment opportunities with advancing age, and thus lost the power to determine the extent and timing of their withdrawal from the labor force. Thus in the urban family older people lost much of their economic function. It is also likely that the tensions increased between them and their adult children because of the generally unsatisfactory living conditions in the cities, compounded by the growing uselessness and economic burden of the older generations.

The length of time an individual spends as an economically active member of the population is a function of several forces, all of which correlate with the economic and social progress of the nation. Prior to industrialization,[70] judgments as to when to work, for how long, and how hard resided exclusively with the individual and the family.

In 1860 this typically meant that such decisions were made by male heads of households, whose authority could be removed only by death. The family unit provided the older worker with virtually the only economic security available. Real property ownership, and ownership in the means of production, were widely distributed along age/status lines, and older people were able to protect their power and defend their interests through ownership and management of private businesses. As noted earlier, such decision-making authority vested in the older generation often exerted a powerful form of economic coercion on the next generation. But such inequities were sanctioned by the power of custom and tradition, were considered part of the natural order, and at any rate gave younger generations (younger males, at any rate) something to look forward to.

Contributing substantially to the economic status of older people had been the fact that they were needed--if not always as decision-makers, then as another pair of hands. In 1860, the U.S. was not yet so wealthy as a nation, nor its inhabitants so prosperous as individuals, that they could afford to dispense with the services of the healthy old.[71] Despite the striking economic and demographic growth that had occurred in the first half of the nineteenth century, the country in 1860 was still undeveloped and short of manpower compared with Europe. Everyone worked who could do so.[72]

---

70 And in the absence of legislation stipulating compulsory school attendance, of accreditation/certification requirements, and of such social constructs as mandatory retirement.

71 Rosow, "And Then We Were Old," p. 23.

72 This is corroborated by recent cross-national studies which demonstrate an inverse relationship between average per capita income and the average number of hours worked per year, or in other words, between the level of industrial development and the proportion of life spent in employment. See, for example, Juanita M. Kreps, Lifetime Allocation of Work and Income: Essays in the Economics of Aging (Durham, N.C.: Duke University Press, 1971), pp. 15, 48, passim.

Most of the population still lived in non-urban environments where economic relations were fairly simple and clear-cut. Markets could be the ultimate arbiter of relative success or failure, but the essential interdependencies among people resided at the level of the family production unit. The much-vaunted individualism of Americans appears not to have penetrated to the level of the individual family member until around the turn of the twentieth century; rather, it was the family that was self-reliant and sought to maintain its autonomy and independence through its economic activity.[73]

In and near the cities, the rupture of the family economy was a more-or-less natural response to competitive pressures. Small, privately-held businesses frequently could not be sustained in the face of spreading changes in the organization of work in factories, which increased efficiency and lowered production costs.

To be sure, the move from the independent shop to the employ of capitalists did not necessarily entail the immediate loss of authority and economic function for the previously self-employed older worker. In the early days of the the period following the Civil War, the father or grandfather sometimes could, as a skilled workman in his own right, take his children with him into the factory and continue to provide training to adult sons and supervise younger children, with only the location of work substantiallly different than before. In this way, his parental authority was transferred into the factory, and traditional ties were preserved among the generations.[74]

However, such circumstances must have been relatively rare, or in any event short-lived, as greater rationalization of production and division of labor were introduced. For the less skilled, or for those whose crafts were rapidly being rendered obsolete by mach-

---

73 Indeed, the traits of independence, self-reliance, etc., had been powerfully reinforced by the mode of production, and were most ballyhooed in political and social rhetoric at precisely the time when the modes of work which they reinforced were being overthrown by industrialization. Such "American" qualities may have been greatly exaggerated and romanticized. Michael Maccoby, David Riesman and others have pointed out that the independence of many Americans in the nineteenth century was antisocial, sternly authoritarian, and emotionally childish; and it was bought at the expense of a compulsive submission to past traditions. See Michael Maccoby, The Gamesman: Winning and Losing at the Career Game (New York: Bantam Books, 1978), p. 85; citing David Riesman, The Lonely Crowd: A Study of the Changing American Character (New Haven: Yale University Press, 1950).

It must be remembered, however, that much of American economic growth and development, so far as individuals and families were concerned, took place on the frontiers of civilized society. Isolation and harsh conditions, before the coming of the railroad, no doubt bred a self-reliance rooted in a fair degree of suspiciousness, stubbornness, and uncooperativeness with respect to "outsiders." To the extent that this was the case, the family unit was all the more important as a source of stability and security. The family was the production unit, consumption unit, school, church, and social safety net all rolled into one. So when work in the home was replaced by wage-work outside the home, what was lost was considerably more than self-employment, it was an entire way of life.

74 Matilda White Riley, "Social Gerontology and the Age Stratification of Society," in Growing Old in America, ed. by Beth B. Hess (New Brunswick, N.J.: Transaction Books, 1976), p. 472.

inery, the separation from the family role served to reinforce the loss of economic independence. As the older worker lost out in the competitive labor market, he lost status in the eyes of those who had looked up to him as a provider, and at the same time he threatened to become a burden on the younger generations.

When families began, even in rural areas, to be fragmented through the work process (although not necessarily immediately in actual living arrangements), the gerontocracy that had granted high stature to older Americans collapsed. Whereas younger family members could still think of their bondage to the factory system as something temporary, to tide them over until they established themselves in business, older factory workers confronted the fact that they had few remaining years in which to realize an improvement in their employment situation. Urban living offered few opportunities for household occupation in retirement as compared to the many chores and responsibilities of the elderly in rural society. In addition, in cities the family as well as former work associates and friends were likely to be scattered, rather than close by as in small towns and rural communities.

Professional dispersion among family members required geographical dispersion, and when the town family itself grew old, it too found itself separated from the children, at least from a housing standpoint.[75] The small size of residences in the city made inclusion of the elderly within the family circle increasingly difficult. Rents were high, so frequently there was no alternative to greater crowding. Yet it appears that older family members still in good health preferred if possible to maintain separate quarters, for this was the final statement of independence.

Early census data on the aged's household status in various localities (Buffalo in 1855, rural Indiana in 1880, and Massachusetts in 1885-1895) indicate that the old placed a premium on separate quarters and typically relied upon kin for assistance only when such an arrangement was no longer possible.[76] The number of older persons living alone, without a spouse[77] began to rise in the country's urban areas in the late nineteenth century.[78] Furthermore, the impact of urban industrial culture on birth and death rates was to magnify the numbers and proportions of the older age groups. The percentage of older people (65 and older) was gradually on the rise, from slightly over two percent in 1860 to 4.7 percent by 1920.[79]

The literature of sociology and social gerontology suggests that something very subtle was going on regarding age relations within the American family, particularly in urban areas, in the late nineteenth and early twentieth centuries. It is possible that a shift from the elder-dominated to the child-centered family was largely an incidental outcome of

---

75 See Ernest W. Burgess, "Family Structure and Relationships," in Aging in Western Societies, ed. by Ernest W. Burgess (Chicago: University of Chicago Press, 1960), p. 272.

76 Achenbaum, Old Age, p. 80.

77 Early widowhood was common.

78 See Havighurst, "Life Beyond Family and Work," p. 303.

79 W. Andrew Achenbaum, "The Obsolescence of Old Age in America," Journal of Social History 8 (Fall 1974):52.

improvements in public health and of contraception which, respectively, reduced infant mortality and ensured that children born were planned for. Hence a phenomenon everywhere apparent with urbanization was a marked decline in birth rates. This is in part because the costs of having children rise in cities, but in late nineteenth-century America it was also influenced by the greater likelihood of children's survival. Parents could invest considerable emotional capital in offspring who were consciously desired and likely to survive to adulthood.

An additional relevant factor was a direct consequence of the industrial revolution. As the workplace became separate from the home with the growth of firms and the transition to wage-labor status, the division of labor within the family became also a division of space. Whether women worked outside the home or not, the household became more exclusively the sphere of the wife/mother than had been the case when the home was the locus of production, while the world of work was more the province of the husband/father who had greater earning power. The result of this labor specialization was a sort of professionalization of motherhood and household management by early in the twentieth century, led off by the families of comfortable means. And this new conception of household management helped to keep the consumer-goods economy growing rapidly.[80]

The development of the child-centered family, alongside a youth-centered labor market, led inexorably to a relative devaluation of the later stages of life. The fragmentation of the family, from its quasi-extended origins into more purely nuclear units, had the effect of decreasing parental authority and leaving elders to fend for themselves. In an age when only a small minority of families earned enough beyond subsistence to accumulate appreciable savings, obsolescent workers who could not under the new rules of the game contribute their share to family income became a serious social and moral, as well as an economic problem.

These trends were reinforced by immigrants' aspirations for upward socioeconomic mobility for their children in the U.S. and by the tendency of many parents to sacrifice for future generations at the possible expense of their own long-run needs. The result was to be an older generation that was economically unproductive, out of power in terms of property relations, and increasingly irrelevant to family life as the years passed.[81]

Effects of Immigration

Analysis of the radical transformation of working and residential life that accompanied and led to the devaluation of older Americans' economic worth must include an assessment of the impact of immigration. Between 1860 and 1920, U.S. population more than trebled, and the labor force grew even more rapidly, nearly quadrupling in the same period. During these years, the median age of the population also was rising rapidly, from 19.4 years in 1860 to 25.3 years in 1920, while the number of children under 10 years of age

---

80 See John Kenneth Galbraith, Economics and the Public Purpose (New York: Houghton Mifflin Co., 1973), pp. 29-37, on the vital role of the "convenient social virtue" of household management in sustaining a high-consumption economy.

81 See Beth B. Hess, "America's Aging: Who, What, When, and Where," in Growing Old in America, ed. by Beth B. Hess (New Brunswick, N.J.: Transaction Press, 1976), pp. 31-32.

decreased from 14 to 11 percent of the population.[82] To some extent this reflected a declining birthrate as the population became more urbanized, but it was chiefly the result of the large inflow of immigrants who were primarily young adults.

Tables 1 and 2 illustrate the dimensions of the additions being made to the population and the labor force, by decade, between 1860 and 1920.

TABLE 1

TOTAL POPULATION AND LABOR FORCE, 1860-1920

Year	Population (millions)	Labor Force (millions)
1860	32	11
1870	40	13
1880	50	17
1890	60	23
1900	76	29
1910	92	38
1920	106	42

Source: U.S. Bureau of the Census, Historical Statistics of the United States, Colonial Times to 1970 (Washington, D.C.: Government Printing Office, 1975), pp. 8, 127, 139.

TABLE 2

PERCENTAGE GROWTH IN POPULATION AND LABOR FORCE ATTRIBUTABLE TO IMMIGRATION, 1860-1910

Decade	Percent Change in Population	Percent Change in Labor Force
1860-1870	17.1	
1870-1880	10.8	16.2
1880-1890	20.1	30.1
1890-1900	8.4	10.1
1900-1910	19.9	24.9

Source: Simon Kuznets and Ernest Rubin, Immigration and the Foreign Born (New York: National Bureau of Economic Research, Occasional Paper No. 46, 1954), p. 45.

---

82 Peterson and Gray, Economic Development of the United States, p. 254.

Immigration fell off in the second decade of the twentieth century, so that population inflows were offset by losses through death and emigration. The population grew by only 2.9 percent between 1910 and 1920, and the labor force actually decreased by 1.2 percent.[83]

The majority of immigrants were of working age, found jobs in industry, and settled in urban areas.[84] The industrial labor force was not an area of government intervention during these years, but governments at all levels fostered an environment that encouraged expansion of the workforce, by refusing to restrict immigration[85] and by making available in the cities the external economies to production to lure businesses and workers to the population centers. The curious shape of the American population and its labor force was to a considerable degree the work of immigration, as the following figures make clear:

From 1840 (when immigration began to occur on a wide scale) to 1930 (when it virtually stopped), the native American population grew sixfold, from 14.2 million to 82.7 million. The population of foreign stock (the foreign-born and the native-born of foreign or mixed parentage) rose from three million to more than 40 million, a thirteen-fold increase. By 1930, one-third of the U.S. population was post-1840 immigrant stock.[86]

---

83 Simon Kuznets and Ernest Rubin, Immigration and the Foreign Born (New York: National Bureau of Economic Research, Occasional Paper No. 46, 1954), p. 45.

84 Both the pull of job opportunities in the United States and the push of socioeconomic conditions abroad were causes of immigration. To the extent that the pull factor was dominant, it reinforced the domestic tendencies toward concentrating populations in large cities. The majority of the jobs filled by immigrants were located in and near urban centers, and friends and relatives who had been in the U.S. for some time were increasingly city-dwellers and served as a further magnet to the cities. Thus, in 1900, 63.1 percent of the nation's rural population but only 40 percent of the urban population were of native-white stock (that is, at least second-generation Americans). In some of the largest cities at the turn of the century (New York, Chicago, Detroit, Boston, Cleveland, St. Louis), the proportions of native white population ranged only between 21 and 35 percent. (Hacker, Course of American Economic Growth, p. 242.)

85 Some restrictions had been set before World War I, but their effects were relatively minor. The Chinese Exclusion Act of 1882 primarily affected California. Succeeding acts outlawed contract labor; the immigration of the physically and mentally ill, vagrants and known anarchists; and Japanese laborers. Only in 1917 did Congress enact literacy requirements--over President Wilson's veto--and in 1929 the National Origins Act set quotas for immigrants from all nations, based upon their representation in the population as of 1920. (Walton and Robertson, History of the American Economy, p. 447; Krooss, American Economic Development, p. 83.)

86 Hacker, Course of American Economic Growth, pp. 188-89.

- The total U.S. population increased by 140 percent between 1860 and 1900, but for the civilian population of working age[87] the growth rate was 170 percent, and for males it was 190 percent over the four decades.[88]

- Between 1860 and 1900, farm population grew by 70 percent; the growth rate of the urban population was 300 percent.[89]

- By 1900 the nation's age composition been significantly altered by immigration; 30.1 percent of all persons over 65 were foreign-born, a proportion not seen before or since.[90]

The "New" Immigration

In the years between 1900 and 1915, two facets of immigration were particularly striking: its great volume, and the continued and pronounced shift in origin which had begun in the 1880s. In the entire history of American immigration, only in the decade 1840-1850 was there a larger inflow relative to the domestic population. In total numbers, the years 1900-1909 showed a greater influx of immigrants than any comparable period. Beginning in 1900, annual immigration exceeded 400,000 and did not fall under that figure until 1915. In six of those years (in 1905, 1906, 1907, 1910, 1913, 1914), there were more than one million new arrivals. More than eight million came in the years 1900-1909 and five million more between 1909 and 1914. [91]

Of all immigrants arriving between 1899 and 1914, 73.7 percent reported having an occupation and can be supposed to have become almost instant additions to the domestic labor force.[92] Even more important for its impact in transforming the nature of work life and reducing older workers' job security, immigration from the late 1890s onward began to come almost entirely from the nations of southern, central, and eastern Europe. This was the so-called "New Immigration," which had begun to be significant in the 1880s.

---

87 Working age is defined here as age 15 and above, although there were well over a million members of the labor force in 1900 who were between 10 and 15. (Walton and Robertson, History of the American Economy, p. 439.)

88 Achenbaum, Old Age, p. 62.

89 Ibid.

90 Ibid.

91 U.S. Department of Commerce, Bureau of the Census, Statistical Abstract of the United States (Washington, D.C.: Government Printing Office, 1919), p. 89. See also U.S. Department of Commerce, Bureau of the Census, Immigrants and Their Children, Census Monograph No. 7 (Washington, D.C.: Government Printing Office, 1927).

92 National Bureau of Economic Research, International Migrations (New York: National Bureau of Economic Research, 1929-1931), 2: 489. See also United States Immigration Commission, Reports, 42 vols. (Washington, D.C.: Government Printing Office, 1911), 1:100-01.

The "Old Immigration" had been mostly from northern and western Europe (in parti-icular the United Kingdom, Germany, and Scandinavia), and had consisted primarily of skilled workers, experienced farmers, and people who owned some of the tools needed to practice a trade. It was these "old immigrants" who so swelled the over-65 population (of which they constituted more than 30 percent by 1900).[93] The members of the labor force from this group in general shared with the native-born skilled workers the experiences of dilution of their skills and occupational obsolescence which accompanied industrialization.

The new immigrants differed from their earlier counterparts in several ways. They were far less likely to be skilled workers, more frequently saw their stay in the U.S. as only temporary, were less inclined to be assimilated by American culture, and were less amenable to unionization. Much of the native workers' degradation and failure as competitors in the labor market was ascribed to the open arms the United States extended to immigrants. And in particular, arrivals at the turn of the century who lacked skills reinforced the trend toward production processes based upon the monotonous repetition of finely-separated tasks. What this trend meant for the older working population was that they were being displaced from many industries and, according to the U.S. Immigration Commission, were forced to "accept lower standards...develop segregated jobs, or find work in other industries."[94] One analyst noted that many older persons were being "utterly scrapped" in the process of displacement by foreign workers.[95]

Immigration and the Division of Labor

By 1910, reports to the Immigration Commission indicated that, for most of the larger industries, from one-half to two-thirds of their workforces were composed of immigrants.[96] While skilled workers from certain northern European countries had been important when an industry was first getting established, and for this reason they were often offered strong inducements to come, with the progress of mechanization and the detailed division of tasks they were increasingly replaceable by the new immigrants of Greek, Polish, Slavic, and Lithuanian background. The older groups were substantially superseded or retained only for key positions.

For example, in the glass factories of western Pennsylvania and Ohio, workers from England, Belgium, and Germany had formed the nucleus of the labor force in the 1880s, but by 1900 they were largely displaced by machinery and unskilled immigrants. In the woolen and worsted trades of New England, German, Scotch, and English workmen consti-tuted the backbone of the industry following the Civil War but were outnumbered by the

93 Achenbaum, Old Age, p. 62.

94 Solomon Barkin, The Older Worker in Industry: A Study of New York State Manu-facturing Industries (Albany: J. B. Lyon for the New York State Commission on Old Age Security, 1933), p. 58.

95 U.S. Immigration Commission, Reports, 1:495. See also John Mitchell, The Wage Earner and His Problems (Washington, D.C.: P.S. Ridsdale, 1913), pp. 37-38.

96 U.S. Immigration Commission, Reports, 1:297-313.

turn of the century by people of less industrial experience--French Canadians, Italians, Syrians, and so forth. The tanneries of Wilmington, Philadelphia, and Milwaukee had been employers chiefly of Germans, Irish, and Scandinavians, but after about 1890 these were supplanted by Italians, Poles, and Slavs who had previously been farmers or farm laborers.[97]

Skill, whether native or imported, continued to count in some trades, such as silk goods manufacturing, clothing, gloves, cigar and tobacco manufacturing, and coal mining. These trades changed little with industrialization because the nature of the work did not allow great opportunities for minute specialization or skill-destroying mechanization. So in these occupations the percentage of the foreign-born who had worked at the same trade prior to immigration was still greater than 50 percent by the turn of the century.[98]

The extractive industries, iron making, and silk and textile manufacturing had become heavily dependent in the post-Civil War years on the expertise of foreign workers, particularly the English, Scottish, and Welsh. Indeed, it was not unusual for employers to meet delegations of such desired workers at the station with brass bands.[99] Reliance on the experience and know-how of particular groups of foreigners was commonplace in the 1880s. Congressional testimony records an American employer being asked why he supported technical schools in the United States and answering, "Because if I want a draftsman or foreman, I want a well- equipped man, and I can't get him in the ordinary workman, unless he has had some opportunities of acquiring knowledge that he cannot get in a shop." To which the questioner replied, "Well, is that the only reason? You could send abroad and get all that in men who have been trained in technical schools already established."[100]

This sort of dependence upon the skill-kits of foreign-born workers was disappearing rapidly at the turn of the century, as skill requirements were being voided by narrow task specialization and greater use of machinery. Yet the proportion of aliens in industries still requiring skills remained significant. In 1870 foreigners accounted for 53.3 percent of the labor force in mining, 37.6 percent in woolen and silk textiles, and 43.4 percent in branches of the iron and steel industry. By 1890 the percentages were 49.1, 42.8, and 37.9, respectively.[101]

---

97 Ibid.

98 Ibid., pp. 505-30.

99 Edward C. Kirkland, Industry Comes of Age: Business, Labor and Public Policy, 1860-1897 (Chicago: Quadrangle Books, 1961), p. 327.

100 Testimony of John W. Britton, Report of the Committee on Education and Labor of the Senate (1885), 2:1129, cited by ibid., p. 327.

101 Charlotte Erickson, American Industry and the European Immigrant, 1860-1880 (Cambridge: Harvard University Press, 1957), Appendix 2, pp. 190-91.

Immigration and Employment Security

Many immigrants, particularly in the first years of the twentieth century, arrived with the intention of staying only a couple of years, accumulating a small stake by benefitting from high American wages, and returning home. They posed the greatest threat to workers already established in this country. This temporary character of immigration (whether in fact the foreigners ultimately left or not) heightened the employment insecurity of the domestic labor force, since such workers by definition shared few of the concerns and values of the pre-existing workforce, and could be more readily manipulated by employers as a reserve army to forestall labor disputes.[102] Workers' hostility was therefore frequently deflected from the employer or organization onto the new arrivals. Although labor force stratification was not a new phenomenon,[103] an undisputed result was increased stratification, from the 1890s onward, along ethnic lines, in addition to the trade, skill, sex, and age-based distinctions already in effect.

The tendency of newer workers from abroad to displace older Americans had received official notice prior to the turn of the century,[104] and the fate of the older industrial worker served to bolster the arguments for restrictive immigration legislation. Relatively free immigration had long served the interests of employers. It maximized their selection from a wide range of skills and experience, disciplined the existing labor force by increasing the threat of unemployment, and placed downward pressure on wage rates.[105] A case against open immigration was put forth in 1896 by Senator Lodge of Massachusetts in arguing for the enactment of literacy standards:

> There is no one thing which does so much to bring about a reduction of wages and to injure the American wage earner as the unlimited introduction of cheap for-

---

102 Jeremiah W. Jenks and W. Jett Lauck, The Immigrant Problem, 6th ed. (New York: Funk and Wagnalls, 1926), pp. 33-40.

103 American blacks were the earliest and most glaring exception to the "melting pot" theory, and the Irish had faced severe discrimination since they began to arrive in large numbers in the 1840s.

104 This was also prior to the peak immigration years of 1905- 1914, when net immigration averaged over one million persons per year. John R. Commons, et al., History of Labor in The United States, 1896-1932, 4 vols. (New York: The Macmillan Co., 1918-1935), vol. 3: Working Conditions, by Don D. Leschohier, p. 15.

105 As noted earlier, although real wages were seldom falling during the 1860-1920 period, and were certainly far higher than those in any other country, they rose less rapidly than either productivity growth or the rate of growth of profits, undoubtedly due to the steady rate of increase in the labor supply owing to immigration. See Clarence D. Long, Wages and Earnings in the United States, 1860-1890 (Princeton: Princeton University Press, 1960), pp. 3-12, 109-18; Albert Rees, Real Wages in Manufacturing, 1890-1914 (Princeton: Princeton University Press, 1961), pp. 3-5; Walton and Robertson, History of the American Economy, pp. 437-38.

eign labor through immigration. Statistics show that the change in the race character of our immigration has been accompanied by a corresponding decline in its quality. The number of skilled mechanics and of persons trained to some occupation or pursuit has fallen off, while the number of those without occupation or training, that is, who are totally unskilled, has risen in our recent immigration to enormous proportions.[106]

In 1895 the Massachusetts Commission on the Unemployed noted that the opportunities for work in this country had been exaggerated:

> Under present conditions the United States is attempting to solve the question of unemployment for Europe as well as for itself....Much of the recent immigration is due, not to a real and permanent demand in this part of the country, but rather to depressed and abnormal conditions abroad.[107]

John R. Commons asserted in 1907 that "the desire to get cheap labor, to take in passenger fares, and to sell land have probably brought more immigrants than the hard conditions of Europe, Asia, and Africa have sent."[108] Writing in 1913 another observer believed that "much of our immigration since 1880...has come in response to inducements of transportation companies and American employers operating through various methods and devices."[109]

Labor bureaus and workers' organizations decried the rates of displacement and unemployment to which massive immigration contributed, while capitalists, manufacturers' associations, and orthodox economists supported free immigration for its value to the community. For if it was possible to get the most menial work done cheaply by people able to do it economically, all the rest of the country benefitted by having the products of immigrant labor at less sacrifice than would otherwise be involved. With immigrants performing low-grade work, their American counterparts faced diminished opportunities for maintaining themselves, but all others were afforded a chance to move up. As one economist put it in 1896, immigration had provided a stimulus to progress

---

106 U.S. Congress, Senate, Senator Lodge speaking for the enactment of restrictions on immigration, 54th Cong., 1st sess., 16 March 1896, Congressional Record, pp. 2817-20, cited by Lescohier, Working Conditions, p. 25.

107 Massachusetts, Report of the Board to Investigate the Subject of the Unemployed, House Document No. 50, part 5 (Boston: Wright and Potter, 1895), pp. 27-28, cited by Lescohier, Working Conditions, p. 26.

108 John R. Commons, Race and Immigrants in America (New York: The Macmillan Co., 1907), p. 108.

109 Frank J. Warne, The Immigrant Invasion (New York: Dodd, Mead and Co., 1913), pp. 47-48. It should be acknowledged that more than compassion for the working classes motivated some of their defenders. Many appeals to protect labor and jobs were thinly-disguised expressions of racism and xenophobia.

by compelling native workers to rise or to die....Much of the opposition to immigration comes from the men who stand in the way of such progress; men who are incapable of rising into the higher grades; men who, if they work at all, are fitted only for such work as foreign immigrants do and who fail to do that work well. There may have been good reasons for putting a stop to Chinese immigration; but the average Chinese immigrant...was far more useful to the community...than the average persecutor who threw stones at him.[110]

Underlying the harshness of the above assessment lay an implicit acknowledgement of the unemployment problems created for some by large-scale unskilled immigration; yet the author concluded that occupational shifts for worthy American laborers could only be to their advantage.[111]

As noted earlier, many immigrants did arrive possessing some skills and training, particularly up until about 1890. However, the act of immigration frequently entailed a change of occupation. The occupational shift might be deliberate, owing to a desire to escape the accustomed type of work, but occupational choice tended to be somewhat circumscribed. First, the circumstances under which the immigrant's old pursuit was carried out in the United States, perhaps coupled with language difficulties, were likely to be so different as to make his former experience largely inapplicable. This was particularly true in the professions and in farming operations.[112] Second, in the usual case, the immigrant arrived in such poor financial condition he was compelled to take the first job that came along, without the luxury to pick and choose.[113]

The percentage of immigrants in the latter category rose with the shift in countries of origin from northern and western Europe to southern and eastern Europe. The most pronounced aspect of any enumeration of immigrants according to their prior occupations is the very large proportion who fell into the unskilled or miscellaneous category.[114] This was particularly the case from 1900 onward, when an overwhelming percentage of immigrants of all nationalities (except English, Scottish, and Hebrew-speaking) could be labelled unskilled: over 80 percent in every case except Germans (66.3 percent) and Scandinavians

---

110 Arthur T. Hadley, Economics: An Account of the Relations Between Private Property and Public Welfare (New York: G. P. Putnam's Sons, 1896), p. 421.

111 Ibid.

112 Warren B. Catlin, The Labor Problem in the United States and Great Britain, rev. ed. (New York: Harper and Bros., 1935), p. 48.

113 Krooss, American Economic Development, p. 86; Harold U. Faulkner, The Decline of Laissez Faire, 1897-1917 (New York: Holt, Rinehart and Winston, 1951), p. 471.

114 Niemi, U.S. Economic History, p. 215.

(77.6), as contrasted with only 43.4 percent English, 38.8 percent Scottish, and 30.5 percent of Hebrew-speaking immigrants who arrived without skills.[115]

Increasingly, the large additions being made to the American labor force comprised people in what, from a manufacturing standpoint, would be called the unskilled labor category; for the most part, such skills as they possessed were appropriate to an agricultural setting. To a considerable extent, this explains why progress in mechanization and minute division of labor was as rapid as it was in U.S. manufacturing establishments. The "New Immigration" contributed directly to the rapidity with which the working classes were dichotomized according to skill, and hence to employers' concern with minimizing the skill required for the performance of the majority of tasks. Insofar as the new immigrants' large numbers made possible and reinforced the production methods and efficiency emphasis which gave rise to superannuation and age-graded employment,[116] immigration contributed substantially, if indirectly, to labor market discrimination on account of age.

Conclusion

In the years following the Civil War, several crucial aspects of the economic and social landscape were transformed by the industrialization process. This chapter has traced those background forces which enhanced the development of large-scale enterprises while diminishing the socioeconomic role to be played by older Americans.

The unification of the national economy, particularly but not exclusively via the railroad building boom of the 1860s through the 1890s, led to a vast increase in market-oriented production; a decline in local and regional autonomy and self-sufficiency; and the establishment of more uniform supply and demand characteristics for merchandise, services, and workers. Additionally, the railroads provided a powerful impetus to capital goods-producing industries which, most notably in the case of steel, would become among the largest and most concentrated of the industrial age. At the same time, the railroads were in themselves an object lesson in the feasibility of conducting an enterprise on a vast scale, covering great distances, incorporating multiple stages of production, and entailing the adoption of sophisticated managerial, financial, and accounting techniques.

Agriculture, which appealed to older people because it allowed for relative independence and a more-or-less gradual withdrawal from work, continued to be an important economic sector, but decreasingly so. Up until the late 1890s, American agriculture provided a relatively worsening standard of living compared with industry because of its inherently competitive structure, its low price and income demand elasticities, and an export orientation that allowed for little recourse to the sorts of protectionist policies that aided

---

115 The figures are for the period 1899-1914, adapted from Walter F. Willcox, International Migrations, 2 vols. (New York: National Bureau of Economic Research, 1929-1931), 2:489-91.

116 "Superannuation" means the early wearing-out of workers under the conditions of work that characterized the industrialization process. Age-graded employment refers to the increasingly common managerial practice of refusing to hire (or firing) workers beyond a certain chronological age, regardless of ability, experience, or health. Both concepts will be discussed in greater detail in the following chapters.

manufacturing. Even with the turnaround in the trend of agricultural prices near the turn of the century, success at farming was increasingly a function of having a large number of acres, considerable business acumen, credit availability, and access to seasonal hired labor to augment the work of family members.

The relative decline in the importance of farming was accompanied by the growth of towns and cities in the closing decades of the nineteenth century.[117] City life separated the generations, with the young family often living in town while the older generation was left in the country. There they might continue to hold onto property, which was vital to their continued well-being and their ability to sustain independence. In the cities, the spread of small-property ownership and the commodity culture diminished the status that property had once conveyed to older Americans. Those who grew old in cities--a growing percentage with the shift toward urban life and slowing birth and death rates--faced increasing dependence on the family for support when they were isolated from old ties and no longer employable.

City life was characterized by competition and expectations of individual self-sufficiency, rather than the helpful neighborliness of more closely integrated rural communities. It was also characterized by much greater economic, occupational, and social mobility than was country life. The price of this mobility, in terms of both economic self-sufficiency and family support, has always been highest for the old and near-old. But in the period of the United States' most rapid urbanization and industrialization, the economic and social strains of becoming old reached new levels. In the 1980s much of what goes by the name of "modernization," "progress," or "technological change" is familiar, if still often disruptive. But a century ago it had no precedent, and for a large percentage of older Americans the changes wrought by industrialization and urbanization must have appeared a sharp break with the past.

It would be simplistic to suggest that increasing concentrations of older people in city ghettos, separated from their families and unable to maintain employment, led directly to negative conceptions about old age, or ageism. The decisive factor has not been whether or not the elderly lived in an urban or rural environment, but whether they were able to be self-supporting or economically productive. This was increasingly not the case in the late nineteenth and early twentieth centuries (although for the elderly in rural areas the most striking losses in self-sufficiency would not be felt until the 1920s and 1930s). The loss of family sustenance was not inevitable, but it was becoming more and more likely. Wealth or substantial property could serve as a cushion against the reduced opportunities for being economically useful. But for the aging individuals faced with propertylessness, joblessness, and uncertain or unlikely family support, the years bracketing the Civil War and World War I were a watershed.

Lastly, immigration was an essential ingredient in the timing, if not the ultimate outcome, of the industrialization process and the devaluation of older workers. The history of the U.S. up to 1860 was one of fairly acute labor shortages that predisposed the nation to be an importer of workers. American living conditions and economic opportunities were a powerful magnet to the economically dispossessed, the socially ostracized, and the

117 The rise of cities has been termed the "demographic counterpart" of the "increased share of the labor force in manufacturing and in trade, service, finance, and government activities." Peterson and Gray, Economic Development of the United States, p. 308.

upwardly-mobile of other lands; and once here, the majority tended to stay. Their importance to an analysis of the economic obsolescence of older Americans lies in the impact
which their arrival in such huge numbers had upon the rate at which industrialization--and
in particular centralization, division of labor, and deskilling--was able to occur.

Especially in the years around the turn of the century, the new immigrants' relative
lack of skills, docility, unfamiliarity with the language and customs, and strong ethnic ties
rendered them assimilable primarily at work, on jobs for which one worker was the same
as any other. The ability to follow simple instructions and maintain a steady pace was what
these mostly young, mostly male workers could most readily demonstrate to American
employers. And so their growing representation in the labor force helped to hasten the
arrival of precisely those conditions of work[118] that placed older individuals at a disadvantage in the labor market. Additionally, the availability of large pools of such workers
hastened the spread of skill-leveling production technologies, which themselves were an outgrowth of the very capital-intensiveness of manufacturing resulting from the nation's
heritage of labor scarcity. These conditions are the subject of the following chapters.

---

118 In particular, much industrial work required great strength and stamina and placed
little or even negative value on traditional techniques and time-tested approaches to production.

CHAPTER 4

GROWING FIRM SIZE AS IT AFFECTED THE EMPLOYMENT
OF OLDER WORKERS

Introduction

This chapter examines the effects on older workers of increasing firm size, the appearance of the corporate form of business organization, and the growing tendency toward economic centralization in the nation's fastest-growing industries between 1860 and 1920. Growing monopoly power and the spread of large-scale production units accelerated the conversion of artisans and craftsmen to wage-labor status in many trades. The majority of American workers were being demoted to a state of subordination to impersonal, hierarchically-structured and bureaucratically-run workplaces. As enterprises grew to larger scale, any individual worker was rendered a less significant part of the productive process. Once workers had to rely upon depersonalized institutions for their economic status, they became subject to the periodic bouts of unemployment that could result from surges in technological innovation and downturns in economic activity.

Mechanization and the concentration of wealth and power in the hands of the few were closing off many of the opportunities for economic self-determination that were once available. While American labor was the freest in the world in being relatively unencumbered by socioeconomic rigidities, its vaunted mobility was being constrained by the dominance of large business establishments. By the 1880s, Henry George was among those who saw the distortion in continuing to speak of mobility as if the United States were still a young nation taking possession of an open continent. George felt that although some few would still advance, the vast majority were fated to be dependent machine-tenders, as small businessmen continued to be pushed out by larger concerns.[1]

A contemporary, Richard Ely, predicted that 99 workers out of 100 would remain in the wage-earning ranks, because industrialization was supplanting small shops with large and impersonal factories. Ely saw the mobility ethic as not only false but pernicious; it proffered as a reality a social doctrine that had become utterly anachronistic.[2] The mobility possible when enterprises were small, when craft or skill was the basis of production, when wealth was fairly evenly distributed, and when living arrangements focused on families and not factories, could not be sustained under conditions of industrial capitalism.[3]

---

1 This process, according to George, was similar to European feudalism in result, because it subordinated small property-holders to the wealthy and paved the way for the ultimate domination of society by the few. Henry George, Social Problems (New York: Doubleday, 1883), pp. 29-42.

2 Richard Ely, The Labor Movement in America (New York: Crowell, 1886), pp. 92-95.

3 At any rate, as Adam Smith had noted in 1776 about mobility, "A man is of all sorts of luggage the most difficult to be transported." Adam Smith, An Inquiry into the Nature and Causes of the Wealth of Nations (New York: Modern Library, 1937), p. 75.

The ubiquity of large institutions today makes it easy to underestimate the importance of this particular transformation in workers' lives and its unique impact on older workers. In the 1860-1920 period, the groundwork was laid for discriminatory practices based on outward characteristics, practices which, then as now, had not just social/psychological meaning but also very real economic consequences. Prior to industrialization, reasonably competent and faithful workers in small shops or firms could anticipate an accommodation in workload, tasks assigned, and length of the workday as they experienced any diminished productive powers with age. For the self-employed--a far larger percentage of the working population then than now--craft production allowed the individual to work with his own small capital and to carry through to completion the entire labor process.[4] Such a system conveyed great freedom as to the hours of labor and the time of beginning and leaving work.

But with the spread of large-scale enterprises, particularly in manufacturing but also in services involving direct dealings with the public, older workers encountered not only the loss of such freedoms, but also a strong disinclination on the part of employers to take them on no matter how fit, willing, or adaptable they might be. The focus of this and tahe two following chapters is on how the conditions of consolidating industrialism became a compelling force for separating older American workers from remunerative employment.

This chapter introduces the following themes: (1) the spread of the corporate form of business organization, which put a distance between employer and employee as it separated ownership from control, and the accompanying decline of the small capitalist firm; (2) the erosion of workers' skills as technological developments and the division of labor made workers increasingly interchangeable with one another from a production standpoint; and (3) the growing instability of the economy, and hence of employment, as large concerns began to dominate market activity. Chapters 5 and 6 will then examine, respectively, the technological and the organizational/managerial functions internal to large-scale firms that made such enterprises uniquely inhospitable to older employees.

Emergence of the Corporate Form

An important element of the shift to large-scale enterprise was the development of the legal concept of the corporation. The corporate form of business organization arose substantially to accommodate bigness, for some businesses required considerably more capital than a sole proprietorship or partnership could generate. As early as 1810, the corporation was well-entrenched in the banking and insurance industries and in turnpike construction, and in the ensuing decades it became commonplace in the canal and railroad industries.[5]

While the corporation had existed in the U.S. before the Civil War, in 1860 the greatest proportion of resources used in manufacturing remained in the control of proprietorships and partnerships. The most modern of rolling mills at that time could be built for $150,000, and the capital needed to establish the largest textile factory was within the means

---

4 Or, more accurately, that portion of the process which he did not contract out to others.

5 Walton and Robertson, History of the American Economy, p. 257.

of a single wealthy individual.[6] It was only following the panic of 1873 that the corporate form of business organization would begin to dominate the nation's industrial structure.[7]

Yet it was clear to contemporary observers by 1860 that "the corporate form would be inseparable from the enterprise of the future; bigness obviously lay ahead."[8] And although the corporate form was not the cause of the increased scale of production, it was undeniably essential to it.[9] The railroads had already shown the merits of incorporation in enterprises for which huge capital outlays were necessary, and technological change was rapidly moving production processes toward larger size, in order to make possible a volume of production that would cover the costs of investment in the new machinery.[10]

From investors' point of view, corporations afforded opportunities for saving for all types of capital owners, from the most conservative investor to the most reckless speculator.[11] A significant point, however, is that control was not similarly dispersed. The controlling influence generally resided with speculative stock, on the principle that those who took the financial risks should have voting responsibility. So it was the owners of speculative capital, not capital owners generally, who directed production, hired and fired managers, and so forth. Although such financiers might individually hold only a small fraction of total capital, they exercised a very real control over the lives of workers and

---

6 Ibid., p. 260. Even prior to 1860, however, some manufacturing firms faced the problem of organizing large numbers of workers. The Pepperell textile mills, for example, averaged 800 workers in the 1850s. Such cases were exceptional before the Civil War but by 1920 plants the size of the Pepperell mills were common. (Peterson and Gray, Economic Development of the United States, p. 309. See also Knowlton, Pepperell's Progress.)

7 Cochran and Brewer, Views of American Economic Growth, 2:16. Thorstein Veblen was to refer to the corporation in the 1920s as "the master institution of civilized life." (Thorstein Veblen, Absentee Ownership and Business Enterprise in Recent Times: The Case of America (New York: B. W. Huebsch, 1923), p. 23.)

8 Walton and Robertson, History of the American Economy, p. 260.

9 U.S. Department of Commerce, Bureau of the Census, The Integration of Industrial Operation, by Willard L. Thorp, Census Monograph 3 (Washington, D.C.: Government Printing Office, 1924), p. 9.

10 In the case of the railroads, increasing firm size was largely a function of technical operating needs; this was less the case in manufacturing, where it was more specifically a strategy for increasing market share. Peterson and Gray, Economic Development of the United States, p. 310.

11 The business world adapted to the various predilections of owners of capital by making available bonds for those seeking a regular income, common stock for those who preferred speculating, and preferred stock for those favoring a middle course. The constantly increasing scale of operations, and the constantly increasing proportion of capital needed for maximum efficiency in production, necessitated a diversity of financial instruments to appeal to all types of investors.

consumers alike, and were the force for binding together the largest of business combinations.

Not only was the typical stockholder not well in touch with the business he partly owned, he was rapidly losing any real control over the few larger stockholders and their agents. One analyst pointed out that by the turn of the century the latter group was rapidly stealing away the rights of the masses of stockholders.[12] This resulted in the decline of the stockholder and the rise to prominence of corporate directors and officers, and hence the concentration of industrial power and wealth in the hands of a smaller number of people.

The small, independently-run shop--proprietorship or partnership--continued to prevail in some fields, notably tanneries, distilleries and breweries, sawmills and grist-mills[13] (and presumably also in the production of items of consumption targeted to the wealthy, such as luxury apparel, fine furniture and glassware, and so forth). But the factory system's rapid and sustained rise to prominence overwhelmed many small shops, for the technology of mass production enabled the production of goods of many kinds nearly equal in quality to what handcrafting had afforded, and at a fraction of the cost.

In addition, the legal protections afforded to the corporate entity put its unincorporated competitors on an unequal footing in cases of disputes over such issues as patent rights, government contracts, and the like. Thus the appeal of large-batch, centrally-managed production was profound, both to the capitalist class and to workers in their role as consumers. The independent artisan or entrepreneur who hoped to preserve his autonomy had to be able to provide a unique, affordable product or service which the factory system was not able cost-effectively to replicate.

Bigness and the Changing Nature of Employments

The significance of the appearance of the corporate form for the working lives of older Americans resides in four phenomena, described here briefly and elaborated on later in the chapter. Although each of these phenomena can readily be seen to have affected workers of any age, they had a particularly powerful effect on the work-lives of older people.

1. The most obvious corollary of the increasing importance of the corporate form of business organization was a relative reduction in the importance of small and medium-sized firms which could not meet the competition from much larger firms within their industries. The disappearance of the small firm also meant disappearing opportunities for employment that provided workers with a high degree of productive autonomy and the scope for a

---

12 They did so by such tactics as limiting shareholders' rights to participate in future issues of securities; allowing management to dispose of new shares on any terms they saw fit; giving management the power to sell corporate assets and enter into new corporate relationships without interference; and successfully exempting themselves from liability for corporate losses incurred in private deals in which officers and directors may have had a special interest. William Z. Ripley, Main Street and Wall Street (Boston: Little, Brown and Co., 1929), pp. 37- 38.

13 Niemi, U.S. Economic History, p. 96.

gradual withdrawal from the world of work tailored to any declining powers with age. These characteristics of pre-industrial capitalism were essential to the continued participation of older workers in the productive realm. To the extent that industrialization eliminated small firms and the jobs they provided, it created the conditions for the appearance of the nation's first class of citizens to experience long-lasting downward economic mobility.[14]

2. The growing average size of business enterprise was to a considerable extent an outgrowth of the need to capture the scale economies afforded by technological breakthroughs. The most outstanding feature of the productive machinery which was increasingly adopted after 1860 was its supremacy over its labor adjuncts. Unlike the tools of the petty-capitalist era, which were developed and utilized to conform to the physical requirements and the rhythms of the human worker, the machinery of industrial capitalism was characterized by its far greater cost and potential productiveness, and hence the need to utilize it at maximum speed to make it profitable.

This entailed both the deskilling of labor[15] and a growing emphasis on the speed at which work was performed, both of which had their greatest impact upon older workers. It further entailed the spread of labor specialization which, while a boon to productivity, profits, and average wages, deprived workers of any real understanding of how their narrowly-circumscribed efforts fit into the overall process. Job specialization asked that

---

14 Apart from their economic losses, the downward mobility experienced by older Americans over the last century and more must also be accounted a social/psychological loss in a country noted for its exaltation of remunerative activity.

15 "Deskilling" is the term coined by Harry Braverman in his Labor and Monopoly Capital to denote the degradation of work as jobs are progressively stripped of any capacity to engage the intellect of those who perform them. Braverman's thesis--to which this work owes a considerable debt--is that at the same time that capitalism has made possible an unprecedented material abundance and feats of technological wizardry, it has managed to subdivide most jobs into petty operations utterly lacking in intrinsic interest. Even tasks requiring considerable "skill" or education are fragmented within large enterprises so as to minimize the uneconomic circumstance of workers' being confronted with new challenges. (Hence, functional corporate divisions separate the processes of design, research, planning, quality control, methods study, maintenance, and so forth.) See Braverman Labor and Monopoly Capital, p. 260.

Skill has become a synonym for mere dexterity, say Braverman and others. See especially M. C. Kennedy, "The Division of Labor and the Culture of Capitalism: A Critique" (Ph.D. dissertation, University of Michigan, 1968). In addition, the concept of education has been narrowed to mean preparation for becoming a certain kind of narrowly specialized worker. On this issue, see, for example, Samuel Bowles, "The Integration of Higher Education into the Wage Labor System," Review of Radical Political Economics 6 (Spring 1974):100-33; Herb Gintis, "Education, Technology and the Characteristics of Worker Productivity," American Economic Review Papers and Proceedings 61 (May 1971):266-79; Ivar Berg, Education and Jobs: The Great Training Robbery (New York: Praeger, 1970). The result is that not only has labor been degraded by capitalist work processes, but so too has the very concept of skill itself.

workers "perfect and value only a few of their simplest abilities,"[16] and hence it stifled creativeness, versatility, and the very potential for exercising autonomy.

3. The growth in the size of enterprises made production workers (and probably, but to a lesser extent, management employees) more interchangeable with one another. Employees could not be valued for their unique personal characteristics within impersonal, bureaucratic, and hierarchical institutions. With bigness there developed the need for concrete rules which would cover all forseeable workplace contingencies, so that employees were valued more according to how well they complied with the governing rules than for their individual traits or talents, which were being de-emphasized through labor specialization and deskilling.

Additionally, the act of incorporation meant to some degree a separation of ownership from day-to-day control of the firm's activities. Employees ultimately worked for the shareholders, but took their instruction from others who were themselves accountable to shareholders. Not only did workers in such circumstances probably never encounter the firm's owners, but they were supervised by individuals whose self-interest mandated that their loyalties be directed to the unseen owners rather than to those in their charge.

4. With larger-scale production units there was a tendency for national economic activity to become more volatile. This business-cycle response to monopoly power has been statistically borne out by various studies of the relationship between the behavior of macroeconomic indicators and the degree of industrial concentration,[17] but it is also understandable intuitively. The response of the small firm to a business downturn was to keep its workers on at reduced hours and pay, allocating the losses more or less equally and enabling the employees' maintenance of at least some degree of purchasing power and putting a floor under the bottom of a recession.

In contrast, the early response to an economic downturn by enterprises employing large numbers of undifferentiated workers was to reduce employment; subsequently, laid-off workers, unable to find other work in the slump, experienced drastic reductions in their ability to make purchases, and so further depressed aggregate demand leading to yet more layoffs. The spread of business giantism corresponded with the national economy's tendency to experience recessions that were longer, deeper, and more frequent than was the case in the pre-industrial period.

---

16 W. J. Heisler, "Worker Alienation: 1900-1975," in A Matter of Dignity: Inquiries into the Humanization of Work, ed. by W. J. Heisler and John W. Houck (Notre Dame: University of Notre Dame Press, 1977), p. 76.

17 See, in particular, Wesley Clair Mitchell, Business Cycles and Unemployment (New York: McGraw-Hill Book Co. for the National Bureau of Economic Research, 1923); Gardiner C. Means, "The Growth in the Relative Importance of the Large Corporation in American Economic Life," American Economic Review 21 (March 1931):10-42; Joseph A. Schumpeter, "The Instability of Capitalism," Economic Journal 37 (September 1928):361-86.

Economic Centralization and Older Workers

Destruction of Small Firms

Mechanization and the rationalization of production revolutionized American industry in the period between the onset of the Civil War and the close of World War I, but obviously not in a consistent manner across all industries. Many industrial pursuits were relatively unaffected by the trend toward integration and incorporation. For example, in the building and construction trades, in clothing, lumber and woodworking, in hardware, bituminous coal mining, and drug manufactures, industry continued to be dominated by small independent firms.[18]

Yet even in these less centralized types of enterprises, new orgnizations began to form. Local and national trade associations composed of producers and wholesalers sought to establish control over prices and output, to standardize marketing practices, and to systematize and enforce some degree of quality control. Hence, such "competitive" industries sought, through vertical alliances and informal rules, to emulate the structure and the market power of the more capital-intensive, highly concentrated economic units in the manufacturing sector.

Ultimately, they were unsuccessful in these endeavors. The problems of such industries lay in their inherently competitive characteristics. Individual firms could not capture the production, distribution, and marketing economies available to the monopolized sector, nor could they individually apply the principles of the division of labor on a sufficient scale to greatly reduce their costs. Their situation had more in common with agriculture than with the rest of manufacturing. As noted in Chapter 3, farmers and farm laborers also sought to stabilize their economic situation in the last decades of the nineteenth century, but since they constituted numerically a very large and diverse group, they achieved even less cohesion than did small business enterprises. The greatest successes were undoubtedly achieved by workers whose trades had not yet been significantly mechanized, deskilled, or factory-based (such as construction, forestry, baking), and thus could not be readily dominated by corporate capitalism.

Since the Civil War a succession of devices had been tried as a basis for promoting monopoly conditions: the pool in the 1870s and early 1880s, the trust in the late 1880s, the simple corporation throughout the last third of the century, and the merger and the holding company (also called a finance company) during the period 1898-1914. [19] The significant increase in the size of manufacturing firms began around 1880. [20] The industries first to

---

18 Alfred D. Chandler, Jr., Stuart Bruchey, and Louis Galambos, "The Industrializing Economy, 1850-1914," in The Changing Economic Order, p. 201. Indeed, a few industries in the late nineteenth and early twentieth centuries--such as silk, lumber, carriage and wagon manufacturing, and shipbuilding--showed tendencies toward a decrease in average firm size. U.S. Bureau of the Census, Integration of Industrial Operation, p. 74.

19 William Z. Ripley, Trusts, Pools and Corporations, rev. ed. (Boston: Ginn and Co,, 1915), p. xiii.

20 Walton and Robertson, History of the American Economy, p. 419.

be characterized by large enterprises were primarily those manufacturing consumer goods, especially those which were processed from products grown on the farm and sold in urban markets.

Progress toward consolidation and centralization in such industries was already substantial by 1893, so that for a wide range of the economy's output, a single business organization (often through pooling arrangements) encompassed procurement, production, distribution, marketing, and finance. This was the case in meatpacking, flour, tobacco, sugar, salt, leather, whiskey, coal and coke, explosives, and rubber production, as well as for such manufactured goods as harvesters, sewing machines, adding machines, and typewriters.[21] In producer goods--primarily iron and steel--and in transportation, such vertical integration was also well established by the 1890s.

Between about 1880 and 1905, the process of achieving bigness was hastened by the attempts of existing firms to combine through sharing markets and linking their financial structures.[22] The passage of the Sherman Anti-Trust Act in 1890 was intended to thwart the various anti-competitive arrangements and practices that had evolved since the Civil War. But what resulted (with a lag owing to the depression of the 'nineties) was the economy's first great wave of mergers, between 1898 and 1902/3.

One student of industrial structure asserts that with monopoly as its goal, the industrial structure of the modern American economy was organized in just these five years.[23] By 1904--when the rate of mergers slackened considerably--the 318 most important manufacturing trusts, covering practically every line of productive industry in the nation, owned 5,288 plants, an average of 17 each (U.S. Steel alone had 785 plants).[24] In that year, approximately two-fifths of the U.S. capital stock was in the control of 300-odd very large firms with an aggregate capitalization of more than $7 billion.[25]

Although by modern standards the average size of American manufacturing establishments was rather small through most of the nineteenth century, Table 3 demonstrates substantial increases in average plant capitalization and output during the 1860-1920 period, and especially after 1880. Real value added per manufacturing plant increased nearly eight-fold between 1860 and 1920, doubling between 1860 and 1900 and almost quadrupling from 1900 to 1920. Real capital expenditures per plant rose over 1,000 percent, almost doubling between 1880 and 1900 and increasing nearly six-fold by 1920.

---

21 Cochran and Brewer, Views of American Economic Growth, pp. 82-83; Walton and Robertson, History of the American Economy, pp. 420,424; Faulkner, Decline of Laissez Faire, pp. 154, 156.

22 Walton and Robertson, p. 419.

23 Averitt, The Dual Economy, p. 14.

24 John Moody, The Truth About the Trusts (New York: Moody Publishing Co., 1904), p. 469.

25 Walton and Robertson, History of the American Economy, p. 428.

The average American worker in 1920 had almost 2.5 times as much capital with which to work as in 1869. [26]

TABLE 3

AVERAGE SIZE OF MANUFACTURING PLANTS AS MEASURED BY REAL CAPITAL STOCK AND REAL VALUE ADDED, 1860-1920

Year	Real Capital Stock per Establishment (1929 dollars)	Real Value Added per Establishment (1929 dollars)
1860	*	$ 8,243
1870	*	6,458
1880	$ 18,991	9,787
1890	31,392	18,197
1900	36,327	17,012
1910	117,557	38,382
1920	215,008	64,795

SOURCE: Niemi, U.S. Economic History, pp. 96-97, citing the following publications of the U.S. Bureau of the Census: (1861-1920) Twelfth Census of the United States, Manufactures, vol. 8, pp. 982-83; (1910) Thirteenth Census of the United States, Manufactures, vol. 8, p. 57; (1920) Fifteenth Census of the United States, Manufactures, vol. i, p. 17.

Value-added figures converted to 1929 dollars by the wholesale price index for all commodities in Historical Statistics, Series E 1-12 and E 13-24; capital stock figures obtained from Historical Statistics, Series P 30-133.

* Reliable capital estimates for 1860 and 1870 not available.

By 1910, the 200 largest corporations (exclusive of banking) had 33 percent of the total assets of all American corporations. By 1920 they controlled 39 percent, and by 1927, although representing less than 7/1000 of one percent of nonfinancial corporations, they would control nearly half of U.S. corporate wealth, leaving 51 percent to be shared by the approximately 300,000 remaining corporations. These 200 giants grew, through reinvested

---

26 Peterson and Gray, Economic Development of the United States, p. 309; Niemi, U.S. Economic History, p. 97; Simon Kuznets, Capital in the American Economy (Princeton: Princeton University Press, 1961), Table 3, pp. 64-65.

earnings and mergers, at more than twice the rate of other nonfinancial corporations throughout the period 1890-1927. [27]

The other side of the story is the relative reduction in the importance of small and medium-sized plants. Firms with an annual output valued at less than $20,000 declined in their percentage of total output and total establishments in the years 1860-1920; and those with annual output valued between $20-100,000 declined as a percentage of total output. But firms with output valued at $1 million or more showed a striking percentage increase in value of product. The more than 10,400 such establishments in 1920 accounted for only 3.6 percent of total firms, yet they manufactured more than two-thirds (67.8 percent) of the value of output.[28]

The trends in business consolidation weakened the position of the small businessman, if they did not put him out of business altogether. They also discouraged potential competitors from entering established industries and prevented people from going into business independently. The turn-of-the-century Industrial Commission of the United States reported that the industrial trusts were in the position of "sapping the courage and power of initiative of perhaps the most active and influential men in the community."[29]

Where cottage industry and small-scale production lingered on, as they did in some industries considerably beyond the Civil War (for example, as subsistence farmers and farm workers sought to augment their incomes via moonlighting), the pace and hours of work may have remained substantially within the individual worker's control. The older worker in such employments could hope to compensate for diminishing vigor by spreading out the work over longer, less intense hours, or by spending part of his time working at more sedentary tasks. However, the trades that allowed for workers' self-pacing were the sunset industries of their day, not the ascendant, centralizing industries spearheading economic growth and prosperity.[30] In addition to farming and carpentry, these sunset

---

27 Means, "Growth in the Relative Importance of the Large Corporation," p. 10; William Z. Ripley, "Our 'Corporate Revolution' and Its Perils," New York Times, 24 July 1932, cited by Epstein, Insecurity, p. 11.

28 Statistical Abstract of the United States, 1922, Table 156, p. 198; Appendix, p. 418. However, no more than one-third of all manufacturing output was in industries for which the four-firm concentration ratio exceeded 50 percent. Peterson and Gray, Economic Development of the United States, p. 313.

29 U.S. Industrial Commission, Report, 19 vols. (Washington, D.C.: Government Printing Office, 1900-1902), 1:34.

30 To the present the generalization still holds. Older workers predominate in trades and sectors on the decline, and when jobs are vacated by attrition, they are frequently eliminated. Harold L. Sheppard, "Aging and Manpower Development," in Aging and Society, ed. by Matilda White Riley, John W. Riley, Jr., and Marilyn E. Johnson, 3 vols. (New York: Russell Sage Foundation, 1968-1972), vol. 2: Aging and the Professions (1969), pp. 165-66. An example from the present is the occupation of typesetting for large metropolitan daily newspapers, now almost exclusively the province of older males with union protection, who are being replaced by machinery when they retire. Whether this phenomenon implies

industries included much of the clothing and hat, wood and leather, watchmaking, metal goods (nailing, cutlery, and blacksmithing), and glass trades.[31]

Erosion of Labor Skills

One major result of the consolidation and centralization of American production and distribution was a machine revolution that transformed the character of working life. During the late nineteenth century, as the factory became the standard operating unit in American manufacturing, mechanized production and the growing reliance on technology created greater separation of the various stages of production. The result was that not only were artisans, craftsmen, and others increasingly found working in centralized locations on a wage-labor basis, but the average skill required in factories was much reduced from what had been typical of craft shop or mill production.

It was not just skilled craftsmen with individual forms of acquired skill who found it difficult to compete with factories that subdivided their trade into numerous parts. A turn-of-the-century economist noted that the growing efficiency associated with the narrow division of labor also crowded out those who had previously "exercised a diversified industry"; the jacks of all trades, who "were the most useful citizens in the past," were "being driven out of existence by the stress of modern competition."[32] Although a staunch defender of the new order, this author acknowledged that "many of the occupations of the modern laborer have a narrowing effect upon those who practise them."[33]

When assessing the impact of technology on employment, it is impossible to disaggregate the effects of the introduction of machinery per se from the results of task specialization. Specialization was most pronounced, and had its most striking effects, when it was combined with the use of rationalized processes and large-scale factory production. From the beginning, the division of labor and inventions had mutually stimulated and reinforced one another. Once a job was divided up into simple elements it became comparatively easy to devise machines or tools for doing that particular work most efficiently, assuming a market large enough to keep the machinery reasonably fully employed. Conversely, more effective use of machinery facilitated ever-greater division of labor. The interaction of machinery and specialization of labor acted in turn upon the development of

---

that the average age of an industry's work force is in part a determinant of that industry's vitality, or whether the reverse is more correct, is a matter of continuing debate in the field of industrial gerontology.

31 See Braverman, Labor and Monopoly Capital, p. 61.

32 Arthur T. Hadley, Economics: An Account of the Relations Between Private Property and Public Welfare (New York: G. P. Putnam's Sons, 1896), p. 351.

33 Ibid.

the factory and the organization of big business, owing to the economic advantages of the continuous use of specialized workers and machines.[34]

As new methods of production and management gained ascendancy, the nature of many jobs was radically transformed. With the substitution of mechanical for intelligent labor, skills were increasingly fitted to the requirements of machines. This contrasted with earlier periods, when the opposite had been the norm in small-scale enterprises geared to local markets. The relationship between the worker and his tools was thus fundamentally altered.

In the preindustrial system of handicraft production, tools had generally been adopted according to their conformability with workers' skills and capacities. However, in large-scale industrial enterprises with substantial physical capital investments, the nature of the tools/machinery determined the skills or attributes that were required of the workers. Rather than operating as a craftsman in any meaningful sense, the worker himself became, in the words of Robert Hoxie, an "animated tool of management."[35]

Machinery did not even have to play a sizable role in this process of skill narrowing. This can be seen in the case of the American meat slaughtering and packing industry of 1905, in which 1050 head of cattle could be moved from the pen to the cooler by a crew of 230 in the course of a 10-hour working day. As Commons noted:

> It would be difficult to find another industry where division of labor has been so ingeniously...worked out. The animal has been surveyed and laid off like a map; and men have been classified in over thirty specialties and twenty rates of pay, from 16 cents to 50 cents an hour. The 50-cent man is restricted to using the knife on the most delicate parts of the hide...; and wherever a less skilled man can be slipped in at 18 cents, 18 1/2 cents, 20 cents, 21 cents and so on, a place is made for him, and an occupation mapped out. In working on the hide alone there are nine positions at eight different rates of pay. A 20-cent man pulls off the tail, a 22 1/2-cent man pounds off another part where the hide separates readily, and the knife of a 40-cent man cuts a different texture and has a different "feel" from that of the 50-cent man. Skill has become specialized to fit the anatomy.[36]

Even in trades requiring highly skilled workers, the processes of manufacture were rapidly to become so subdivided, and so reduced to the simplest units, that a man or woman could spend an entire working life continuously performing a fractional part in the construction of the whole. Following by nearly a century and a half Adam Smith's description of the division of labor in a pin factory, a student of industrial fatigue marvelled at "this

---

34 See Philip S. Florence, Economics of Fatigue and Unrest and the Efficiency of Labour in English and American Industry (New York: Henry Holt and Co., 1924), pp. 31-34.

35 Robert F. Hoxie, Scientific Management and Labor (New York: D. Appleton and Co., 1915), pp. 131-32.

36 John R. Commons, "Labor Conditions in Meatpacking and the Recent Strike," Quarterly Journal of Economics 19 (November 1904):3-4.

minutest subdivision of work" in the making of shoes.[37] (The boot and shoe industry was the nation's third largest in 1860 and tenth largest by value added in 1910.)[38] In 1902 the United States Industrial Commission, in looking into the question of the conditions and hours of work in various industries, mentioned specifically the intensity of labor in boot and shoe factories "where the operator is required to handle thousands of pieces a day and guide them through the machine." [39]   Goldmark provides the following description:

...a well-built shoe has passed through the hands of about 100 workers and through the operations of about 60 different kinds of shoe making machinery. These figures do not include the workers in the stitching room, where a separate force sews together, on specially constructed sewing machines, the pieces of leather and lining which make up the so-called "uppers." From the stitching room, the flat, sewed uppers are sent to the making or "bottoming" room, where they are shaped over lasts fastened to the soles, and made up into the forms which we recognize as shoes.[40]

Under such conditions, workers wore out at an early age, after a relatively short period of industrial activity, of which they understood only a tiny part; and that age was apparently falling. Exhaustive subdivision of even those tasks requiring some degree of skill worked to the particular disadvantage of older workers whose reflexes might be slowing down, especially so if they had been subjected to some years of such body- and mind-numbing rigors.

The impact of the scientific regularization of production on the working classes was giving rise to the phenomenon of economic superannuation. Waning physical powers were hastened by the strains of the industrial workplace to deprive the worker of the very qualities demanded by industry; or they so impaired his efficiency that he was no longer capable of satisfying the minimum requirements for any employment. On the eve of World War I, economic old age in many of the industrial trades was commonly thought to set in at about 30 for women and 40 for men,[41] leading one scholar of the period to state that under the conditions of modern industry "middle age is old age."[42]

---

37 Josephine Goldmark, Fatigue and Efficiency: A Study in Industry (New York: Russell Sage Foundation, 1912), p. 64.

38 U.S. Department of Commerce, Bureau of the Census, Eighth Census of the United States, 1860, 3:733-42; Thirteenth Census of the United States, 1910, 8:40, cited by Walton and Robertson, History of the American Economy, pp. 403-04.

39 Goodyear Welt Shoes, How They are Made (Boston: United Shoe Machinery Company, 1909), p. 11, cited by Goldmark, Fatigue and Efficiency, p. 64.

40 Goldmark, Fatigue and Efficiency, p. 64.

41 Barkin, The Older Worker, pp. 59-67.

42 Edward T. Devine, Misery and Its Causes (New York: Macmillan Co., 1909), p. 125.

Even where some skill was still required, the capitalist employer had scant motivation to hire an older (presumably slower) worker in preference to a younger (presumably quicker) one. Evolving age limitations on people's economic usefulness served to reinforce the negative stereotypes about older workers' productivity that had begun to surface as early as the 1870s. As an example of such thinking, George Beard, an influential psychologist, had put forth the theory in 1874 that at least 70 percent of the world's work had been done by men before the age of 45, and that the most useful stage of life fell between ages 30 and 45. [43]

Quite apart from the way factory methods devalued older people's worth, there was another, less tangible sense in which older workers were particularly affected by the adverse consequences of industrial technology and business consolidation. Older Americans had the strongest attachment to, and the greatest investment in, the disappearing economic order. Merely because of their years they had more thoroughly internalized the values of hard work, initiative, independence, socioeconomic mobility, and individual success. While many of these traditional values would continue to hold sway in the popular imagination well into the twentieth century,[44] the reality was beginning to be altogether different by the final third of the nineteenth century. The psychic strain that such a value system created for the large and growing numbers who failed to meet its criteria must have been very great.

The years between 1860 and 1920 witnessed a sharp erosion of skill levels in all types of work that were susceptible to narrow specialization and mechanization, the linchpins of mass production. Although reliable data for most of the period are unavailable on the age distribution of workers in large firms versus small shops, it is logical to suppose that the self-employed and craft occupations requiring skills with a long gestation period were those in which individuals were older than the average for the labor force as a whole. One of the unmeasurable appeals of possessing a skill has always been the productive role that one can continue to play with advancing years.

Once these crafts had been rendered redundant by machinery and division of labor in large-scale enterprises, older workers faced the greatest difficulty in obtaining employment in establishments geared to narrow skill specialization, speed, and monotony.[45] A lifetime of developing and practicing a skill could be rendered meaningless by the arrival of production processes relying upon specialization of function. For those with a well-developed skill, the substitution of brute energy for that skill threatened both economic and psychological security.

---

43 George Beard, Legal Responsibility in Old Age, Based on Researches into the Relationship of Age to Work (New York: Russells, 1874), cited by Fischer, Growing Old, p. 141n.

44 For that matter, they are touted down to the present. Civics and history texts continue to explain the nation's economic and political successes by reference to these virtues; and they have at all times served to buttress the nation's claim to being the land of opportunity for the dispossessed and disenchanted of other cultures.

45 See, for example, Catlin, The Labor Problem, chapter 5 on "Overstrain and Superannuation," pp. 155-92, esp. pp. 159-66. See also Abraham Epstein, The Challenge of the Aged (New York: Vanguard Press, 1928).

Impersonality of Employment

Workers earning a living in large-scale enterprises faced yet another phenomenon which devalued them, and that was their relative anonymity and increasing interchangeability with any other workers capable of performing their jobs. This was to some extent a result of the narrowing of the tasks assigned to any one individual and of the erosion of skills as workers became tenders of machines, but it was also an outgrowth of the increases in the absolute size of business units.[46]

In most instances, increased firm size was not necessary solely on the grounds of the technological economies of large-scale production. Rather, it arose in part as a consequence of mass marketing,[47] and because severe price competition or price wars led to losses which pushed manufacturers to seek protection in various forms of monopoly.[48]

In manufacturing, the major part of increased firm size was in the number of plants directed by a single firm, rather than in the size of the production unit at the plant level. With the plant expansion necessary to accommodate new technologies cost-effectively, firms had to invade each others' markets to achieve sufficient volume. This led to a problem of overcapacity, which was solved by horizontal combinations in which competing enterprises merged to create multi-plant operations.[49] Even at the plant level the average number of employees was on the rise. The average increased slowly in the late nineteenth century, falling slightly as a result of the retrenchments imposed by the Civil War and later as a result of the depression of the 1890s. But in the first two decades of the twentieth century, the average manufacturing plant's employment more than quadrupled.

Despite the fact that census statistics prior to 1900 are heavily weighted by very small "hand and neighborhood industries,"[50] they nonetheless reveal an increase in the average number of workers per manufacturing plant of about one-third between 1870 and 1900.

---

46 There doubtless were workers, as there are today, who preferred to be treated with impersonality on the job, just as some probably preferred working by the steady rhythms of machinery over working at tasks requiring mental effort and seasoned judgment. See, for example, Margaret Duckles, Robert Duckles, and Michael Maccoby, "The Process of Change at Bolivar," Journal of Applied Behavioral Sciences 13 (Summer 1977):387-99.

Marx considered the alienation of undifferentiated workers from each other to be as great an evil of capitalist production as workers' alienation from their products through mechanization and specialization. The very real psychological costs of such alienation for the mass of workers should not be underestimated, but the focus here is the fundamental impact that growing anonymity of employment had on the job prospects of workers as they aged.

47 Alfred D. Chandler, Jr., Strategy and Structure: Chapters in the History of the Industrial Enterprise (Cambridge: Harvard University Press, 1962), p. 19.

48 Peterson and Gray, Economic Development of the United States, pp. 310-11.

49 Ibid., p. 310.

50 Ibid., p. 309.

Between 1900 and 1920 the increase was approximately 50 percent if the hand industries are not included.[51] By the end of the period, half of American workers were employed in fewer than four percent of all plants,[52] a transformation of startling proportions.

While corporatism is important in explaining workers' progressive loss of control over working conditions, labor found it almost as difficult to cope with the power exercised by large employers operating single plants as with that of corporations owning a number of facilities.[53] Employers in the former category might be nearby and ostensibly accessible to workers, but their position was often nearly impregnable and they generally maintained an autocratic control over labor conditions. Good working conditions might exist only to the degree that public sentiment, labor legislation, and employers' tendencies dictated. Employers' mutual cooperation in confronting their workforces could be almost as effective as centralized control of an industry.[54]

The trends in consolidation and incorporation of businesses clearly affected workers' interests by concentrating operating policy in the hands of persons completely inaccessible to employees in scattered plants.[55] By 1904, 70.6 percent of American factory workers were employed by corporations in which day-to-day control rested with hired managers; in 1915 the percentage was 80.3, [56] and by 1920, 86 percent of industrial wage earners worked in such manufacturing corporations.[57] While absentee ownership with its attendant evils was not new in American economic life, it became the norm with the growth of the giant corporations.[58]

---

51 Ibid.

52 Krooss, American Economic Development, p. 436.

53 Lescohier, Working Conditions, p. 297.

54 See Commons et al., History of Labor, vol. 4, chapter 10.

55 A 1905 study by John R. Commons' provides numerous examples of what accessibility to management could mean to workers, even in industries with a record of fairness. For instance, in the meatpacking industry, cattle typically reached the stockyards at night but seldom got to the killing floors until 9:00 a.m. or later. The workers had to be at the plant at 7:00 but got no pay until they started work. To minimize inventory costs, they had to kill all the cattle that had arrived, which often entailed working late into the evening, but they were paid only for an ordinary working day. When a committee of workers arranged a meeting with the president of one of the companies, he said he had no knowledge that such conditions existed and saw to it that overtime was abolished, work began at 7:00, and any cattle not processed were carried over to the next day. John R. Commons, Trade Unionism and Labor Problems (New York: Ginn and Co., 1905), p. 233.

56 Florence, Economics of Fatigue and Unrest, p. 40.

57 Faulkner, Decline of Laissez Faire, p. 155.

58 Ibid., p. 176.

In this context, employers as a class were making decisions of far-reaching importance to workers, based largely upon cost accounting data, reports from lower management, graphic analysis of business trends, and a concern for dividends.[59] Hired managers were given rules of thumb to follow in their hiring, placement, work pace, and firing decisions. Although hiring and firing "by the book" rather than "by the person" was a time-saver and could lower costs by reducing misjudgments, it was not a very great step from such a practice to hiring and firing according to group characteristics, or outright discrimination.[60] In fact, industry by the late nineteenth century did maintain discriminatory hiring practices and generally specified maximum hiring-age limits regardless of background (see Chapters 5 and 6). Furthermore, as noted in the previous section, the age at which workers were being let go and facing employment barriers in large firms was moving downward in the opening years of the twentieth century, from 50 to 45 according

---

59 Lescohier, Working Conditions, p. 295. Furthermore, the efficiency of the local management was measured by its ability to show a profit. Each plant of the corporation had its costs compared with other plants', and the local manager who increased his costs because of a concern for his workers was in danger of losing his job. Ibid., pp. 295-96.

60 While we know relatively little about explicit age discrimination in employment in this era, there exists considerable documentation of racism, sexism, and ethnic differentiation on the part of employers. Ageism in our period is reflected indirectly by data on employment, and by the prevailing social/political attitudes of the time. Economic discrimination on the basis of sex, race, and ethnic origin, particularly the latter two, was much more freely acknowledged by employers. With exceptions, this was perhaps less out of innate prejudice than a desire to keep the wages bill as low as possible while forestalling unionization.

Sex roles in economic activity were gradually changing for pragmatic reasons (young women domiciled in factories, mothers pursuing cottage industry); and ethnic priorities in hiring were being altered for the same reason, but perhaps even more rapidly because of the shifts occurring in immigration demographics. Older workers, by contrast, were still for the most part considered "one of us" in the sense that they were mostly male and mostly "native" Americans. Hence there exists less in the way of damning statements from industrial and financial magnates on the necessity of being discriminating in hiring from this group.

Quite the contrary, in fact. Industrialists appear to have been influenced by a sort of nostalgia for the past that pervaded popular culture as a whole and included paying lip service to the usefulness of older people. For example, Henry Ford repeatedly expressed in the popular media a preference for men between 35 and 60 years of age, and stated that those over 40 had in general greater tolerance and tenacity than their juniors. See Henry Ford and Samuel Crowther, My Life and Work (Garden City, N.Y.: Garden City Publishing Co., 1922). Yet the age distribution of workers in Ford plants appears not to have reflected this philosophy of employment. Catlin, The Labor Problem, p. 165.

to some writers, and from 45 to 40 according to others.[61] The periodicals of worker organizations expressed the phenomenon as "the crime of 45" and "the scrapheap at 50."[62]

Business thinking and impersonality came to overwhelm employers' sense of responsibility to workers for steadiness of employment, wages, and working conditions.[63] Older workers' economic security hinged on all three. Steadiness of employment was important because older workers had greater difficulty than others in finding work following a layoff, particularly if not protected by seniority in unions, which remained rare. Wages were of course a vital concern because pensions were uncommon and inadequate. Working conditions mattered because the pace and unhealthful character of industrial employments were progressively wearing out workers at younger and younger ages, while wage-labor status placed the retirement decision beyond the individual's control.

Irregularity of Employment

The employment insecurity of older workers during the 1860-1920 period was part of the larger phenomenon of the economy's increasing susceptibility to recessions and depressions. When the economy had been mostly agrarian and oriented toward local markets, bad times seldom spelled catastrophe. People could usually get enough to eat and did not usually lose their homes. Even workers living in cities (with the exception of the crowded tenement districts of the largest urban areas) commonly owned, or had relatives who owned, plots of land nearby, on which they could raise some food to tide them over during economic downturns.[64]

But with growing economic concentration in an increasingly urban society dominated by large business units, the ups and downs of business activity came to be more sudden and extreme. When times were good, increasingly efficient factories spewed out torrents of goods. When demand collapsed they closed down abruptly--often virtually overnight--and remained closed until the surplus disappeared. The result was massive unemployment, on

---

61 Isaac M. Rubinow, Social Insurance. With Special Reference to American Conditions (New York: Henry Holt and Co., 1913), p. 306; B.J. Hendrick, "The Superannuated Man, Labor Pensions and the Carnegie Foundation," McClure's Magazine , December 1908, pp. 115-27, cited by ibid.

62 Rubinow, Social Insurance, pp. 301-07.

63 Consolidations in manufacturing also undoubtedly reinforced resistance to workers' attempts to organize around such issues. This was because bankers were beginning to have a large influence on the directorates of corporate mergers, and bankers as a class had even less understanding of and sympathy for unions than did industrialists. Lescohier, Working Conditions, p. 297.

64 As late as 1890, Queens County and much of Brooklyn, only a few miles from the nation's largest metropolis, were still semi-rural, and many families continued to be as reliant upon small-scale agriculture as upon industrial or commercial employment. (Robert W. Smuts, Women and Work in America [New York: Schocken, 1971], cited by Braverman, Labor and Monopoly Capital, pp. 273-74.)

an entirely new scale, mirroring the new scale of business enterprise and interdependence of markets.

Reliable unemployment data for any population group in the period under investigation are either unavailable or unreliable, as Chapter 5 will show. Yet it was becoming widely recognized that at periodic intervals the trough of a business cycle appeared and, in Kirkland's words, "a palsy seized industry, production was curtailed, and workers had to shift as they might until a slow cure was effected." But "in the nineteenth century there was no accurate means of measuring this unemployment."[65] The panic of 1837 had first called public attention to the phenomenon of cyclical unemployment, and the panic of 1893 was the first for which even partial figures exist. These are "well-meaning estimates" of between one million and 4.5 million persons out of work in 1893. [66]

The economy began to experience significant spells of unemployment in the final third of the nineteenth century, in no small part because American business had come to rely heavily upon borrowed capital to finance expansion. Whereas prior to the Civil War, those who owned capital had typically been the same people who managed it, the post-war structure of bankers, brokers, and other money and credit middlemen possessed an altogether new degree of power and importance. When, for whatever reason, a sizable proportion of these lenders began to suspect that their clients had become overextended, panic set in.[67]

Thus the economy experienced the "Jay Cooke panic" of 1873, the less severe "railroad panic" of 1884, and in 1893 the "Cleveland panic," the most severe depression the country had yet encountered. There followed the "rich men's panic" of 1903, the "Roosevelt panic" of 1907, and an unnamed recession in 1914; followed in the post-war years by the "Harding panic" of 1921 and the "prosperity panic" of 1929. [68] Epstein calculated that between 1885 and 1920 there were 16 alternate periods of prosperity and depression;[69] according to Wesley Mitchell, there were 15 "business crises" between 1812 and 1920."[70] The magnitude of the distress these crises caused was attested by numerous studies, sufficient to warrant the conclusion that unemployment and recession were attendant evils of

---

65 Kirkland, History of American Economic Life, p. 523.

66 Ibid., pp. 523-24.

67 See A. Ross Eckler, "A Measure of the Severity of Depressions, 1873-1932," Review of Economic Statistics 15 (May 1933):75-81; Charles Hoffman, "The Depression of the Nineties," Journal of Economic History 16 (June 1956):137-64.

68 Abraham Epstein, Insecurity: A Challenge to America, 2nd revised ed. (New York: Random House, 1938), p. 191.

69 Ibid.

70 Mitchell, Business Cycles and Unemployment, p. 5.

industrial life.[71]   Far from being merely a temporary occurrence, unemployment was proving to be a chronic malady of industrial capitalism.

The explanation lay both in the transformation of farmers, shopkeepers, and craftsmen into wage laborers and in the increasing size of business units, in which decision-making authority resided with individuals and institutions that were not accountable to the ultimate producers. Layoffs could be sudden, massive, and imposed at arm's length without regard to individual circumstance. Yet Lescohier noted that public opinion before 1920 had "not yet fully grasped the preponderant significance of industrial and economic factors as contrasted with the peculiarities of individuals as causes of unemployment."[72] Americans persisted in viewing joblessness as a reflection on the individual, on the one hand, and on the other as being peculiar to a particular year, attributable to a change of administration, a fluke, and so forth.

Challenges to such a view existed but failed to enter the mainstream until after World War I. Wesley Mitchell published the first of his numerous volumes on business cycles in 1913, [73] in which he lay the groundwork for his later work linking severity of unemployment to trends in industrial consolidation. Also in 1913, economist John Mitchell explained the insecurity of employment of the American worker in the context of a monopolistic industrial structure.[74]

But the relationship between extent of unemployment and firm size would not be addressed rigorously for the first time until the early 1920s. In September 1921 President Harding convened the Conference on Unemployment,[75] for which the National Bureau of Economic Research and cooperating organizations conducted extensive investigations of the impact of the industrial structure on the business cycle. Among the findings was that

---

71   See, for example, William H. Beveridge, Unemployment: A Problem of Industry (London: Longmans, Green and Co., 1909); Henry George, The Condition of Labor (New York: United States Book Co., 1891); Frances Kellor, Out of Work: A Study of Employment Agencies (New York: G.P. Putnam's Sons, 1904); John Mitchell, The Wage Earner and His Problems (Washington, D.C.: P.S. Ridsdale, 1913); Ralph G. Hurlin, "Three Decades of Employment Fluctuation," The Annalist, October 24, 1921; Massachusetts, Board to Investigate the Subject of the Unemployed, Report, House Document No. 50 (Boston: Wright and Potter, 1895); Chicago, Mayor's Commission on Unemployment, Report (Chicago: Cameron, Amberg Co., March 1914); New York, Mayor's Committee on Unemployment of New York City, Report (New York, 1917).

72   Lescohier, Working Conditions, p. 129.

73   Wesley C. Mitchell, Business Cycles (Berkeley: University of California Press, 1913).

74   John Mitchell, The Wage Earner and His Problems.

75   This was the first conference on the subject ever called by the Federal government. Lescohier, Working Conditions, p. 134.

the unemployment rate among employees of large establishments appeared to be far worse than that among employees of smaller firms in the same industry.[76]

It was reasoned that in a downturn, large establishments had a much greater trendency to cut production sharply and protect their products' market prices rather than trying to maintain output and sell at lower prices, or maintain employment by sharing the available work--the response typical of small-scale, decentralized economic units.[77] In addition to the cyclically-induced contractions of employment in large establishments, the savings and often greater efficiency of business consolidations yielded some duplication of labor which also could throw many out of work at one time.[78]

Following by a year the release of the Conference findings, economist Philip S. Florence remarked on a corollary phenomenon with even more direct bearing on the subject of this study. Florence's interest in the unemployment generated by the collapse of 1921 led him to examine the impact of industrial employment upon workers' health and hence their worklife expectancy. He concluded that there appeared to be an inverse relationship between average firm size and degree of industrial concentration, and the average age of an establishment's workforce. "As a rule," he wrote, "the average age of men seems lower in the factory...than in trades less centralized."[79]

Conclusion

Florence was articulating something that had concerned only a few other social scientists during the nation's industrialization: the circumstances of the older worker. The

---

76 National Bureau of Economic Research, Business Cycles and Unemployment (New York: McGraw-Hill Book Co., 1923), p. 97. The year 1921 was one of severe unemployment, which is what instigated the conference. The estimated jobless rate in manufacturing and transportation in that year was put at 21.2 percent. Douglas, Real Wages in the United States, p. 445.

77 This is one of the principal differences between the business cycle responses of the manufacturing and agricultural sectors. Manufacturing has reduced output and employment when the market showed signs of weakening, whereas agriculture, locked into an externally-imposed product cycle, has maintained production and employment levels and accepted lower prices.

78 Business consolidations were detrimental to labor whether it was organized in unions or not, but where workers were able to organize they fared better in the decentralized or smaller industries (railroad transportation being the major exception). Faulkner, Decline of Laissez Faire, p. 175. Many of the largest consolidations--in particular, U.S. Steel--were able to prevent unionization of their workers until the union-enabling legislation of the 1930s. There is no evidence that workers in centralized industries were better paid than workers in industries less centralized, although the large firms could better afford certain welfare projects which benefitted workers. Jeremiah W. Jenks and Walter E. Clark, The Trust Problem, 5th ed. (New York: Doubleday, Page and Co., 1920), pp. 138-56.

79 Florence, Economics of Fatigue and Unrest, p. 315.

economic transformation which had put the majority of the labor force at the mercy of impersonal market forces and the machinations of powerful capitalists was even more acutely damaging to the security older Americans. The techniques of modern industry exhausted workers at an early age because the new requirements of industrial employment led to an early decline of powers. Rapid technological change created a climate in which skills, experience, and seasoned judgment were de-emphasized as criteria for employment; in their place, speed, strength, and adaptability to hierarchical working relationships became valued employee attributes in the era of industrial capitalism. Workers of middle age and beyond were less likely to possess these qualities than were their younger counterparts,[80] and were far more likely to possess the attributes and skills whose importance was being eroded through technological and organizational change.[81]

For the first time in the American experience, macroeconomic transformations were creating a downwardly mobile group of people who faced diminished prospects for employment at a time when the national labor force was expanding rapidly with pell-mell economic growth. Growing firm size, rationalization of production, and economic concentration after 1860 were the foundations of the proletarianization of the labor force and the transformation of older Americans into a lumpen-proletariat.

A society in which production was ruled by blind economic forces was being eclipsed by one in which production lay in the ultimate control of only a relative handful of individuals. This economic power in the hands of the small number of bankers and industrialists who controlled the large corporations was a potent force which could harm or benefit millions of Americans, affect entire districts, alter the currents of trade, bring ruin

---

80 To be sure, older workers committed to the old order might be less tractable employees during periods of rapid changes in production techniques and workplace relationships. To the extent that this may have been so, their diminished economic circumstances over time can be seen as a personal problem rather than the social problem that is of concern here. Unquestionably speed and endurance decline with age to some degree in all workers. The weight of the evidence from studies in industrial gerontology supports the view that such physical changes do not cause a decline in productivity in those employments which afford the individual an opportunity to build upon skill and experience. See, for example, Jon Hendricks and C. Davis Hendricks, Aging in Mass Society (Cambridge, Mass.: Winthrop Publishing Co., 1977), p. 177; Alan T. Welford, Skill and Age, An Experimental Approach (London: Oxford University Press, 19510, p. 147 passim; George Telland, ed., Human Aging and Behavior (New York: Academic Press, 1968); Jerome A. Mark, "Comparative Job Performance by Age," Monthly Labor Review 80 (December 1957):1467-71; Alastair Heron and Sheila M. Chown, "Expectations of Supervisors Concerning Older Workers," in Processes of Aging, ed. by Richard H. Williams et al., 2 vols. (New York: Atherton Press, 1963), 1:282-83.

81 Overall demand for skilled workers was not falling. It continued to grow throughout the period under discussion, but at a rate that was far slower than the demand growth for unskilled and semi-skilled workers. And the content of skilled jobs was shifting at the same time it was being narrowed, with the consequence that the skills most likely to be unique to older workers were diminishing in importance.

to some communities and prosperity to others. Large enterprises were passing far beyond the realm of private enterprise to become very nearly social institutions.

In the following chapters, the concentration issue as it affected older people's economic security will be broken down according to its mutually-reinforcing technological and organizational imperatives. Economic consolidation for technological reasons may theoretically be separated from consolidation for organizational reasons, but in fact they produced many similar, overlapping consequences for older workers' economic viability. For example, both led to a division of labor, deskilling, loss of workers autonomy, automation, a changing occupational structure, increasing bureaucracy, and a move toward age-based employment practices. Nevertheless, it is possible to dissect the underlying industrial conditions impelling age-graded labor market behavior according to technological and organizational criteria. Chapter 7 then provides an analysis of the political/social climate which reflected a persistent, ideologically-based failure of the state to address the singular distress of the aged until long after it had become widely evident.

CHAPTER 5

TECHNOLOGICAL CHANGE, MACROECONOMIC INSTABILITY, AND OCCUPATIONAL OBSOLESCENCE

Introduction

The mechanization of production which characterized the 1860-1920 period was of two kinds: (1) that which merely expanded output, and (2) that which directly displaced workers. Both kinds typically lowered unit costs, enabling lower selling prices and/or higher profits. In the case of a technologically-induced increase in the demand for labor, the lag could be substantial between the introduction of a more productive, labor-saving technique and its trickle-down impact on (expanding) employment elsewhere in the economy (as in the need for workers to make the new machines). This would especially be the case in instances in which new methods were introduced with sufficient rapidity in some firms to undermine the competitive position of other firms in the industry. Such a circumstance effectively foreclosed for a time the widespread adoption of the new technology and hence its potential for generating new jobs.[1]

Furthermore, once a firm or group of firms gained a competitive advantage within an industry,[2] other firms, which were still functioning according to the older mode of organizing production and workers, were forced to make changes to keep up. This in turn restricted the employment choices of workers who remained employed, because they were forced to submit to mechanized, segmented, and rationalized production methods as other forms of work in that industry disappeared.[3]

The tremendous growth of the paid labor force between 1860 and 1920 (owing to mass immigration and the release of surplus labor from agriculture) testifies to the explosion in production which characterized the American economy during its industrialization. Mechanization clearly led to an increase in the total demand for labor in a

---

1 Lescohier, Working Conditions, p. 146. Economies of size could substitute for or augment the benefits of capturing a new technology, especially if the size differential between a firm and its rivals was very large. Innovational advantages coupled with those of size enabled the lengthy domination of their respective industries of such firms as Baldwin Locomotive Works, Boston Associates (textiles), Swift and Armour (meatpackers), Anaconda (mining), U.S. Steel, and Standard Oil. (Gerald Gunderson, A New Economic History of America [New York: McGraw-Hill Book Co., 1976], p. 311.)

2 Perhaps the most striking as well as best-known example is that of Henry Ford's innovations in the automobile industry. Although the concept of the automobile had long existed, and a few cars were built to order by tinkering mechanics by the early 1890s, Ford combined moving assembly lines, interchangeable parts, low cost, and mass marketing to revolutionize and for a time dominate the industry by the second decade of the twentieth century. Hacker, Course of American Economic Growth, p. 280; Peterson and Gray, Economic Development of the United States, p. 279; Faulkner, Decline of Laissez Faire, pp. 228-32. Ford thus exemplified Schumpeter's theory of innovations (see Chapter 3).

3 Braverman, Labor and Monopoly Capital, p. 149.

dramatic way. Employment in all of manufacturing (production workers) rose from less than 1.5 million in 1860 (accounting for $815 million in value added) to more than 8.5 million in 1919 ($23.8 billion in value added).[4]

However, rapid adoption of new technology, coupled with the shift toward larger-scale production units with some degree of monopoly power, placed new strains on the operation of the labor market. As pointed out in Chapter 4, labor was simultaneously confronted with several destabilizing phenomena resulting from the ascendancy of the wage-work system itself. Workers faced task specialization, potential displacement by machinery (or displacement by newly-arrived, more docile immigrants accustomed to a lower standard of living), repetitive work routines, arms' length and bureaucratic dealings with employers/managers, and a rapidly changing structure of demand for labor.

This chapter examines the employment effects on older workers of increasing firm size and economic centralization as these twin forces enabled the diffusion of labor-saving technology, rapidly rising productivity, and a transformation of the nation's occupational structure. The following chapter focuses on the other major aspect of consolidating capitalism's impact upon older Americans: the complex of changes in industrial manage-ment and administration, including the rise of a managerial class, growing reliance on rigid rules of thumb in employment and layoff decisions, and the increasingly negative impact of industrial occupations upon worklife expectancy.

Technological Change

The pattern of the introduction and diffusion of new technology for the period 1860-1920 can be roughly divided into two phases. Up to the 1890s, the major industries serviced an economy that was still preponderantly agrarian. With the exception of a few companies supplying the rapidly expanding railroad network, the nation's leading industrial firms processed agricultural output and provisioned farmers and craftsmen with food and clothing.[5] Firms tended to be small, and they purchased their inputs and sold their output locally. Those that produced for markets more than a few miles distant worked through commissioned agents on contract to several small firms.[6]

By the nineties, also, the U.S. economy had approached a state of near maturity with respect to profitable opportunities in coal, iron, railways, steamships, textiles and clothing.[7] These industries (together with those that had practiced the "American system" of using

---

4 U.S. Bureau of the Census, Historical Statistics of the United States, Colonial Times to 1970, 2:1-12.

5 Chandler, "The Beginnings of 'Big Business,'" p. 81.

6 Ibid.

7 Lewis, Growth and Fluctuations, p. 26. Up until the 1890s, it could reasonably be argued that for all the disparities of detail produced by cultural and geographic differences, the U.S. had essentially followed, in a shorter time, the path of the British economy.

interchangeable parts[8] since before the Civil War) were declining in importance by late in the nineteenth century, both in terms of contribution to GNP and in terms of their technological precocity. Inventions in these pre-Civil War industries had a decidedly practical bent and had their origins primarily in empirical testing.[9]

By the end of the century, technological breakthroughs began to be mainly a result of applications of advancements in scientific knowledge--advancements which were beyond the capabilities of a system based upon crude empiricism.[10] These advances, which began to be most intensively exploited after the 1880s (in organic chemicals, electricity, steel, rubber, power machinery, machine tools, and automobiles)[11] required a higher degree of productive organization and larger amounts of working capital than had earlier technological breakthroughs; and hence companies in these industries were in the forefront of the consolidation movement.

The shift in the source of new technology was accompanied by a shift toward producers' goods to be used in industry, and a relative decline in industries producing for the farm and for the ultimate consumer.[12] Of the ten leading industries in 1900, three manufactured food, drink, and allied products; two were in textiles and clothing; one was in the processing of raw materials; and four were in producers' goods (three of these producers' goods industries were in the top four industries by value added in 1900).[13] Most of the major industries had come to be dominated by a few enterprises possessing a technological edge which they sought to maintain by instituting, among other innovations, the nation's first formal research and development departments.[14] These giants had their own national purchasing and marketing organizations, obviating any role for the middleman/agent relied upon by smaller firms in less concentrated industries.

---

8 These included firearms production, followed by clocks and watches, sewing machines, locks and hardware, farm implements, ammunition, and bicycles. (Niemi, U.S. Economic History, pp. 180-81.)

9 See Alexis de Tocqueville, Democracy in America, 2 vols. (New York: Century Company, 1898), 2:40-53.

10 Niemi, U.S. Economic History, p. 181; A. P. Usher, A History of Mechanical Inventions (Boston: Beacon Press, 1959), p. 56, cited by Rosenberg, Technology and American Economic Growth, p. 119.

11 Lewis, Growth and Fluctuations, p. 26.

12 Chandler, "The Beginnings of 'Big Business,'" p. 81.

13 Krooss, American Economic Development, p. 434.

14 Chandler, "The Beginnings of 'Big Business,'" pp. 96-97. Particularly after the emergence of the electrical industry in the 1890s, it became necessary for firms to systematize attempts to develop new products to stay ahead of the competition. Walton and Robertson, History of the American Economy, p. 317.

Output Growth Due to Technology

The acceleration in invention and innovation that occurred in this period is attested to by the phenomenal growth in national income, from $6.5 billion in the 1869-1878 decade to $36.3 billion for 1909-1918 (in current dollars; in 1929 dollars the growth was from $9.4 billion to $50.3 billion).[15] The nation's increased capacity to produce wealth is even more forcefully demonstrated by reference to the differences in output attributable to machine production as opposed to hand production. As an example, in 1852, printing and folding 480,000 newspaper pages took 3660 hours of labor at a (labor) cost of $447, whereas by 1896 the same quantity of output required only 18.5 hours and cost $6.27. [16] In 1855 the production of 40 bushels of corn took 38.75 hours of work at a total labor cost of $3.63, while in 1894, just over 15 hours of labor at a cost $1.51 produced the same quantity.[17]

Virtually any area of manufacturing tells a similar story. Steel production, almost nonexistent in 1850, was over 10 million tons in 1900, a more than 10,000 percent increase; pig iron output rose from 631,000 tons to 15.4 million tons in the same period;[18] crude petroleum output rose by 9,060 percent between 1860 and 1900; bituminous coal from 9 million to 212 million tons in those four decades.[19] By way of comparison with other industrializing nations, in the 1850s the industrial output of the U.S. was far below that of Great Britain. By 1894 the value of American production nearly equalled that of Great Britain, Germany, and France combined; and by 1915 American manufacturing output had trebled its 1894 level, with the U.S. contributing more than a third of global industrial production.[20]

Yet another indication of the rate of technological innovation and occupational transformation can be gleaned from the caseload of the U.S. Patent Office in the last half of the nineteenth century. Six thousand patents were granted between 1851 and 1855; in 1875-1880 the figure was 64,000; and in 1901-1905, 143,000. [21] Altogether, nearly 780,000

---

15 Simon Kuznets, "Changes in the National Income of the United States of America Since 1870," Income and Wealth Series II (London: Bowes and Bowes, Ltd., 1952), p. 30.

16 Thirteenth Annual Report of the U.S. Commissioner of Labor, cited by Ely, Evolution of Industrial Society, pp. 65-66.

17 Ibid.

18 John A. Garraty, ed., Labor and Capital in the Gilded Age: Testimony of the Times, Selections from Congressional Hearings (Boston: Little, Brown and Co., 1968), p. vii.

19 U.S. Bureau of the Census, Historical Statistics of the United States, 1860 passim, cited by Hacker, Course of American Economic Growth, p. 175; Victor S. Clark, History of Manufactures in the United States, 3 vols. (New York: McGraw-Hill Book Co. for the Carnegie Institute of Washington, 1929), vol. 2: 1860-1893.

20 Chandler, Bruchey, and Galambos, "The Industrializing Economy, 1850-1914," p. 200.

21 Epstein, Insecurity, p. 229.

patents were issued in just over 50 years, almost 25 times the number granted in the preceding 60-year history of the Patent Office.[22]

Clearly the nature of work was being radically altered by a technological juggernaut that had its origins in the uniquely American propensity to tinker and the economy's historic condition of relative labor scarcity. By the end of the nineteenth century, the growth of productivity was rapidly reducing the demand for labor per unit of output; few trades were unaffected by mechanization.[23] The combination of technologically-induced reshufflings of occupations and more pronounced macroeconomic fluctuations triggered the country's first encounters with widespread technological unemployment.

Technology and Macroeconomic Instability

Technological unemployment was one of the earliest forms of unemployment to be recognized and receive formal treatment by social scientists.[24] From at least the middle of the eighteenth century onward in the U.S., machinery's effects upon labor had been debated, but through the first half of the nineteenth century Americans were so busily and successfully exploiting the new technological possibilities that their philosophical or ethical aspects were scarcely considered.[25] Labor was in short supply, the frontier remained to be settled, markets were widely dispersed, and unemployment as a social problem was virtually nonexistent. This state of affairs lasted until the Civil War which, as noted earlier, provided a powerful stimulus to production and distribution on a theretofore unprecedented scale. In addition, with the defeat of the South and the dismantling of the highly efficient plantation system, the implausibility of the nation's economy remaining based upon agrarian values became evident; with industry, the North's great advantage, lay the prospective future.[26]

As noted in the previous chapter, at least from the 1870s onward, American workers were increasingly subjected to severe and lengthy periods of unemployment.[27] In 1873 and again in 1882, the economy underwent serious business depressions that were primarily national, and indeed international, rather than regional in their effects. American attention began to be focused as never before on the machine as the potential enemy of stable employment, once it was realized that these depressions took their severest form where

22 Thomas V. DiBacco, "Viewpoint," <u>American Magazine</u>, July/ August 1979, p. 19.

23 Yellowitz, <u>Industrialization</u>, p. 45.

24 Catlin, <u>The Labor Problem</u>, p. 119.

25 Ibid.

26 Walton and Robertson, <u>History of the American Economy</u>, pp. 306, 308.

27 Lewis, <u>Growth and Fluctuations</u>, p. 126. The 1893 slump was termed the "Great Depression" by historians until the 1930s gave new meaning to that epithet. Robert C. Puth, <u>American Economic History</u> (New York: Dryden Press, 1982), p. 303.

machinery use and efficiency-of-labor criteria were most fully developed.[28] John Commons asserted that these technologically-precocious, nation-spanning corporations created more unemployment than smaller firms, and thus by the turn of the century, the behavior of the distant stock market became by the turn of the century one of the most important labor problems.[29]

Although the majority of workers had not yet begun to organize around the issue, there was a growing awareness that labor-saving devices were not merely a method of relieving toil, that within centralized, bureaucratic enterprises, saving on labor also translated into widespread unemployment. Whereas ten years before the Civil War approximately 70 percent of manufactured goods were produced in handicraft workshops, by the turn of the century more than 80 percent of such goods were turned out in factories making standardized products.[30] Thus, to the farmers of the South and West who had been suffering from the great downward swing in prices since the Civil War, were added industrial laborers and small businessmen who bore the brunt of declining economic activity during the major depressions.[31]

While short periods of revival and uneasy prosperity separated the depressions from one another, in 1878-1882 and less surely in 1886-1892, stagnation increasingly characterized the world's most mechanized economy.[32] The depression of 1893-1896 culminated more than two decades of disquieting cyclical fluctuations.[33] Subsequently, following the first great merger wave of 1898-1902 with its enormous expansion of output and profits, there occurred the mild 1903-1904 depression, a sharp panic and deep depression in 1907-1908, a mild depression in 1910-1911 and a short but severe depression in 1914. [34]

The years after the 1873 recession were also increasingly characterized by labor-management strife. Disharmony prevailed, among other reasons, because even the most basic and stable of industries experienced intermittent unemployment brought about by

---

28 David A. Wells, Recent Economic Changes (New York: D. Appleton and Company, 1899), p. 61.

29 Commons, "Introduction," History of Labor, 3:xxvii.

30 Laura Katz Olson, The Political Economy of Aging: The State, Private Power, and Social Welfare (New York: Columbia University Press, 1982), p. 29.

31 Walton and Robertson, History of the American Economy, p. 458.

32 Lescohier, Working Conditions, p. 127. A glimpse at the trend of prices is illustrative. If the price index is established by 1873 prices, it stood at 77 after the 1873 panic; in the mid-1880s it fell from 87 to 76, and in the 1890s from 78 to 71, in both 1894 and 1896. Four years away from the turn of the century, the price index stood at a level not seen since Lincoln's first election. Bureau of the Census, Historical Statistics of the United States, 1789-1945, pp. 231-32.

33 Walton and Robertson, History of the American Economy, p. 458.

34 Lescohier, Working Conditions, p. 127.

seasonal or market conditions. As an example of this, Kirkland records that although the blast furnaces of the iron and steel industry constituted one of the most regularized industrial processes, its employment fluctuations could be extreme. In a two-year period, 1908-1910, the number of blast furnace workers ranged between 18,485 and 46,810. An investigation in 1910 into the conditions of labor in the iron and steel industry found that the strongest and most frequent worker complaints had to do with the extreme irregularity of employment.[35]

In the wake of the panic of 1873, the idea of "underconsumption"--or, alternatively, "overproduction"--had begun to surface in the analysis of some financiers and economists. In 1886 the Bureau of Labor, under its first Commissioner, Carroll D. Wright, released its study of the "alleged causes" of depression, which examined 71 separate possibilities and concluded that the major cause of the "industrial disease" was underconsumption. The farmers' chronically low returns, the slowing of railroad construction, the rise of bankruptcies and consequent unemployment--all reduced people's capacities and willingness to make purchases.[36]

As to the overproduction explanation, most Americans refused to accept that it was possible.[37] After all, the U.S. with its huge resource endowment had made a god of production, the problem always having been how to get enough of it. The nation's best-known economic thinker of the day, Henry George, along with the profession's more orthodox members, rejected this explanation for unemployment, saying, "I do not think there can be any such thing as an overproduction until everybody has more than enough."[38]

But David A. Wells, a Treasury Department tax and tariff reformer of the 1870s and 1880s who influenced George and other economists, demurred. Wells was the outstanding theorist of overproduction as the primary cause of unemployment. In his capacity as a "publicist" for the constellation of views embraced by economic orthodoxy and Protestant theology,[39] his opinions carried a disproportionate weight in the last quarter of the century. Wells argued that the primary reason for the growing problem of cyclical unemployment lay in technological advances which, in a time of rising immigration, depressed the demand for labor well below its supply.

Unlike in earlier periods, he reasoned, when laborers had the option of occupying public land, and thus rather readily becoming independent (if not always prosperous)

---

35 Kirkland, History of American Economic Life, p. 523.

36 U.S. Bureau of Labor, First Annual Report of the Commissioner of Labor (Washington, D.C.: Government Printing Office, March 1886), pp. 76-79, 243-46.

37 An important exception were labor leaders and their allies.

38 Testimony of Henry George, Report of the Committee on Education and Labor of the Senate, 1885, I:471, cited by Kirkland, Industry Comes of Age, p. 10.

39 Through the 1880s, economist and churchman were very often the same person, as "the search for a providential intelligence at work took those trained in theological seminaries into an examination of the laws by which social arrangements were effected." (Hacker, Course of American Economic Growth, pp. 194, 197.)

businessmen, such an alternative had all but disappeared by the last quarter of the nineteenth century. With the growth in efficient, labor-saving methods of production, there would inevitably come into existence a permanent pauper class, unless new wants were discovered whose satisfaction would lead to an increase in the demand for labor.[40]

Yet Wells' and Wright's sympathies lay preponderantly on the side of progress at almost any cost. Indeed, their prescription for the amelioration of the pains of mechanization might be said to conform to the theoretical economic defense of machinery (in its effect on labor, and on employment in particular) that had been worked out by Jean-Baptiste Say and others by 1830. While both men felt that all help and sympathy should be extended toward those unfortunates who were being displaced by machinery (this would primarily be in the form of universal extension and improvement of education, and a voluntary and informed paternalism on the part of manufacturers), they cautioned against governmental interference with the "free action...of industrial social forces."[41] The solution to the individual problems created by the rapid growth of technology lay in even faster growth, to spur demand and re-employ the idled.

This free action of industrial forces--the classical economists' theoretical defense of labor-saving technology--operated as follows: Granted, in the case of individual workers and specific industries, there was a diminution of skill and, less certainly, an immediate contraction of the demand for labor relative to output, as a result of the adoption of machine methods. In the short run, unemployment appeared to signal the economy's need for a redirection of its available labor force toward other areas where employment was growing more quickly. For at least some period of time, economic theory conceded, a displaced worker in one occupation might be forced to take a job at less than his previous wages and thus be compelled to live at a standard below that to which he was accustomed.[42]

In the long run, however, there was a virtually inexhaustible supply of job openings in the "blotting paper" industries[43] that would more than absorb all displaced workers, thus eliminating unemployment difficulties. A great deal of economists' attention by the turn of the century was directed to the "temporary" character of most instances of unemployment; it was thought that no one who did not choose it could be permanently unemployed because of technology. Social reformers decried this refusal to face up to the possibility of permanent technological displacement of labor, particularly in view of all the admissions and concessions circumscribing the arguments put forth by the proponents of unrestrained technology. In the words of Epstein,

...it may be logically asked whether the entire debate regarding temporary versus permanent technological unemployment is anything more than metaphysical hair

---

40 Wells, Recent Economic Changes, pp. 70-113.

41 Ibid., pp. 437, 466; Carroll D. Wright, The Factory System as an Element in Civilization (Boston: Little, Brown Co., 1882), p. 30.

42 Epstein, Insecurity, p. 233.

43 Ibid., p. 236.

splitting. To the man who is unemployed for two or three years it makes very little difference whether he will ultimately be assigned a job in a statistical table. After a prolonged period of unemployment he may be unable to hold the job even if he should get it.[44]

The Extent of Unemployment

The historical record does not support the contention that the newly emerging occupations in the late nineteenth century were capable of absorbing the technologically unemployed. Most industries in the 1880s and 1890s did not ultimately rehire all skilled workers displaced by machines, even in a less skilled capacity and even when product demand was expanding. According to the First Annual Report of the Commissioner of Labor in 1886, which was based solely on employers' estimates of job loss through mechanization, rates of displacement ranged anywhere between 25 and 75 percent of the skilled work force in industrial trades.[45]

If it did not put him out of a job altogether, the substitution of mechanical for intelligent labor in modern manufacturing deprived the worker of independence and reduced him to the position of a machine. Not only were individual forms of acquired skills (for example, hand-loom weaving) rendered useless by the introduction of machinery, but, according to economics textbook author Hadley,

...large classes of men who were the most useful citizens in the past are being driven out of existence by the stress of modern competition. The increasing efficiency connected with the division and organization of labor has crowded out those men who exercised a diversified industry. It is not merely the jack-of-all trades, but the master of one trade, that finds it difficult to compete with the employers who subdivide his trade into a hundred different parts. The village blacksmith finds his occupation gone when so large a part of his product can be made by machinery at one-tenth of the old cost. We have secured diversification of consumption through the cheapening of products, but it has been obtained at the sacrifice of diversified industrial activity on the part of the men who make those products. It is undeniable that labor is becoming more and more specialized, and that many of the occupations of the modern laborer have a narrowing effect upon those who practise them.[46]

Yellowitz states that "by the end of the nineteenth century, there were few trades that had not been affected by mechanization, yet the continued improvement of machinery periodically renewed the threat to the existing level of skill." This clearly revealed "the capacity of mechanization to divide workmen along lines of competing self-interest" because

---

44 Ibid., p. 232.

45 See First Annual Report of the Commissioner of Labor, pp. 80-90. These figures were not subject to independent verificaton by the Labor Bureau, nor was it ascertained whether or where the displaced had found work, or in what trades, or at what wages.

46 Hadley, Economics, p. 351.

"the skilled viewed the unskilled as competitors."[47] Even if the number of jobs in an industry ultimately rose owing to mechanization, unskilled or semi-skilled labor took the place of the older skilled labor force.[48] This was harmful not only to the displaced individual but also to his union, if one existed. Employers often saw machines as a way to rid themselves of the craft unions to which their skilled workers belonged. Thus the impetus toward deskilling was accentuated, because it could increase profits directly by boosting productivity and indirectly by reducing the share going to labor.[49]

Occupational Distribution

The depression of 1893-1896 culminated more than two decades of violent cyclical fluctuations in the American economy. In this depression the human toll was unprecedented, and the problems of relief reached enormous proportions in both large and small cities. Yet there continued to be more interest in debating the depression's causes and cures than in determining who was unemployed or discussing the merits of various relief plans.[50] As a reflection of such attitudes, it was not until the 1910 decennial census that any systematic attempt was made even to answer the most fundamental question of employment, that is, what percent of the labor force were wage-earners, what percent employers of labor, and what percent independent producers.[51]

Nevertheless, attempts were made to estimate these magnitudes from the sketchy data from censuses of the last half of the nineteenth century. While different researchers' figures varied widely, the trends were unmistakable. The American people at the end of the century were rapidly becoming a wage-working people, dependent for their subsistence upon workplaces over which they had little control.

Up until the 1910 census, all work was classified under one of five very broad headings: (1) agriculture,[52] (2) professional service, (3) domestic and personal service, (4) trade and transportation, and (5) manufactures and mechanical industries. The percentage of the American labor force among these pursuits in the final three decades of the nineteenth century were reported in the 1900 census as shown in Table 4.

---

47 Yellowitz, Industrialization, p. 45.

48 The steel industry was a classic example of this. See Katherine Stone, "The Origins of Job Structures in the Steel Industry," Review of Radical Political Economics 6 (Summer 1974):113-73.

49 See Robert Ozanne, A Century of Labor Management Relations at McCormick and International Harvester (Madison: University of Wisconsin Press, 1967).

50 Walton and Robertson, History of the American Economy, pp. 458-59.

51 Rubinow, Social Insurance, p. 29.

52 Agriculture also included the extractive industries such as lumbering, mining, and quarrying. The census data do not break out these categories.

TABLE 4

OCCUPATIONS OF AMERICAN LABOR, 1880-1900

Class of Occupation	Percent of Labor Force			
	1820*	1880	1890	1900
(1) Agriculture	71.9	44.3	37.7	35.7
(2) Professional Service		3.5	4.1	4.3
(3) Domestic & Personal Service		19.7	18.6	19.2
(4) Trade & Transportation	2.5	10.7	14.6	16.4
(5) Manufactures & Mechanical	12.2	21.8	25.0	24.4

SOURCE: U.S. Department of Commerce, Bureau of the Census, <u>Twelfth Census of the United States, 1900, Population,</u> Part II, p. 133, cited by Ely, <u>Evolution of Industrial Society,</u> p. 104.

* Included for comparison purposes. This is the earliest year for which any such sttistics are available for the United States. See Pascal K. Whelpton, "Occupational Groups in the United States," <u>Journal of the American Sociological Association</u> 21 (September 1926):339-40.

The proportional decline in agriculture is evident; in manufactures the trend is less clear-cut, probably owing to the shake-out from the depression of the 1890s, during which unemployed manufacturing workers might have tried to make a go of it in one of the first three categories.[53] If the last two groups are combined and compared to agriculture, then in 1880 agriculture was considerably larger, whereas in 1900 the opposite was true.

Data derived from the Census Bureau's <u>Historical Statistics</u> for the 1860-1920 period elaborate on this trend. The estimated percentage of the labor force engaged in agriculture, forestry, and fishing fell from 59 percent in 1860 to 27.4 percent in 1920; the percentages in manufacturing and construction; and in trade, transportation, and finance, rose in those years from 18.3 to 31.4 percent and from 7.4 to 21.7 percent, respectively.[54]

The latter categories (classes 4 and 5 of Table 4), were those being most radically transformed by economic growth and consolidation; were preponderantly the occupations of wage-earners; and were, as will be seen in the next section, those with a diminishing

---

53 As mentioned in Chapter 3, a back-to-the-land movement has accompanied all lengthy recessions. Attempts at self-employment have been another response to widespread urban unemployment up to the present.

54 The data for the earlier decades, 1860 in particular, are not strictly comparable with later years. U.S. Department of Commerce, Bureau of the Census, <u>Historical Statistics of the United States from Colonial Times to 1970</u>, 1:138.

component of older workers. Their growth was fueled by immigrants with few or no usable skills, the "New Immigration." Between 1890 and 1910, the number of gainfully employed persons in the U.S. rose from 23.3 million to 38.2 million, owing largely to immigration from the nations of southern and eastern Europe.[55] By 1910, immigrants of prime working age comprised 34.5 percent of all mining employees and more than 25 percent of manufacturing workers.[56]

Although at the turn of the century there were no census distinctions among wage-earners, employers, and the self-employed, a member of the Census Bureau subsequently undertook to estimate these data on the basis of available material.[57] Using very conservative assumptions, the study concluded that, once account was taken of farm laborers (not farm family members), salaried employees, and salespersons on payrolls, fully 52 percent of the 29 million gainfully employed in 1900 could be considered wage-laborers; only one-seventh of the producing population fell into the three classes of employers, independent producers, and strictly professional people.[58] The class of specifically industrial (manufacturing) wage earners had risen, according to this analysis, to 34.8 percent of the workforce in 1900, up from 27.4 in 1880.[59]

Unemployment by Labor Force Status

Data on rates of unemployment are inadequate for most of the 1860-1920 period. As stated in Chapter 4, the panic of 1893-1896 was the first for which even partial figures exist; in the first year of that depression, estimates ranged from as few as one million to as many as 4.5 million out of work.[60] Using admittedly unsatisfactory data, Douglas and Director estimated unemployment among wage-earners in manufacturing and transportation to be 9.6 percent in 1893, 16.7 percent the following year, and between 11.9 and 15.3 percent through 1898.[61]

---

55 U.S. Department of Commerce, Bureau of the Census, Fifteenth Census of the United States, 1930 (Washington, D.C.: Government Printing Office, 1933), 5:37.

56 Puth, American Economic History, p. 299.

57 Isaac A. Hourwich, "The Social-Economic Classes of the Population of the United States," Journal of Political Economy 19 (March 1911):205.

58 Ibid.

59 Rubinow, Social Insurance, p. 30.

60 Kirkland, History of American Economic Life, p. 523.

61 Paul Douglas and Aaron Director, The Problem of Unemployment (New York: Macmillan Co., 1931), p. 26. Lebergott estimated that in the peak unemployment year of 1894, 18.4 percent of the labor force were unable to find jobs. See Stanley Lebergott, Manpower in Economic Growth: The American Record Since 1800 (New York: McGraw-Hill Book Co., 1964), pp. 164-90. There are no estimates of how many of those who

The best statistics were kept for occupations that had become broadly unionized, such as in printing, bricklaying, or stonemasonry,[62] where the union's administrators could be counted on to keep fairly accurate tallies. Such occupation-encompassing unions were rare, however; besides which tight union organization implied a relatively greater ability to control their numbers, hours of work, and so forth, and thus minimize members' employment dislocations.

Furthermore, an occupation such as printing, for example, is easily defined, even during periods of technological innovation. The introduction of the Linotype did not at first, as the printers feared, eliminate skilled workers, but rather made them immensely more productive and far preferable to employers than the unskilled. The profession itself did not have to be redefined as a result of capital deepening. Because no significant deskilling accompanied increases in productivity, the job classification (if not its description) remained intact.[63]

But many innovations did not similarly increase the demand for the same type of worker, even in the short run; indeed, as noted above, machinery might be introduced precisely for the purpose of ridding an employer of skilled workers and their unions.[64] In such cases--the majority during the period under examination--occupational classifications outside of agriculture were fluid, intensifying the problems of data collection.

Consequently, for the unorganized or weakly organized workers who bore the brunt of technological and cyclical unemployment, available statistics are highly impressionistic. Some of the individual cities and states (especially Massachusetts, New York, and Wisconsin) did attempt to keep employment and unemployment data by type of occupation for those within their jurisdictions, but even these data were frequently casually assembled. As an example, from a 1911 report by the New York Commissioner of Labor:

> We find in the industrial centers of this state, at all times of the year in good times as well as bad, wage-earners, able and willing to work, who cannot secure employment....Private employment offices can find work on the average for but one out of four of those who apply to them....The census of 1900 found 25 per cent of those engaged in manufacturing and mechanical pursuits in New York state

---

retained their jobs in high-unemployment years suffered reduced wages because they had only part-time work, but the numbers may have been substantial. See Puth, American Economic History, p. 197.

62 Catlin, The Labor Problem, p. 547.

63 However, printing did become a "younger" occupation, apparently because older workers found the adjustment to the Linotype machine difficult to make. Furthermore, printing was a notoriously unhealthful occupation, for which morbidity and mortality rates of practitioners aged 30-59 were quite high. Catlin, The Labor Problem, p. 197.

64 Yellowitz, Industrialization, p. 28.

unemployed at some time during the year; over one-half of these were unemployed from one to three months, 37 1/2 per cent from three to six months.[65]

Such figures, while imprecise, are striking. The report continues, "We want to know not so much how many are without work, as how many <u>need to be</u> without work....The problem must be approached from the standpoint of industry."[66] The implication seems to be that counting the unemployed was a useful exercise to the extent that it provided prospective employers with information on labor availability, a peculiar stance, by present standards, for a department of labor.

Isaac Rubinow, primary American theoretician of social insurance, made an independent estimate of national unemployment according to length of idleness for 1900 (at which time the labor force numbered over 29 million), shown in Table 5.

TABLE 5

ESTIMATED NATIONAL UNEMPLOYMENT IN 1900 BY DURATION OF JOBLESSNESS

Unemployment Duration	Number Unemployed	Percent Unemployed
Less than 3 months	3,177,753	49.1
3-6 months	2,554,925	39.5
6-12 months	736,286	11.4

SOURCE: Rubinow, <u>Social Insurance</u>, p. 445.

Since 1899-1900 was not a year of industrial depression, as were 1893-1894 or 1907-1908, this conveys an impression of the magnitude of the problem of idleness not traceable specifically to the workings of the business cycle.

In 191,8 a careful study of non-agricultural, urban employment fluctuations since 1902 was published by the Helen S. Trounstine Foundation. The study concluded that for the 16-year period, 1902-1917, the unemployment rate fluctuated between 4.7 percent (1.4 million) in 1916-1917 when the economy was booming; and 16 percent (4.6 million) in

---

65 New York, Commissioner of Labor, <u>Unemployment and the Lack of Farm Labor</u>, Third Report of the Commission appointed under Chap. 518 of the Laws of 1909 to inquire into the question of employers' liability and other matters (Albany, April 26, 1911), p. 2, cited by Lescohier, <u>Working Conditions</u>, p. 130. It should be noted that 1900 was not a recession year.

66 New York Commissioner of Labor, <u>Unemployment</u>, cited by ibid., p. 131. Emphasis in the original.

1914-1915, the period of a short but deep recession. The average number of unemployed persons for the period was 2.5 million, or nearly 10 percent of the non-agricultural, non-rural labor force.[67] Because the study was an amalgam of varyingly incomplete state and federal data using differing criteria for their definitions of joblessness, it, too, is merely suggestive of the scale of employment disruptions from manufacturing innovations and growing business consolidation.

As long as the United States lacked a formal, uniform system of unemployment insurance, there was no reasonably accurate measure of who was out of work, where, or for how long.[68] A further problem, of course, and one that remains to this day, is that of the discouraged worker. One cannot count the person who has dropped out, fails to register, or cannot be located, even today, when counting has become a national pastime. As will be seen in the next section of this chapter, it is probably reasonable to suppose that by 1900 discouragement characterized the majority of older displaced workers.[69]

---

67 Hornell Hart, Fluctuations in Employment in Cities of the United States, 1902 to 1917 (Cincinnati: Helen S. Trounstine Foundation, 1918). The data were gathered from the U.S. Census of Manufacturers, Occupations, and Population; Reports of the United States Geological Survey; the Bureau of Mines; the Interstate Commerce Commission; the U.S. Bureau of Labor Statistics; the U.S. Commissioner of Education; the Eight-Hour Commission; and the reports of many state departments of labor and state industrial commissions.

68 The argument of economic and political conservatives may, however, be at least partially granted. They suggest that the mere availability of such insurance can distort (that is, inflate) the figures. The "moral hazard of liberalism" is that people behave differently in the presence of some form of insurance than they otherwise would. If one can receive any benefit from not working, according to this view, there is reason to suspect that unwillingness to seek work is at least as likely to be responsible for unemployment as is inability to find work. See, for example, George Gilder, Wealth and Poverty (New York: Basic Books, 1981) for a concise expression of this view. If it is accurate, then the choice is between no statistics and misleading ones, yet in this period there is not even a choice.

The conservatives' argument is as old as the debate over social insurance. In Great Britain and the United States at the turn of the century, it was widely alleged that the protection granted by state pensions and insurance destroyed the sense of watchfulness and the independent spirit of the working classes, and actually increased the total of economic disasters against which it was directed. This issue will be taken up in greater detail in Chapter 7.

69 As late as 1930, the paucity of data was to remain a serious problem. As noted by economist Bryce Stewart:

> No important industrial nation has such inadequate statistics of unemployment as the United States. Except for the preliminary data supplied by the census of 1930, there are no figures on unemployment for the country at large, for any state, or for any industry within a state, except a broken record of trade union unemployment percentages for the building trades in Massachusetts. In the past two decades, interest has been directed to statistics of employment rather than unemployment, and

Age, Occupation, and Labor Force Participation

By the turn of the century the ubiquity of unemployment helped to direct attention to the particular employment problems of older workers. Because the prevailing explanation of unemployment continued to be expressed in terms of the personal causes of idleness, old age was included as one of these causes. Simultaneously, middle age came to be seen as an employment handicap when it was perceived that the new standards of industrial production caused the less-young to be categorized among the relatively inefficient. It was widely felt that older workers were destined to be a marginally employed group, one whose ability to work would depend largely on employers' fluctuating "demand for inefficient workers."[70]

Despite the fact that mechanization by no means eliminated the skilled and semi-skilled from the labor force (their numbers actually increased with technology), their proportions inevitably dwindled in the old industries as certain old skills were eradicated and the value of others was reduced.[71] Because there were variations in the rates of displacement and the degree to which skill was diluted in different occupations, workers forced from one craft often sought work in other trades that perhaps had also experienced some deskilling, but which still paid wages above what could be earned as machine tenders in their original industry.[72] It was partly in response to this occupational movement and underbidding by the displaced that trade unions increasingly formed in the 1890s to keep out interlopers.

Yet a further problem for skilled older workers was that many were experienced in only a small portion of the larger craft. Some became so specialized in their duties that they were not able to follow their craft into another trade when they became unemployed, as happened to skilled workers in railroad shops after the end of the railroad boom, and also to glass workers, cigarmakers, and meatpackers.[73]

Men 65 and older comprised 12 percent of the unskilled, non-agricultural labor force at the turn of the century; many of these were underemployed, having been shifted out of self-employment and the older skilled trades by the competition from large-scale enterprises and by the rapid advances in technology and division of labor.[74] Such older workers were forced from their jobs and found it difficult to enter new trades. Overall,

---

in periods of business recession the government has had to rely on estimates of unemployment based on records of shrinkage and expansion in employment, which are available only for a few industries. Bryce M. Stewart, Unemployment Benefits in the United States (New York: Industrial Relations Counselors, Inc., 1930), p. 77.

70 U.S. Industrial Commission, Final Report of the Industrial Commission, 14:37, 19:747.

71 Faulkner, Decline of Laissez Faire, p. 265.

72 Yellowitz, Industrialization, pp. 28-29.

73 Catlin, The Labor Problem, p. 548.

74 Rubinow, Social Insurance, p. 306.

probably fewer than half were reabsorbed to help meet the increased demand for their product resulting from mechanization, mass production, and lower prices.[75]   The Massachusetts Board to Investigate the Subject of the Unemployed reported in 1895 that "unquestionably many are permanently out of work."[76]

Thus, as the percentage of older people in the U.S. population was gradually increasing, from about 2.5 percent for those over 65 in 1860 to approximately 4.7 percent in 1920,[77] their labor force participation rates and occupational status apparently were dropping rather consistently. As will be seen, the same thing was happening to workers aged 45-65 in mechanized industry.

By late in the nineteenth century more people were surviving to old age because of improvements in sanitation, hygiene, and infant and maternal health earlier in the century (yet in 1900 life expectancy at birth was still under 48 years).[78] Midcentury immigration of young adults also helped to swell the older population by the turn of the century.[79] Furthermore, the birth rate declined sharply through the nineteenth and early twentieth centuries as a concomitant of industrialization and urbanization.[80] Little improvement was made in adult longevity between 1800 and 1900; [81] yet in the latter year an average person of 40 could expect to live for another 28 years,[82] and average life expectancy at 65 was another 12 years.[83]

Some professions were for a long time little affected by the arrival of factory mechanization and the concentration of the forces of production, but the professions for which this was the case were for the most part of decreasing or only marginal relevance to the emerging industrial order. It was in precisely these occupations that older workers

---

75 Yellowitz, Industrialization, p. 26.

76 Massachusetts, Board to Investigate the Subject of the Unemployed, Report (Boston: Wright and Potter, 1895), 4:39-40, cited by Yellowitz, Industrialization, p. 26.

77 W. Andrew Achenbaum, "The Obsolescence of Old Age in America," Journal of Social History 8 (Fall 1974):52, 56.

78 It had risen from about 35 years in 1800, 38 years in 1850. Krooss, American Economic Development, p. 58.

79 Because the greatest influx of young working-age immigrants came between 1898 and 1914, the most rapid growth of the aged population occurred in mid-twentieth century.

80 Niemi, U.S. Economic History, p. 13.

81 Ibid.

82 U.S. Department of Commerce, Bureau of the Census, The Statistical History of the United States from Colonial Times to the Present (Stamford, Conn: Fairfield Publishers, 1965), p. 24.

83 Neil Cutler, "Population Dynamics and the Graying of America," Urban and Social Change Review 10 (Summer 1977), p. 4.

were disproportionately represented after 1860. Foremost among these were jobs in the agricultural sector, in traditional services, and in some of the older manufacturing and mechanical trades producing established products.

Agriculture

The economic fortunes of the agricultural sector during the 1860-1920 period, and the age-demographics of farming, have been discussed in Chapter 3. As to the impact of technology in agriculture, it was shown that the results were primarily labor-saving rather than increases in yield per acre, and yet the labor force in agriculture continued to increase until the turn of the century (growing 47 percent just between 1860 and 1890, owing to immigration) and only began to decline absolutely by 1910. [84]

Increased market activity, coupled with technological advances, encouraged greater specialization of output in agriculture, much as it did in industry. Unlike industry, however, technological changes in farming led to neither greater average farm size nor greater average economic concentration. Mean farm size, approximately 200 acres in 1860, fell to 133 acres in 1880 (largely because of the breakup of large plantations following the Civil War), then rose slightly to 147 acres by 1920; [85] while the number of farms grew steadily from 2 million in 1860 to 6.5 million in 1920. [86]

Such trends were deleterious to the economic security of middle-aged and older Americans who were disproportionately engaged in agricultural pursuits. Achenbaum has calculated that in 1890 approximately 43 percent of all men over 65 continued to be engaged in agriculture.[87] Agriculture--along with forestry and fishing, and personal and public service--was then and has continued to be one of the occupational groups with a less rapid and pronounced rate of decline in gainful employment above the age of 40 than the average "drop-off rate"[88] for all occupations taken together.

What these "agricultural" occupations shared was a tolerance toward the older worker, offering him/her a refuge from the more exacting demands and the prejudices of

---

84 Lewis, Growth and Fluctuations, p. 63. It has been estimated by one authority that in the 1870s and 1880s, 20 farmers moved to the city for every city worker who took up farming. (Shannon, The Farmer's Last Frontier, p. 357.)

85 Niemi, U.S. Economic History, p. 225.

86 Ibid.

87 Achenbaum, Old Age, p. 98. Demographer John Durand points out that national rural-urban classifications were not available for that year, but his calculations for industry in 1890, and for agriculture and industry from 1920 to 1940, suggest that this is a reasonable estimate. See John D. Durand, The Labor Force in the United States, 1890-1960, reprint ed. (New York: John Wiley and Sons, 1968), pp. 12-13, 197-200.

88 The "drop-off rate" refers to the rate at which an occupational category shows a marked decline in its practitioners with advancing age.

other employments.[89] Age per se was not a serious obstacle to continued engagement in agriculture, whereas this was not the case in the manufacturing and mechanical pursuits. Of those in agriculture in 1900, 6.1 percent were at least 65 years of age, compared to 5.5 percent in professional occupations and 3.5 percent in manufacturing and mechanical jobs.[90] In agriculture, a person could remain active later in life than in other pursuits, so it tended to be a haven for older workers.[91]

Services

Throughout the final third of the nineteenth century, men over 65 continued to be employed in the traditional jobs in services, primarily as transportation agents and collectors, middlemen, merchants and hucksters. In this period the percentage of men over 65 in such occupations was about twice as great as the percentage of all males over 10 so employed.[92] These categories of employment were classified by the Bureau of the Census as "Trade and Transportation" occupations, employing 10.7 percent of the work force in 1880, 14.6 percent in 1890, and 16.4 percent in 1900. [93] However, the "older workers' jobs" mentioned above comprised but a small portion of those in both trade and transportation. Only three percent of the jobs in transportation and trade in 1900 were filled by workers 65 or older.[94] "Trade" included everything from the Rockefeller trust activities abroad to bookkeepers, clerks, and copyists,[95] to corner grocers; "transportation" encommpassed not just agents and collectors but also the work of construction and operation and repair of roads, canals, and railroads, jobs occupied by a larger percentage of younger than older men.[96]

Hence the apparent extent of older people's potential for employment in these rapidly-growing occupations is somewhat illusory.[97] Older women in particular faced

---

89 Barkin, The Older Worker in Industry, p. 285.

90 Rubinow, Social Insurance, p. 306.

91 Barkin, The Older Worker in Industry, p. 285.

92 Achenbaum, Old Age, p. 68.

93 U.S. Department of Commerce, Bureau of the Census, Twelfth Census of the U.S., 1900, Population (Washington, D.C.: Government Printing Office, 1902), 2:133.

94 Rubinow, Social Insurance, p. 306.

95 These were primarily occupations of younger men. Achenbaum, Old Age, p. 68.

96 Ibid.

97 The picture is further complicated by the evolution of census classifications over time with changes in statistical practice. As pointed out by Braverman, "service" occupations are those that do not result in tangible, vendible objects for which the capitalist serves as an intermediary between producer and consumer. But by this modern definition there are

difficulties in service employment. In an 1896 report by the superintendent of the free employment office in New York City, it was observed:

> We find it very hard to get employment for women [in domestic service] after they reach 35 years of age as the demand is for young women. And in this respect the age limit for men, as far as we can judge, appears to be 45 years.[98]

When in 1899 the number of women available to perform domestic work fell short of demand, the report for that year noted that employers were nonetheless reluctant to hire older women. Only those willing to accept a small wage and "what is called a 'good home' in lieu of compensation" could get jobs.[99]

Manufacturing

More than a third of the over-64 population in 1900 were employed as wage-earners in the manufacturing sector.[100] When one examines the manufacturing and mechanical trades, an interesting feature of older workers' employment patterns emerges. Of those occupations in which older workers were most heavily represented--masonry, carpentry, blacksmithing, marbleworking, cement-making, boot- and shoe-making--none except for the last was significantly altered by century's end, by either technology or the move to centralized production in factories.[101] These were essentially the trades that had existed in

---

workers who today would be called service workers who at the turn of the century were included in manufacturing, such as those repairing and servicing carriages, bicycles, automobiles; power laundry workers; maintenance workers; and so forth. Citing Stigler, Braverman notes that the difference in actual occupation between a fabricator and a maintenance/repair worker is frequently negligible; but the former works in a manufacturing plant (and is typically far better paid) while the latter works for a small service or repair shop and is part of the services sector. Braverman, Labor and Monopoly Capital, pp. 359-61, citing George J. Stigler, Trends in Output and Employment (New York: National Bureau of Economic Research, 1947), p. 23.

Thus, although services at present constitute a vital economic sector, they were much less important to the economy as defined by the census statistics of a century ago, when they primarily had reference to the most menial class of occupations, those in domestic and personal service. Ely, Evolution of Industrial Society, p. 104.

98 New York, Bureau of Labor Statistics, Fourteenth Annual Report (Albany, 1897), p. 1028, cited by Barkin, The Older Worker, pp. 63, 76.

99 Idem, Seventeenth Annual Report (Albany, 1900), p. 1230, cited by Barkin, The Older Worker, pp. 63, 76.

100 Rubinow, Social Insurance, p. 306.

101 See Victor S. Clark, History of Manufactures in the United States, 3 vols. (1929; reprint ed. New York: Peter Smith, 1948), vol., 2: 1860-1893, and vol. 3: 1893-1928.

the United States since colonial times, and thus were the jobs into which older Americans had grown. Such jobs were in the sunset industries of their time.

Not only were these trades in general only minimally susceptible to deskilling and displacement by machinery, they were insulated from another feature of segmented industrial labor, which was the tendency (since the mid-1800s) to replace prime-age males with female and child labor. With the progressive leveling of skill requirements throughout much of the economy, many factory jobs requiring little talent or experience were filled by children, who could be paid less than adults, and by females whose wages were below those of males. Women could be paid on average one-third to one-half as much as men; children, one-half to three-quarters as much as women.[102]

It is conceivable that the middle-aged and older men in the more "protected" lines of work had chosen them precisely because of their evident staying power as occupations that would permit maximum long-term security. Yet it should be remembered that despite the much-vaunted freedom and mobility that has characterized occupational choice in U.S. history, these concepts are only relative. Even 50 years ago, and certainly a century past, the majority of Americans selected occupations that corresponded closely to what their parents before them had done for a living.

In the first place, there were certain groups of occupations among which there had always been very little chance of moving, for workers of any age. These occupational groups were largely reserved for, or else relegated to, distinct social grades. Economists and students of the structure of the labor force variously distinguished four or five grades, or as many as eight or ten, but there were three broad groupings which had quite distinct employment and employee characteristics: (1) manual wage earners, skilled and unskilled; (2) clerks, shopkeepers, and employer-farmers; and (3) professional workers.[103] There was little movement among these groups, which were distinguishable from one another in several respects: average incomes; rigors of work; autonomy; incidence of sickness, accidents, unemployment, and poverty; and opportunities for worklife longevity.[104]

In addition, assuming occupational selection by the most fortunate older workers involves imputing to them a remarkable degree of prescience. The late-century "old worker trades" of masonry, carpentry, smithing, and so forth, relied on substantial skill and experience. Thus if a person were going to be a carpenter or a blacksmith, the decision to do so would have been made by about the age of 25. For workers of middle or old age by, say, the 1870s or 1880s, such a path was chosen before the economy's massive shift to industrial capitalism had begun to be evident. The logical explanation is that these workers were merely the lucky ones.

Such an interpretation is reinforced when one examines those skilled occupations that were most radically transformed by industrialization. In such jobs (such as iron and steel production, plumbing, steamfitting, printing, and machine tooling), the proportion of

---

102 Krooss, American Economic Development, p. 456.

103 Florence, Economics of Fatigue and Unrest, pp. 309-14.

104 Ibid.

all males over 10 exceeded the proportion aged 65 and over throughout the final third of the nineteenth century.[105]

Similar results are evident for female employment. Most women employed outside the home in manufacturing worked as seamstresses, dressmakers, milliners, and so forth, but older females were more likely to be in jobs little altered by machine technology. They were, for example, underrepresented in the cotton, wool, and silk mills, the knitting industry, shoe/boot/hosiery manufacture, and tobacco processing. These occupations were being revamped by new machines and methods, and they were notable for being physically tiring and hence suited to younger, more able-bodied workers.[106]

The influence of occupation on extent of unemployment was established by the 1900 census. In that year, the jobless rate ranged from a low of 1.9 percent for physicians to a high of 59.9 percent for glassworkers (who were disproportionately older workers, many of them northern European immigrants after the Civil War.) If the professions are excluded and only mechanical trades considered, the low was 11.2 percent for confectioners/bakers.[107] Some of the unemployment percentages in 1900 were particularly striking, especially for the skilled construction trades and extractive industries. The census gave approximate unemployment percentages in representative occupations, shown in Table 6.

TABLE 6

**THE INFLUENCE OF OCCUPATION ON RATES OF
UNEMPLOYMENT, 1899-1900**

Occupational Group	Percent Experiencing Some Unemployment
1. Plasterers and masons	55
2. Carpenters, joiners, paper-hangers, ordinary laborers	40-50
3. Miners	44
4. Marble-workers	40 (approx.)
5. Iron, steel, lumber workers	30 (approx.)
6. Textile and clothing workers	20-30
7. Transportation workers	15-20
8. Food workers	10 (approx.)
9. Commercial employees	<10

SOURCE: U.S. Department of Commerce, Bureau of the Census, Twelfth Census of the United States, 1900, Occupations, pp. 225-26, 232-33.

---

105 Achenbaum, Old Age, p. 69

106 Ibid.

107 Rubinow, Social Insurance, p. 447.

Based upon what little is known with certainty from this period about age-specific employment patterns, the older worker was more likely to be employed in the first four categories, with the greater employment fluctuations, than in the final five. Hence their experience with unemployment was probably greater than the average because they were concentrated in these relatively declining occupations.

Primary among these are the extractive industries (mining, lumbering), which censuses before 1910 lumped together with agriculture, a pursuit favoring older workers. All of the first six categories were occupations for which the demand for skilled foreign labor had been strong since the end of the Civil War (see Chapter 3). Many of their skilled practitioners had arrived in the U.S. as prime-age workers in the 1860s and 1870s, and thus would have been classified as "older workers" by the turn of the century.

Edward Devine noted in 1909 that older workers were disappearing in almost all factory occupations, where human beings were scrapped in the same way machinery was:

The young, the vigorous, the adaptable, the supple of limb, the alert of mind, are in demand. In...the professions maturity of judgment and ripened experience offset, to some extent, the disadvantages of old age; but in the factory and on the railway, with spade and pick, at the spindle, at the steel converters, there are no offsets.[108]

Tables 7 and 8 provide further evidence of older Americans' diminishing aggregate rates of labor force participation.

TABLE 7

PERCENT OF AMERICANS 65 AND OLDER IN THE POPULATION AND IN THE LABOR FORCE, 1870-1920

Year	Percent of Population 65 and Over			Percent of Over-64 Population in Jobs	
	Total	Male	Female	Male	Female
1870	2.99	2.97	3.02	80.6*	5.8*
1880	3.43	3.40	3.47	76.7*	5.8*
1890	3.87	3.86	3.88	73.8	7.7
1900	4.06	4.02	4.11	68.4	8.5
1910	4.30	4.18	4.43	63.7*	8.6*
1920	4.67	4.61	4.73	59.9	7.9

SOURCE: Achembaum, "Obsolescence of Old Age," pp. 52, 56, calculated from Bureau of the Census, Historical Statistics of the United States, Colonial Times to 1957, p. 10.

* Estimated. Data not available prior to 1870. The 1890 (eleventh) census was the first to provide reasonably reliable age-specific employment statistics. In the 1910 census, however, all employed persons 45 and over were classified together.

---

108 Devine, Misery and Its Causes, p. 125.

TABLE 8

PERCENT OF MALES AGED 65 AND OVER IN THE OVER-15 MALE POPULATION AND IN THE MALE LABOR FORCE, 1880-1910

Year	Percent Males 65 and Over are of Males 15 and Over	Percent Males 65 and Over are of Employed Males 15 and Over
1880	5.4	5.2
1890	6.0	5.0
1900	6.1	4.7
1910	6.3	n.a.*

SOURCE: Adapted from Rubinow, Social Insurance, p. 305.

* Not available. As noted in Table 7, the gainfully employed aged 45 and over were lumped together in one group in the 1910 census. This practice itself suggests something about the age at which workers were presumed to be "old" by early in the twentieth century.

But the declining labor force participation of the 65-and-over population is only part of the story. Middle age was becoming old age in the world of employment, and people in their forties and fifties were experiencing increasing labor market difficulties, as shown in Table 9.

TABLE 9

DECLINE OF GAINFULLY EMPLOYED MIDDLE-AGED AND OLDER MALES, 1890-1910

Percent Gainfully Employed at Ages:	1890	1900	1910
45-54	96.6	95.5	n.a.*
55-64	92.9	90.0	n.a.*
65 and over	73.8	68.4	63 (est.)
55 and over	85.0	80.7	76.4 (est.)
45 and over	n.a.*	87.9	85.9

SOURCE: Adapted from Epstein, Facing Old Age, p. 10.

* Not available. See notes to Tables 7 and 8.

All of the evidence points to a diminishing labor force participation rate around the turn of the century for workers beyond the age of 45. Those aged 65 and older had not yet begun to experience significant unemployment in 1870, when 80.6 percent were employed, compared to 54.7 percent for the male population over 10 years of age.[109] The impact of the depression decades of the 1870s and 1890s on older males' employment is unmistakable. In the latter decade alone the labor force participation rate for those 65 and older fell by 5.4 percentage points, from 73.8 to 68.4 percent. According to Rubinow, the number of over-64 males gainfully employed in 1900 was 1.065 million, and the economic changes in the previous decade had thrown 100,000 of these individuals out of work during a time when the total number of gainfully employed males rose by almost six million, from 23.3 to 29.1 million.[110]

Although the Thirteenth Census of 1910 gave no breakdown of employment status by age for workers beyond age 44, the percentage of 45-and-older workers in the labor force fell from 87.9 in 1900 to 85.9 in 1910. (Recall that although 40-45 was at this time apparently considered an industrial old age, the average individual of 40 in 1900 could anticipate another 28 years of life.[111]) If we assume the same rate of decrease between 1900-1910 as obtained for the 1890-1900 decade for employed males 55 and over and 65 and over, the result is a 20-year drop-off in the rate of labor force participation for these groups of 8.6 percent and 10.8 percent, respectively. Epstein concluded that of the nearly 4,660,400 males 55 and older in 1910, considerably more than one million had been eliminated from the ranks of the gainfully employed since 1890. [112]

Given the prevailing trends in urbanization and family unit fragmentation, a growing inequality in the distribution of wealth, and the near-total absence of any uniform protection against summary dismissal and resulting poverty, these admittedly crude calculations represent a serious reduction in economic security for older Americans.[113] Furthermore, as shown earlier, the emerging occupational distribution was placing them at a disadvantage relative to other working Americans. The jobs they held onto were becoming a smaller percentage of total jobs available because they were not in general the jobs that were vital

---

109 Achenbaum, "Obsolescence of Old Age," p. 56.

110 Rubinow, Social Insurance, p. 306.

111 See Bureau of the Census, The Statistical History of the United States From Colonial Times to the Present, p. 24.

112 Epstein, Facing Old Age, p. 10. These computations are obviously unscientific. 1900-1910 was not a "depression decade" as was 1890-1900, and thus the drop-off in labor force participation rates of older males is perhaps overstated. Yet by the first decade of the twentieth century the strenuousness of industrial working conditions was reaching extreme levels, and the rate of superannuation was great, as discussed in Chapter 6. Also, in the first decade of the 1900s the rate of immigration reached an all-time high, so there was an ample supply of labor available to replace those whose physical powers may have been declining.

113 Chapter 7 will elaborate on the growing destitution of dispossessed older Americans.

to the new economic conditions. Older workers' continuation in the more traditional and less dynamic jobs caused a decline in their relative earnings compared to the mechanized sector, including younger members of their own families.[114]

The emphasis here has been on the employment patterns of older males. The trend for older female workers is quite different but probably not very meaningful. Women had not constituted a sizable presence in the paid workforce until after the Civil War, when a combination of economic and social forces raised their participation rates. This was particularly the case for girls and young women who helped provide family support through their work in the factories of the North.

Urbanization was reinforcing a trend toward later marriages and smaller families which helped to increase female labor force participation.[115] Women were in demand because they could be hired more cheaply and were viewed as more easily controlled than males for the majority of manufacturing jobs requiring little skill, training, and strength. Employers might also transform jobs into "female jobs" in order to thwart possible attempts at unionization. A saying of the early twentieth century was that "when a job becomes mechanical it is a woman's job; when it becomes automatic, it is neither man's nor woman's."[116]

Also, as a part of the suffragist movement, the early feminists had been breaking down barriers that had previously made it unthinkable for a woman to work outside the home. And by the turn of the century middle-aged and older women, particularly the widowed and single, were increasingly likely to be forced into the paid labor market by the changing nature of family life in urban areas. By 1920, at any rate, older women's labor force participation rates had begun to fall and they continued to do so for the next several decades, although for females in general they have continued to rise for reasons both economic and sociological.

For older males, the trend in labor force participation was steadily downward after 1860. It would rise again only briefly under the extremely tight labor market conditions of the World War II era. By 1920, for the first time, the percent of the older male population gainfully employed (59.9) had fallen below the percent for the population of males 10 and older (62.7). This occurred despite the fact that the growth of the latter group had been slowed by the near-disappearance after 1910 of workers aged 10 to 15. Child labor laws combined with the introduction of machinery reduced the value of the sort of labor children

---

114 Factory workers' wages early in the period could in fact be two-to-three times higher than those of independent producers. Indeed, the most skilled factory workers might earn as much as or more than some professionals, especially teachers. Normal Ware, The Industrial Worker, p. 52. Large-scale enterprises often found it necessary to pay above-market rates to attract the requisite labor pool, or to forestall unionization, but the differential would soon disappear once the mission had been accomplished. See John R. Commons, "Introduction," History of Labor, 3:xxv.

115 Puth, American Economic History, p. 294.

116 Catlin, The Labor Problem, p. 70.

could contribute, and the spreading habit of longer years of schooling reinforced the trend.[117]

Conclusion

As industrial capitalism, fuelled by technology, got fully underway, older Americans appear to have disproportionately experienced a contraction in opportunities for employment as compared with younger workers. For some, the most logical explanation for such a phenomenon in a system based upon profits is that such workers' productivity was lower than the average. This argument has had widespread currency in the twentieth century, based to a considerable extent upon the relatively low levels of education possessed by older members of the population. But the education gap that may have existed between older and younger workers by, say, 1900 was probably not enough to affect significantly the employability of the elderly (particularly given the millions of immigrants who found work with virtually no schooling or even a working knowledge of English). In fact, the contribution of formal education to nineteenth-century American economic growth has perhaps been overrated.[118] Public secondary schooling was still rare in the U.S. until after 1900, free public colleges rarer still. In 1871, 2.0 percent of 17-year-olds were graduating from high school; in 1900 the figure was 6.4 percent;[119] only one in nine persons of high school age or older was a graduate.[120]

A somewhat more compelling explanation for the declining percentage of the older population engaged in remunerative work lies in the economy's evolving institutional arrangements. In addition to its impact on the occupational structure and on macroeconomic stability, the rapid pace of technological change described in this chapter made possible a new and massive scale of economic organization. To an increasing extent the capital of large firms was composed not of tangible goods but of organizations constructed

---

117 See Lescohier, Working Conditions, pp. 40-41. The number of working children aged 10-15 reached a peak of about two million in 1910, representing approximately 20 percent of all children in this age group and five percent of the total labor force. Thereafter the incidence of child labor declined rapidly. Puth, American Economic History, p. 294; Walton and Robertson, History of the American Economy, p. 324.

118 Krooss, American Economic Development, p. 461; Peterson and Gray, Economic Development of the United States, pp. 382-83.

119 Hacker, Course of American Economic Growth, p. 215.

120 Lance E. Davis and John Legler, "The Government in the American Economy, 1815-1902: A Quantitative Study," Journal of Economic History 26 (December 1966):514-52. Furthermore, a point stressed by labor economists is that while education may be an important background characteristic, it is seldom a productive skill per se. It is jobs that provide skills and their accompanying rewards, so how the economy allocates jobs determines the distribution of human capital and labor income. See Lester C. Thurow, The Zero Sum Society: Distribution and the Possibilities for Economic Change (New York: Basic Books, 1980), pp. 202-03.

in the past to operate in perpetuity. Even the value of goods and services tended to become increasingly dependent upon their organized relationship to other goods and services comprising the property of the giant corporations.

Capitalists seeking to maximize profits in the 1860-1920 period might legitimately have argued that evolving conditions of work, favoring strength, speed, and endurance, required that they consider only workers below a particular age who could rapidly adapt to the new technologies intensifying the work process. Yet the profit-maximizing behavior of employers predisposing them to seek agility and strength in their workforces tended to become calcified into an ethic that young is better than old, youth more productive than age. It was but a small step from a technologically-based calculus to the imposition of age norms in hiring and retaining employees, or ageism.

The altered production relationships of large-scale enterprise led to a progressive distancing of employees from those they served, enabling the development of workplace practices and conditions that were harmful to older workers in two major ways alluded to previously. First, the intensification of the work process to get maximum use of short-lived capital equipment (often within dirty and dangerous environments) speeded up natural aging and made people physiologically old and economically obsolete before their time. Second, the institutional arrangements which permitted this disregard for individuals' well-being in the context of competitive production resulted also in bureaucratic approaches to hiring and retaining employees based upon assessments of group characteristics, rather than upon individual traits. And age was a characteristic as obvious to prospective or current employers as sex and race.

Chapter 6 explores the institutional discrimination against categories of workers that affected older Americans in the 1860-1920 period. In doing so, the labor conditions confronting workers of all ages are examined to see how they led to a premature waning of productive powers and hence a reduced presence of older workers in the U.S. labor force.

CHAPTER 6

ORGANIZATIONAL AND INSTITUTIONAL IMPEDIMENTS TO THE EMPLOYMENT OF OLDER WORKERS: INCREASING INTENSITY OF WORK AND THE EMERGENCE OF MANAGERIALISM

Introduction

It has been shown how middle-aged and older workers in the years 1860-1920 were experiencing occupational obsolescence through the introduction of machinery, the trend toward deskilling, and the heightened macroeconomic instability that accompanied corporatism and growing firm size. The widening gap between the nation's proportion of older people and their representation in the workforce reflected three major changes in the nature of work within American firms having uniquely negative consequences for workers of middle age and beyond.

The first of these has already been dealt with: the growth in firm size to enable efficient implementation of the most up-to-date plant and equipment, which translated into a diminished emphasis upon older workers' skills and experience. Technology and large size led to two other major obstacles to such workers' ability to maintain their labor market presence. First, an increased emphasis on worker speed and agility to maximize the productivity of short-lived, costly capital meant that machinery became the driver of labor, often at a pace sustainable only by the most hardy; and second, machine-intensive production drove a wedge not only between workers and their product, but also between workers and the overseers/managers/owners of capitalist enterprises. This greatly reduced opportunities to establish or maintain the personal workplace relationships that had provided a measure of job security in smaller, decentralized, and more labor-intensive economic units.[1]

The requirement that machinery be used to its utmost capacity before being scrapped had obvious repercussions for the physical condition of workers. Critics of machine methods maintained that mechanized industry impelled physical exhaustion at an early age, raising the criteria of individual performance beyond the capacities of older members of the labor force.[2] As mechanization led to an emphasis on speed rather than seasoned

---

1 It should be pointed out that such relative security did have its less appealing side. Employment in small enterprises could be oppressively paternalistic, and many employers made it their business to try to influence their employees' conduct off the job as well as on. They might, for example, set rules on church attendance and contributions, on physical appearance, and on smoking and drinking behavior. Such rules were enforceable in small towns, where escaping attention was difficult. Puth, American Economic History, p. 193.

But this sort of paternalism in fact also prevailed in some of the largest enterprises. For example, steel mills were frequently the hubs of entire communities whose citizens were expected to rely upon the mills for their recreational and housing needs, in addition to providing employment.

2 See, for example, George L. Bolen, Getting a Living: The Problem of Wealth and Poverty--Of Profits, Wages and Trade Unionism (New York: Macmillan Co., 1903), pp.

judgment, and on alertness and quick reflexes rather than an artisan's skills as the most desirable personal qualities, older workers were coming to be at a distinct disadvantage in the labor market.[3]

In addition, as the new enterprise bureaucracies and their attendant managerial practices began to develop in much of the economy's growth sectors late in the nineteenth century, the principles of firms' organization increasingly embodied a bureaucratic form of managerial control over workers and work standards, which might have little or no basis in the technologies that had spawned the new structures. To promote worker identification with business goals, some of the largest firms imposed sets of highly differentiated job ladders and pay scales, even though technological advances had already virtually eliminated meaningful skill distinctions.[4]

In other words, capitalist industrialization rested not only on a technological imperative--the need to remake labor to conform to the more efficient machine methods--but also upon a greater degree of hierarchy and bureaucracy than could have existed in petty capitalism. Such attributes of the division of labor were most pronounced within the largest establishments, but they increasingly characterized market relationships more broadly. Thus, as a by-product of technology, the nature of interpersonal working relationships became more ordered and precisely defined.[5]

This chapter explores the effects upon older American workers of the natural tendencies of capitalist enterprise in the direction of long hours; monotonous and frequently unhealthful working conditions; an emphasis on rapid flow-through to spread fixed capital costs over the greatest possible volume of output; and staffing by the often-arbitrary decisions of foremen, and later by bureaucratic regulations, rather than according to individual merit. It will be shown how these phenomena gave rise to economic superannuation as, for the first time in human history, there came to be a substantial supply of people who were

---

80-81; U.S. Industrial Commission, Final Report, 14:377.

3 G.R. Stetson, "Industrial Classes as Factors in Racial Development," The Arena 41 (February 1909):177-89. To be sure, the rising bias against older workers was not necessarily grounded in inaccurate perceptions by employers. As has been pointed out, as the nature of work became transformed, so too did many individuals' ability to meet work requirements, and while possession of stamina was not a guarantor of success, the lack of it was all too often a concomitant of economic failure.

4 The iron and steel industry is a well-documented example of this phenomenon. See Katherine Stone, "The Origins of Job Structures in the Steel Industry," Review of Radical Political Economics 6 (Summer 1974):113-73. The meatpacking and shoe-making examples cited in Chapter 4 also reflect internal job classification schemes of great intricacy.

5 Whereas today we are practiced at acknowledging the trade-off between increasing material comfort and productive autonomy, this was a relatively new notion in the period under examination, although productive self-sufficiency had been eroded considerably in both rhetoric and incidence since pre-Civil War days.

surviving beyond their economic usefulness,[6] and who were being denied employment for both practical and ideological reasons.

The chapter concludes by examining the earliest formal analyses of older workers' declining labor force participation. These studies indicate that by the turn of the century, an institutionalized bias against age was widespread and growing; and that the industrial wage system was creating a problem of "economic old age" that, for "the vast majority" of workers, arrived "very much earlier than physiologic old age."[7]

Specifically, in this chapter we wish to ascertain how older workers fared once most of the competition for success among individuals had begun to take place within the context of the broader depersonalized competition among large firms and industries.[8] How did the bureaucratization and hierarchicalization of working life lead to a preference, on an institutional level, for youth over age, for the new over the traditional, for the unknown over the known quantity? The tendencies of industrial capitalism--toward narrow job specifications, long and intensive workdays, and an increasing component of managerial as opposed to production work--fostered the phenomenon of what might be called "bureaucratic displacement" of labor. Such displacement is based upon external characteristics of, and widely held biases against, certain groups, irrespective of individual talents and circumstances. This trend had its most lasting deleterious impact upon older members of the labor force. Although older workers were but one class of workers to experience difficulties arising from the progressive depersonalization of the employment contract,[9] they appear to have been unique in the overall direction taken by their economic fortunes

---

6 Peter F. Drucker, "Demographics and American Economic Policy," in Toward a New U.S. Industrial Policy?, ed. by Michael L. Wachter and Susan M. Wachter (Philadelphia: University of Pennsylvania Press, 1983), p. 241.

7 Rubinow, Social Insurance, p. 304.

8 Depersonalized, that is, with the exception of the highly personalized style of the legendary capitalist entrepreneurs.

9 Some of the most overt forms of employment discrimination reflected a divide-and-conquer strategy on the part of the hiring classes, to minimize the wages bill. Large concerns in particular frequently sought national diversity in their work forces for the rivalry it inspired, which made it a form of "strike insurance." Commons termed such discriminatory practice a "fascist-like" attempt to prevent labor organization. He recounted a scene from 1904 when he visited a Swift and Company employment office in Chicago and noticed only Scandinavians in the waiting room. When he asked the employment agent why only Swedes were being considered, he was told that such a condition was for the present week only; that the previous week only Slovaks were employed; that the explicit Swift and Company policy was frequently to change about among the different nationalities and languages to prevent them from getting together; and that this practice had become systematized through weekly luncheons of the employment managers of the major Chicago-area firms, at which they discussed their labor problems and exchanged information supplied by men in the field who had infiltrated established or nascent labor organizations. Commons, "Introduction," History of Labor, 3:xxv.

and their reputation as workers--from being in demand for their know-how, to being seen as a liability to productivity and profits. An anonymous commentator in 1913 expressed the older workers' dilemma this way:

> In the search for increased efficiency, begotten in modern time by the practically universal worship of the dollar...gray hair has come to be recognized as an unforgivable witness of industrial imbecility, and experience, the invariable companion of advancing years, instead of being valued as common sense would require it to be, has become a handicap so great as to make the employment of its possessor, in the performance of tasks and duties for which his life has fitted him, practically impossible.[10]

The Hours and Intensity of Work

The decades following the Civil War marked a pronounced shift in employers' attitudes toward their workforces. Early American entrepreneurs, as noted above, had held a paternalistic attitude toward their employees, and concerned themselves with what went on in their lives outside as well as in the shop. But this paternalism was greatly weakened by the factory system and the pressures of competition, and workers came increasingly to be viewed more as productive inputs and less as individuals. A particularly telling illustration of the new stance of employers regarding their employees is this remark by a small factory owner in Fall River, Massachusetts, in mid-nineteenth century:

> I regard my work-people just as I regard my machinery. So long as they can do my work for what I choose to pay them, I keep them, getting out of them all I can. What they do or how they fare outside my walls, I don't know nor do I consider it my business to know.[11]

Employment within the factory system provided workers with "but a feeble and uncertain bond"[12] when they began to have arms' length dealings with bosses. Although commonplace today, this separation of the employer from the employed was quite alien to most workers in the latter part of the nineteenth century. This was no doubt particularly true for those in the older age groups, who had begun their working lives at a time when co-workers were "family" and when it was not yet uncommon for a laboring man to be able to aspire to managing a business of his own. That a relatively small proportion may actually have succeeded in such undertakings, even then, is somewhat beside the point. To many observers it was clear by the turn of the century that such a prospect was out of the question for all but a few of the most energetic and fortunate workers. In Ely's words:
The few may rise, as the few may draw prizes in a lottery, but it is foolish for an

---

10 "Independent Opinions," Independent 75 (August 28, 1913):504, cited by Achenbaum, Old Age, p. 48.

11 Cited by Norman Ware, The Industrial Worker, p. 77.

12 Catlin, The Labor Problem, p. 5.

ordinary workman to look forward to...the ownership of an independent business. There are, for example, over a million persons engaged in the railway business in the United States, but less than one per cent of them are officers of any sort, let alone being president of the railway.[13]

The Hours of Work

A feature of industrial working life in late nineteenth-century America which undeniably contributed to the early aging of workers was the length of the workday and the workweek, which also surely exacerbated the extent of unemployment due to injury or illness. In the U.S. the hours of work were longer as a rule than in other industrialized nations, and they did not begin to shorten perceptibly until after the first decade of the twentieth century (with the exception of the hours of child and female labor, which were regulated by statute as early as 1867 in Wisconsin).

Although some unionized skilled workers had attained the 10-hour workday in the 1830s, midcentury was generally characterized by workdays running dawn to dusk, six days a week (as many as 75 hours per week), with vacations unknown and holidays rare. But the pace of work, by contemporary standards, was comparatively slow prior to the Civil War, and neither capitalist nor laborer appears to have given much thought to productivity in this period.

The pace of work was speeded up noticeably in many lines of work in the 1860s and 1870s[14] as entrepreneurs attempted to cut costs to cope with increasing competitive pressures and scanty reserves. The belief was that the longer and more rapidly a worker toiled the more he produced; there appears to have been no awareness of the possibility that reducing hours and speed of work might actually boost productivity. (The first known attempt to ascertain the relationship between productivity and the length and intensity of the workday was not made until 1893, by an Englishman, Sir William Mather.[15]) It was not until after the turn of the century that annual holidays could be taken without loss of pay in most lines of work, so industrial workers usually worked a full 52 weeks in a year out of economic necessity.[16]

Hours of work had been a source of controversy in the U.S. at least since 1822 when the journeymen millwrights and machinists of Philadelphia met to decide "that ten hours of labor were enough for one day, and that work ought to begin at 6 A.M. and end at 6

---

13 Ely, Evolution of Industrial Society, pp. 79-80.

14 This had occurred earlier in some industries: the 1830s and 1840s in textiles, the 1850s in shoemaking.

15 Krooss, American Economic Development, p. 459.

16 In 1909, 76 percent of factory wage earners were found to be working between 54 and 60 hours per week; in 1922, the National Bureau of Economic Research calculated the average number of hours worked per week to be 50.3 when every type of industry was considered. Florence, Economics of Fatigue and Unrest, pp. 67-68.

P.M., with an hour for breakfast and one for dinner."[17] Progressively through the nine-teenth century, the hours issue grew to be as large a cause of controversy as wages. Its discussion became entangled with machinery, speed, efficiency; with health, fatigue, accidents; with output restriction, unemployment, and business depressions.

By the turn of the century the worst "hours situation" was in the steel and railroad transportation industries, which had become, by the second decade of the century, among the industries with the lowest proportions of older employees,[18] an unsurprising finding in light of the rigors of the work compounded by long hours. In the 1890s the average week in the steel industry was 65-66 hours. This average included the thousands of "turn men" who labored 72-84 hours per week at the blast furnaces and open hearths, a practice which continued with only minor modifications until the eight-hour day was adopted in 1923.[19] Railroad trainmen in the 1890s worked seven 10-hour days per week, the standard since about 1840. Although in 1890 locomotive engineers and conductors worked only a 60-hour week on average, in 1898 in Virginia the standard week of engineers still stood at 84 hours.[20]

The rationale for long hours in American industry was based upon employers' belief, in Florence's words, that "the added sum paid in wages [for a longer as opposed to a shorter workday] was not to be compared with the added gain in net value of output."[21] In other words, the hours spent at work might have little connection with workers' pay, but duration of work was seen to be intimately bound up with the profitability of an enterprise. Some employers' associations in the late nineteenth century put forth the argument that the reduction of the working day from 11 1/2 to 10 1/2 hours would take away all the employer's net profit.[22]

Such a view had received theoretical legitimacy in the work of Nassau Senior. Senior hypothesized a four-to-one ratio of business fixed capital in plant and equipment to circulating capital, representing current requirements in raw materials and wages. This led to his formulation of the long-lived economic fallacy that profit derives from the output of the last hours of work, and hence "profits would be destroyed if the eleventh or even the twelfth hour of work were curtailed."[23]

After industrialization was well-entrenched, the probable determining factor in the minds of employers when they insisted on long hours was the relatively large amount of fixed capital the application of the new technologies necessitated. As Senior concisely put it, "The great proportion of fixed to circulating capital makes long hours of work desir-

---

17 John B. McMaster, A History of the People of the United States, 8 vols. (New York: D. Appleton Co., 1914), 5:84.

18 As established in Chapter 5.

19 Lescohier, Working Conditions, p. 99.

20 Ibid., p. 102.

21 Florence, Economics of Fatigue and Unrest, p. 69.

22 Ibid.

able."[24] "Interference" with fixed capital via state regulation, such as limiting work hours, would lead to a cessation of business activity, to the detriment of capitalists and workers alike, for

> ...ten hours paid only the expenses of the "plant" and the wages of labor, and...if work stopped at ten hours, there would be no profit on the capital invested. The surplus, then, whether it was one, one and a half, or two hours beyond ten hours, was the only time from which a remunerative return for capital could be made, without which it could not be expected that men would carry on business.[25]

The capital invested in an industry was valued according to its productiveness, which generated the economic imperative to keep such properties working. Recurring costs such as interest, rent, insurance, and taxes, of course had to be paid at regular periods regardless of the amount produced in the interval. In addition, apart from depreciation through wear and tear, there was a physical loss of value through the mere passage of time, that is, from exposure plus the further loss of value owing to the rapid obsolescence of machines under conditions of incessant competition and rapid technological change. As the material equipment for production became ever more costly, the view developed that the factory existed primarily to house this equipment, and the human workers simply had to adapt themselves--to fumes, noise, humidity, and temperature extremes either caused by the machinery or required for its optimal use--as best they could.

An extreme case of loss of value was in the continuous industries using chemical processes. If the work were to suffer any interruption, the material in process had to be scrapped and the equipment might be damaged as well. Such industries near the turn of the century included steel-making, blast furnace works, sugar-refining, and glass, cement, and chemical manufacturing. In all of these a concerted effort was made to keep the capital equipment at work around the clock. In consequence, employees had to work either three shifts of eight hours or two of twelve hours, with American manufacturers opting for the latter when they could.

Most of the important controversies about the hours of work revolved around these continuous-process industries. American manufacturing workers in general were experiencing a gradually diminishing work week, but work at night and on Sundays was the norm in the continuous industries, and the "vogue in American steel plants" was that "one shift must work twenty-four hours on end before being relieved!"[26] By 1886, according to Andrew Carnegie, "every ton of pig iron made in the world, except in two establishments,

24 Nassau Senior, cited by Florence, Economics of Fatigue and Unrest, p. 126.

25 Testimony of Joseph Hume in Parliament, Hansard's Parliamentary Debates, 3rd series, February 10, 1847, cited by Goldmark, Fatigue and Efficiency, p. 127.

26 Florence, Economics of Fatigue and Unrest, p. 70.

was made by men working in double shifts of twelve hours each, having neither Sunday nor holiday the year round."[27]

The Intensity of Work

In many industries there began, by mid-century, to be a dramatic increase in the number of machines served by the individual worker. This form of the "speed-up," as Kirkland has noted, made it

> ...difficult to apportion the causes of these increases [in output] between the use of improved and automatic devices and the more intensive application of human labor....Although the machinery undoubtedly lightened heavy labor, it substituted an emphasis upon precision, attention, nervous vitality, which was extremely wearing. In spite of the numerous attempts at statistical measurement of fatigue, no very specific generalization can be made as to whether the worker was more or less tired after the eight-hour day of 1920 than after the eleven-hour day of 1850.[28]

As the hours of labor were gradually reduced, under the impact of collective bargaining and state legislation, particularly after the economy's recovery from the depression of the 'nineties, employers turned their attention to increasing the intensity of work. This could be done either by increasing the speed of work, the constancy of work, or the load of work per operative. The first of these, the speed of work, depended both on the speed at which machines were set and the particular piece-wage system in effect (to be explained later in this section).

Increased constancy of work could be an automatic result of greater efficiency in routing materials and more diligent attending to machines, leaving less chance for rest on account of mechanical breakdowns or materials bottlenecks. The load of work could be increased in several ways: by increasing the number of machines (automatic looms, furnaces, and so forth) that an individual worker had to monitor; by increasing the number of tools, or the amount of work to be performed simultaneously by any one machine; or by the introduction of cheaper, lower quality materials which required greater attention on the part of the worker.

Thus the augmentation of productivity through the continuous application of labor-saving machinery could be further reinforced by the disciplining effects of machinery on the workforce. As Charles Babbage had observed in 1832, "one of the most singular advantages to be derived from machinery is the check it affords against the inattention, the idleness, or the knavery of human agents."[29] When all such manipulations of work standards are taken into account, there can be little doubt that what workers were able to gain from the 1870s onward in reduced hours of work was substantially offset by increases in the intensity

---

27 Andrew Carnegie, "Results of the Labor Struggle," The Forum 1 (1886):544, cited by Lescohier, Working Conditions, p. 101.

28 Kirkland, History of American Economic Life, p. 521.

29 Charles Babbage cited by Florence, Economics of Fatigue and Unrest, p. 71.

of work. As a consequence, by the early 1900s workers' councils were focusing less upon the issue of the hours of work than upon the evils of the speed-up.

The competitive pressures in most establishments forced employers to give little regard to the welfare of individual workers. The strains of industry--its intensity (not merely speed, but also noise and monotony) and long hours--were a natural accompaniment of employers' heavy investment in fixed capital, a rapid rate of technological change, and a weakly organized working class. Capitalists were confronted with the likelihood that equipment would depreciate at least as rapidly through obsolescence as through wearing out, so they sought both continuous operation of their plants and the most rapid operation consistent with the desired quality of output. Each machine had to earn its replacement plus an income on the capital it embodied before being thrown on the scrap heap. With appropriate maintenance the machines, however, were tireless, even at rapid speeds. The only limiting factor to the speeding-up process lay in the capacities of the operatives.

These capacities were themselves influenced by the incentive structure of the production process. In particular, opportunities for speeding up work were afforded through an enterprise's system of remuneration. For example, under the "task system," a group of workers performed different processes as a unit, and were thus effectively linked together. Although ostensibly "cooperating" with one another, team members would actually be in competition because each was expected to keep up with the worker ahead of him, and it was the quickest who set the pace.[30] (It might be thought that the slowest workers set the pace by holding up the line, but they would not long be tolerated in so interfering with both managerial goals and the remuneration of the other workers.) With improvements in power production and transmission and with ever-increasing automation of the machines themselves, the average rate of speed could be raised, and consequently so, too, the strain on the workers.

However, it was the piece-rate system that was responsible for the vast majority of instances of feverish haste in manufacturing establishments. A system that caused a worker's pay to depend directly on the size of his output might seem, on the face of it, to be fair to all parties concerned. Employers could argue that if any employees overworked under this system, it was their fault and they should take the consequences.

But if the time-wage system was not independent of the volume of output, neither was the piece-rate system independent of time. The employer's first concern was that the machinery be efficiently used, so any employee who failed to keep pace was an encumbrance and would be let go. The tendency in most American manufacturing establishments was initially to fix piece rates according to the tempo of the quicker workers. But upon slight improvements in the machinery, or when it was deemed that the operatives were earning excessive wages, there was a tendency for the rate to be reduced.[31]

The premium/bonus plan combined these two methods of paying workers (piece-time and time-wage) and would become a common feature of scientific management and kindred

---

30 See David F. Schloss, Methods of Industrial Remuneration (New York: G.P. Putnams, 1892), chapter 3.

31 Catlin, The Labor Problem, p. 168. Marx had presented an extended discussion of this phenomenon. See Karl Marx, Capital: A Critique of Political Economy, 3 vols. (New York: Modern Library, 1906), 1:447-66.

efficiency schemes. A certain minimum standard was set for a particular time period, and the worker was spurred to meet or exceed it either by the threat of a fine or the promise of a small addition to his pay. The net effect was a system which more closely approximated piece-rate reimbursement in its promotion of exertion by the operatives.

Examples of these various systems of promoting speed, and of the enormous strain they created in the workforce, could be found in almost every industry by the early 1900s:

- The textile trades used the piece-work system in almost all branches, and also exhibited a constant tendency to speed up the machinery and increase the size and number of machines tended by each worker.[32]

- Before the introduction of the dial system, the experienced telephone operator was expected to handle 225 calls per hour.[33]

- Conveyor belts in canneries and other food-processing establishments supplied containers at pre-set rates of flow to the young women staffing them, thus enforcing speed.[34]

- The glass industry, before it was largely automated in the 1920s, gave striking evidence of all types of speeding. In the making of incandescent lamps, a minimum output was required; piece rates were kept low and were subject to reductions with little or no notice; bonuses were offered for increased output; and the fastest workers set the pace.[35]

A report by the U.S. Commissioner of Labor in 1910 found that there was "...a nervous strain, manifesting itself in a feverish concentration on the work, to be seen in most of the establishments and particularly in the larger and more modern plants."[36] A classic example of the pressures of speed is John A. Fitch's 1911 description of work in the steel mills:

> In the first place, the men engaged in the processes are all paid piece rates, an incentive in itself to output; but this in the steel industry has never been strong enough to produce the results secured by other methods. It is augmented by the fact that each man's rate is paid on the tonnage gotten out by the crew, so that his fellow

---

32 The number of looms per cotton operative was steadily increased, from one or two in the mid-nineteenth century to 12, 16, and 36 looms by the early 1930s; and under the "stretch-out" system in the South (so-called by labor, referred to by management as the "extended labor" or "multiple-loom" system), to over 100. ("Report of the Board of Inquiry for the Cotton Textile Industry to the President," New York Times, 21 September 1934, pp. 18-19; U.S. Industrial Commission, Report, 19:817-18; Goldmark, Fatigue and Efficiency, p. 57.)

33 United States Bureau of Labor, Investigation of Telephone Companies (Washington, D.C.: Government Printing Office, 1910), pp. 56-61.

34 Elizabeth B. Butler, Women and the Trades: Pittsburgh, 1907-1908 (New York: Russell Sage Foundation, 1911), pp. 36, 64.

35 Goldmark, Fatigue and Efficiency, p. 57.

36 U.S. Commissioner of Labor, Women and Child Wage-Earners (Washington, D.C.: Government Printing Office, 1910),3:478 et seq.

workers are interested in the effort he puts into his part of the job....In all the different departments of mill work there are gangs, each man dependent upon the others in his gang, and each gang dependent upon other gangs. From the wages standpoint the strain is great, for if one man is slow he reduces the tonnage and hence the earnings of a hundred other men. From the production standpoint the strain is perhaps greater, for on each man rests the necessity for handling the steel as fast as it comes. The procession must not be halted. Put a strong, swift man at the head of the first gang and the steel does its own driving.[37]

The system of bonuses and appeals to the spirit of rivalry were used to establish "records" which thereafter became the norm. But it was the reductions in the tonnage rate that had the greatest influence in increasing daily production in the mills.[38]

Admirers of the assembly line method argued that the timing was synchronized with average ability, and that in the last analysis it was the workers themselves who set the pace. However, this did not appear to be the case according to the testimony of an avowedly sturdy young man who spent a summer working in a Ford plant:

> The conveyors are speeded up to the maximum of a man's endurance, and once in a while they must be stopped for the workers to catch up....A man can stand this speed for a while but it gradually tells on him and the Ford factory has trouble keeping men on the "line"....Lunch hour comes about the middle of the shift. It lasts from fifteen to twenty minutes....Often men have their mouths crammed full of food when they start to work again.[39]

Such examples might be endlessly multiplied. Employers of wage-workers were more or less enlightened and adopted workforce policies of greater or lesser benevolence; but humane treatment of workers could carry a high price in an era of cutthroat competition. Offering higher wages or requiring fewer hours than the prevailing norm raised an enterprise's costs as compared to competitors' costs, threatening the firm's viability. (It was this fact of the brutalizing effects of competition which led many to support combinations that would result in nearly purely monopolistic industries, which could then be regulated by statute.[40]) Consequently, the trend was toward ever-increasing speed, monotony, partitioning of duties, and hiring and firing according to inflexible and often unreasonable criteria.

---

37 John A. Fitch, The Steel Workers (New York: Charities Publication Committee, 1911), pp. 184-85.

38 Ibid., pp. 187-90.

39 Walter E. Ulrich, "On the Belt" (pamphlet; New York, 1929), pp. 4, 6, cited by Catlin, The Labor Problem, p. 170.

40 Among the well-known economists who thought regulated monopolies would probably be preferable in human welfare terms to wide-open competition were Richard Ely and Henry George.

The New Managerialism and the
Redivision of Labor

The technological basis for the division of labor addressed in the previous chapter provides only a part (and perhaps the less important part) of the rationale for specialization of tasks. A vital impetus to the division of labor came from firms' attempts to introduce greater organizational rationality so as to maximize the economies of large-scale production. To ensure the success of giant enterprises, an altogether new degree of sophistication in administration and management was crucial. Not only did production workers have to be handed their instructions and closely supervised, but an equally thorough division of duties took place to facilitate purchasing, transportation, accounting, and planning procedures for national marketing. Jobs were more narrowly defined to take advantage of the economies of repetitive tasks, and the division of labor between workers and management was more clearly established.

Most important, when employers no longer were personally acquainted with those they employed, it became possible, even necessary, to alter the relations of authority and control within the firm.[41] From employers' perspective, labor--with its indifference or outright hostility to the interests of capital, and its usually vague but periodically explosive unrest--was becoming distinctly a "problem" to be "managed."

In those large firms and concentrated industries for which detailed evolutionary studies exist,[42] it is evident that conscious strategies of labor force control were operating to downgrade the role of skill in the production process, while giving greater scope to managerial functions. At first, managerial control essentially amounted to replacing skilled craftsmen with foremen. According to Robert Reich, the number of foremen in American manufacturing and construction firms increased fourfold between 1890 and 1900, from 90,000 and 360,000.[43] Foremen were given complete responsibility for their segments of production, and were usually free to manage their workers any way they cared to, so long as they coordinated production goals with other foremen. They could hire, fire, promote, demote, reward, and punish workers with relative impunity.[44]

---

41 For extensive discussions of the late nineteenth and early twentieth century managerial revolution, see Daniel Nelson, Managers and Workers: Origins of the New Factory System in the United States, 1880-1920 (Madison: University of Wisconsin Press, 1975); and Richard C. Edwards, Contested Terrain: The Transformation of the Workplace in the Twentieth Century (New York: Basic Books, 1979). See also Michael Reich, David Gordon, and Richard Edwards, "Dual Labor Markets: A Theory of Labor Market Segmentation," American Economic Association Papers and Proceedings 63 (May 1973): 359-65.

42 Among them, steel (U.S. Steel), the railroads, automobiles (Ford), farm implements (International Harvester, McCormick), sewing machines (Singer), meatpacking (Swift, Armour), petroleum (Standard Oil).

43 Robert B. Reich, The Next American Frontier (New York: Times Books, 1983), p. 37.

44 Ibid.; Lescohier, Working Conditions, p. 304.

This new "input" in the production process was a development of great consequence. Although within his sphere of accountability the foreman was as autonomous as the skilled craftsman had been within his, the craftsman's control over subordinates had been sanctioned by his superior skills, which were directed toward making a product. By contrast, the foreman's control stemmed from his formal position in an organizational hierarchy, and his task was to supervise and discipline the producers.[45]

Such oversight responsibility on the part of the foremen/managers revolutionized the methods by which employees were trained, making it possible to remove knowledge about the production process from the province of workers, skilled as well as unskilled. With growing control over how knowledge about production got disseminated, firms' owners could better guard against the possibility that their workers would go off on their own to compete through their own organizations.

Management began to come into its own as a legitimate job category and field of study in the first decade of the twentieth century. The New York Public Library's Technology Division registered no titles on management prior to 1881. Between 1881 and 1900 there were only 27; but in the next decade there were 240, with rapid increases thereafter.[46]

Scientific Management

As part of the process by which firms sought to consolidate control over all aspects of production, physical, or hand work, came to be separated from mental, or head work. The apostle of this distinction was Frederick W. Taylor, who early had recognized that the mandate for the factory was at least as much managerial as it was mechanical, or how else could one explain the ability to dilute skill by subdividing tasks that could be done by hand, that is, without the introduction of labor-saving machinery? Although Taylor's name has become synonymous with the managerial revolution, in fact he merely systematized and codified the inchoate set of administrative/organizational practices that had been developing within large firms for some time.

Taylor's contribution to hastening the trend toward large-scale production is difficult to assess, but where Taylorist principles were followed they decidedly reinforced the prevailing trends in task specialization upon which capitalist industrialization depended. A trained machinist, Taylor turned his attention in the 1880s to the continuing risk of production failures faced by firms that had managed to solve quite well the problems of financing and sales.[47] Like others before him, he pointed out that the volume of output was fairly independent of overhead costs such as depreciation, interest, rent, salaries, insurance, taxes, and other operating costs. Thus, a large volume of output should be the aim of the rational producer seeking to lower unit costs.

Taylor's first essay to gain widespread attention was a lecture in 1895 before the American Society of Mechanical Engineers entitled <u>A Piece Rate System, being a Step</u>

---

45 Reich, <u>Next American Frontier</u>, p. 37.

46 Lescohier, <u>Working Conditions</u>, p. 303.

47 Kirkland, <u>Industry Comes of Age</u>, pp. 172-74.

towards a Partial Solution of the Labor Problem. This foreshadowed his major technical work of 1906, On the Art of Cutting Metals, as well as the more popular books, Shop Management (1903) and Principles of Scientific Management (1911). Over a period of three decades Taylor undertook his time and motion studies in the steel fabricating industry, studies which essentially sought to prove that rising wages were not necessarily incompatible with rising profits so long as unit-time (unit cost) was falling.[48]

Yet Taylor's early writing revealed an undisguised interest in increasing the rate of labor exploitation, with the result, according to one Taylor scholar, that "Taylorism aroused the opposition and revulsion of the workers [and of many foremen and managers] to an extent which threatened to defeat its own objectives," and thus, in the interests of expediency, it was "modified and wrapped around with a medly of 'sciences'--physiology, psychology, sociology and so on."[49]

Fundamentally what Taylor had in mind was a replacement of the traditional confrontational relations between employers and the employed by a wedding (though not necessarily harmonious) of their mutual concerns. To do this required, according to Sohn-Rethel, that the worker be converted "from a machine-operator into a part of the machinery itself,"[50] for

> ...the concepts of time and motion used in its [Taylorism's] job analysis are technological categories and no true terms of human labour at all. Taylorised labour, therefore, is human labour made into a technological entity, homogeneous with the machinery, directly adaptable and can be inserted or transformed into it without any difficulty of conversion [sic]. Here labour is not only subsumed economically to capital (to use Marx's expression), i.e., by the act of the workmen selling their labour-power to the capitalist, but also physically and technologically.[51]

In order for the majority of laborers to be effectively converted into appendages of machinery, there had to be created a decision-making class. In Taylor's words,

> ...we propose to take all the important decisions and planning which vitally affect the output of the shop out of the hands of the workmen, and centralize them in a few men, each of whom is especially trained in the art of making those decisions and in

48 F. B. Copley, Frederick W. Taylor, Father of Scientific Management (New York: Harper and Bros., 1923).

49 Alfred Sohn-Rethel, Intellectual and Manual Labour: A Critique of Epistemology (Atlantic Highlands, N.J.: Humanities Press, 1978), p. 150.

50 Ibid., p. 156.

51 Ibid., pp. 155-56. Emphasis in the original.

seeing that they are carried out, each man having his own particular function in which he is supreme, and not interfering with the functions of other men.[52]

Taylor's investigations would lead directly to the introduction of some valuable inventions and scientific discoveries--such as more efficient designs for machine tools, and self-hardening and high-speed steels. But Taylor himself felt that one of his most inspired contributions lay in "the development of the slide rules which enable the shop managers, without consulting the workmen, to fix a daily task with a definite time allowance for each workman who is running a machine tool, and to pay the men a bonus for rapid work." [53]
The slide rule made possible

...the original object for which in 1880 the experiments were started; i.e., that of taking the control of the machine shop out of the hands of the management, thus superseding the "rule of thumb" by scientific control.[54] Under our system the workman is told minutely just what he is to do and how he is to do it; and any improvement which he makes upon the orders given him is fatal to success.[55]

Throughout the post-Civil War period, factory superintendents and mechanical engineers had increasingly been preoccupied with the problem of securing internal economy within the workplace and with performing industrial operations with maximum efficiency.[56] Taylorism was the apotheosis of all such efforts. The appeal of his theories to the owning and managing classes was straightforward and unmuddied by any romantic sentiments about self-sufficiency or noble labor. The unskilled, physical work should be handled by the "gorilla type" of worker,[57] and the skilled worker should be separated from his skills to the extent required to ensure managerial hegemony.

---

52 Frederick W. Taylor, On the Art of Cutting Metals (New York: American Society of Mechanical Engineers, 1906), para. 124.

53 Ibid., para. 51.

54 Ibid., para. 52.

55 Ibid., para. 118. Note that even "improvements" were considered undesirable if they arose outside of established channels.

56 See, for example, "The Engineer as an Economist," Transactions of the American Society of Mechanical Engineers 8 (1885-1886): 428- 29.

57 Taylor cited by Kirkland, History of American Economic Life, p. 520. Particularly desired by American employers were recent immigrants, primarily southern Europeans, whose "sturdy physiques, low standard of living, relative docility, and cheapness" uniquely fitted them for the hardest, most disagreeable, least-skilled, and lowest-paid tasks. Catlin, The Labor Problem, p. 52.

In The Principles of Scientific Management (1911), Taylor's best-known work, the importance of taking judgment and discretion (that is, "mental" skills) away from the skilled worker was succinctly stated:

> Now, in the best of the ordinary types of management, the managers recognize the fact that the 500 or 1000 workmen, included in the twenty or thirty trades, who are under them, possess this mass of traditional knowledge, a large part of which is not in the possession of the management. The management, of course, includes foremen and superintendents, who themselves have been in most cases first-class workers at their trades. And yet these foremen and superintendents know, better than anyone else, that their own knowledge and personal skill falls far short of the combined knowledge and dexterity of all the workmen under them.[58]

Even shop-floor managers were to be discouraged from independent thought. In the pamphlet, Shop Management, Taylor urged, "All possible brain work should be removed from the shop and centered in the planning or laying-out department, leaving for the foremen and gang bosses work strictly executive in nature."[59]

The result of the application of Taylorist principles to production was an attempt at complete separation of planning from execution. The thinkers (managers and superintendents) would plan the work and establish the procedures, and the workers would do what they were told. The original "managers," the foremen, were now more of a worker elite than a separate class. Maximum efficiency required that foremen's range of action be limited to very specific duties. The substitution of formal rules for individual discretion in such jobs probably protected workers in general by greatly reducing the proportion of workplace decisions or arrangements that were arbitrary or based upon whim or personal prejudice. Older workers, however, as will be seen in the next section, now increasingly faced iron-clad rules which hampered their finding employment.

The distinction between thinking and doing did not necessarily mean that all production work was unskilled. The work of machine maintenance and repair was ongoing, and there continued to be aspects of machine-based production that required considerable, if narrowly-defined, skill and experience (such as many aspects of meatpacking and shoe-making, for example). Nonetheless, much skilled labor by the turn of the century had altogether different attributes from the traditional skilled labor that had characterized production prior to industrialization.

What had been lost was an overall understanding on the part of the worker of how the production process unfolded, from procurement of raw materials, to contracting out of ancillary tasks, to getting the output to its ultimate purchasers. The loss of this understanding reduced the workers' power to the threat of the strike over hours and wages, because most workers no longer had any effective appeal to the self-employment option. Even strikes became less of a threat as larger numbers of workers experienced deskilling

---

58 Frederick W. Taylor, The Principles of Scientific Management, in Scientific Management (New York: Harper and Bros., 1911), p. 32.

59 Taylor, Shop Management, in ibid., pp. 98-99.

or skill-narrowing, and as immigration rates reached an all-time high in the first decade of the twentieth century.

In 1914-1915 the United States Commission on Industrial Relations appointed a committee to carry out a thorough study of the theory and practice of scientific management. The conclusion they reached was that scientific management at its best had greatly benefitted industry through its emphasis on systematization, coordination, and accurate knowledge; and that it seemed to "enormously add to the strength of capitalism." But, the committee added,

> ...neither organized nor unorganized labor finds in scientific management any adequate protection to its standard of living, any progresive means for industrial education, or any opportunity for industrial democracy by which labor may create for itself a progressively efficient share in efficient management.[60]

The committee found the goals of scientific management and those of labor to be "equally vital, equally indestructible, and equally uncompromising."[61] Only after World War I did organized labor and proponents of scientific management even begin to see that their respective purposes might be harmonized.[62]

Superannuation and Ageism

Industrial efficiency along the lines of Taylorist principles meant using up human energy at greater speed and within a shorter time, and dispensing with workers as soon as their efficiency began to decline. Rapid increases in investment in fixed capital and the resulting increases in fixed and overhead charges created a situation whereby only an intensification of the work process would allow for profit margins to be maintained. This was all the more true because of the shortening of hours and restrictions on night work enforced by the spread of organized labor and labor laws.[63]

From the vantage point of the working classes, already threatened by unemployment of a technological, structural, cyclical or seasonal nature, the intensification of work became another potential cause of unemployment, through overstrain and superannuation, or economic old age. In the words of Rubinow,

> The constant speeding up of the industrial processes, the almost inhuman intensity of effort which grows even more than in direct proportion to the shortening of the

---

60 Robert F. Hoxie, Scientific Management and Labor (New York: D. Appleton Co., 1915), Appendix I, p. 137.

61 Ibid., p. 138.

62 Lescohier, Working Conditions, p. 315.

63 For a time, many feared that machine industry would be ruined by the advent of the eight-hour day, which forced millions of dollars' worth of investment to remain idle for two-thirds of the time. Rubinow, Social Insurance, p. 305.

workers' hours, the work at great depth in mines, or dizzy heights in building operations, the ever-present danger of bodily injury, all these facts have their effects. We have scarcely begun to study the problem of pathological effects of fatigue, but that it must result in producing premature old age is quite evident. The result is the pathetic problem of the man at fifty,...which threatens to become the problem of the man at forty-five. Modern tendencies in industry all work together to aggravate this situation.[64]

Industrial working conditions (particularly when coupled with such typical living condition hazards as poor housing, nutrition, and sanitation) made young persons middle-aged, the middle-aged old, and the chronologically old person of 60 or 65 expendable. Economic superannuation, virtually unknown before the advent of the factory system, was the most serious threat of all to continuing employment, because its arrival tended to be permanent.

The poor health conditions of factory workers who had to accommodate themselves to the requirements of machinery were a refutation of the contention that machines were enhancing life by reducing drudgery.[65] In the years between 1880 and 1920 overstrain from machinery rhythms became the most notable trait of American industrial work, far more widespread in the U.S. than in Great Britain or Europe. Irving Fisher noted in 1909 that the majority of the American population, even including many children, suffered at least partial disability on account of excessive fatigue.[66]

Chronic fatigue predisposed its victims to the onset of disease. While infant mortality was reduced through the conquest of infectious diseases, the death rate increased for those over 40 (whereas in Great Britain, for example, where the work pace was less hurried, death rates were falling for all age groups.)[67] This led many to wonder if there were not something radically wrong with the American manner of work and living.

Within the factory, fatigue manifested itself in decreased levels of efficiency and output, and in absenteeism and high rates of labor turnover. Ultimately, chronic fatigue and overstrain caused premature aging, rendering workers unfit to hold jobs of any kind. The result of such occurrences was an anti-age bias in hiring workers in many occupations, "a premium put upon youth and agility, and...a handicap upon age and maturity."[68]

The average worker attained his maximum earning power early in life, both because of fatigue and because of the dwindling importance attached to acquired skills and seasoned

---

64 Ibid., pp. 304-05.

65 John Stuart Mill had noted that "it is questionable if all the mechanical inventions yet made have lightened the day's toil of any human being." Mill, Principles of Political Economy (New York: Augustus M. Kelley, 1919), p. 751.

66 U.S. Conservation Commission, Report, Bulletin of the Committee of One Hundred on National Health, being a Report on National Vitality, its Wastes and Conservation (Washington, D.C.: Government Printing Office, 1909), 3:669.

67 Catlin, The Labor Problem, pp. 157-58; Barkin, The Older Worker, p. 109.

68 Catlin, The Labor Problem, p. 161.

judgment. There were never many executive or managerial positions for older workers to aspire to, and at any rate such jobs were increasingly filled by people whose employment backgrounds were in clerking, sales, and related occupations, not in factory-based work. Such occupations involving direct dealings with the public appear to have been particularly discriminatory against older workers, as will be documented later in this chapter.

Factors Working Against the Employment
of Older Workers

The older worker confronting large enterprises, regularized according to Taylorist managerial principles, was in a tenuous situation for five principal reasons: (1) possession of pre-industrial attitudes and habits of thought; (2) heightened susceptibility to tiring from industrial rhythms; (3) possession of the wrong skills, whether altogether outmoded or merely of diminished value; (4) a short remaining worklife expectancy; and (5) powerlessness in confronting relatively inflexible hiring bureaucracies. The last of these difficulties affected working-class people of all ages, but even so it probably had the greatest effect on older workers over time. These aspects of older workers' dilemma will be discussed in turn.

(1) The skills which the older worker had acquired, within the traditional system of moving up from apprentice to journeyman to master, were in particular the sorts of skills which the techniques of management were explicitly designed to destroy, because they gave the worker a degree of power or influence in decisions as to how to produce that threatened managerial hegemony. Such an individual was accustomed to exercising a considerable degree of independent judgment--"thinking"--when turning out his product. He thus had the potential to interfere with the planning functions of those higher up in the corporate hierarchy, as well as perhaps being inclined to slow down the lines while he pondered an insight or a problem that might arise.

However, not only did older skilled workers possess the very skills which the new industrial order was eliminating in the process of centralization, but in particular they possessed pre-industrial attitudes, a mindset that made them perhaps less willing than their younger colleagues to follow orders simply because they were orders. This independence of thought undoubtedly handicapped them when seeking employment in large establishments. A younger applicant, and especially a newly-arrived immigrant eager to work at American wages, could be supposed to accommodate himself far more readily and rapidly to accept routinized, uninteresting wage-work than the individual with an old-fashioned approach to production, and with ideas of his own. Older workers disproportionately possessed the "wrong" attitudes.[69]

(2) Even if still quite hale, the older worker was likely to find that the unceasing rhythm of repetitive tasks performed according to the machinery's tempo quickly exhausted

---

69 A point frequently made then and today by corporate executives and personnel managers, in defense of age bias in hiring, is that older employees are loath to change their ways and accept new ideas. They are often seen to be slow learners, for reasons both physiological and psychological. A voluminous literature on industrial gerontology has not fully resolved this issue, but the weight of the evidence supports such a view only for jobs demanding speed, strength, and endurance--surely a rapidly growing proportion of jobs in the period being examined--but not for reasons of nonadaptability.

him.[70] This of course happened not only to older workers but to those of all ages, yet advancing age almost inevitably is accompanied by reduced vigor. It was not merely a question of rapid pace per se, but of a pace utterly unrelieved by the accustomed freedom of movement from one task to another, with the mental diversion such variation allowed. In addition to no longer being master of his job, the aging worker coped as best he could with the swifter pace and the greater nervous strain of factory production which wore out all workers more rapidly than ever before.

The conditions of the wage contract served to accentuate the normal disabilities of old age. Under normal physiological conditions, old age led to a gradual failing of productive powers, unless preceded by a chronic illness. As the independent producer grew old, he worked less, but he continued to work so long as he could produce something; and thus in pre-industrial times, the economic usefulness of old people did not end until actual senility was established, a rather rare phenomenon. But under a wage system, the economic disability of age could arise suddenly--and at a relatively young age, particularly if the intensity of the work process had always been great--while the older individual was still fit for productive activity, albeit at a slower pace than previously.

(3) As scientific management gained ascendancy, the process of hiring came increasingly to determine which workers would and would not have the relevant skills. When the acquisition of particular skills had been largely an individual matter, whereby the young man starting out apprenticed himself to a master and worked his way up through the ranks to a hoped-for competence, the distribution of skills in general dictated the distribution of positions within the labor force.

Once corporate establishments had become rationalized along the lines prescribed by the new managerial principles, management not only determined the skills it sought but also the process of acquiring them. With the development of internal labor markets and carefully-specified job ladders, none of the traditional skills had an economic value independent of the dominant method of organizing production. The skills that were valued in employment were those transmitted by the corporate hierarchy.

Furthermore, the greater economy and efficiency to be had from consolidation and specialization had the effect of driving smaller and less efficient competitors out of business, and discouraging new competition from entering, thereby reducing employment opportunities outside of large enterprises. Skilled workers were now effectively barred from entering the entrepreneurial class because the newer establishments depended not so much on the craft and experience such workers possessed as on large agglomerations of capital and the managerial/financial skills of promoters.

(4) At the same time, within large enterprises, with training now in the hands of employers rather than individual workers, worklife expectancy for the first time became an

---

70 A large literature, including debates in both learned and popular journals, arose to assess whether, or to what extent, machine production ruined the health of the laborers. See, for example, Florence, Economics of Fatigue and Unrest; Felix Frankfurter and Josephine C. Goldmark, The Case for the Shorter Work-day (New York: National Consumers' League, 1916); Frank B. Gilbreth and Lillian M. Gilbreth, Fatigue Study (New York: Macmillan Co., 1919); Goldmark, Fatigue and Efficiency; Thomas Oliver, ed., Dangerous Trades: The Historical, Social and Legal Aspects of Industrial Occupations as Affecting Health (London: J. Murray Co., 1902).

important hiring criterion. In a system of petty capitalism, workers who acquired necessary skills on their own time or at their own expense might compete with one another for employment based almost exclusively on the basis of who possessed the greater or more appropriate skills. An employer had no prima facie reason to prefer one applicant over another on account of age, because the cost of turnover was very low in any case, and what minimized it was an optimal skill-to-wage ratio, without regard to the number of years of productive life remaining to the employee.

Hiring costs in hierarchical establishments threatened to become a significant component of the wages-bill, however, when training became an internal function of the firm. Thus the work process which was governed according to the stopwatch came increasingly to be accomplished by workers who were selected according to the calendar. One's age at the time of hiring became a primary determinant of anticipated cost, even where there existed no basis for the belief that a younger job-seeker would stay on past the period of training.

If management was to do the training, it had to maximize its return on that training insofar as the return could be predicted, and the most ready predictor was an applicant's chronological age. And where training was to be minimal, for the unskilled positions requiring purely manual labor, the preference for youth over age was, understandably, equally great for reasons having to do with physical strength and endurance.

(5) A final impediment to continued employment for older workers also relates to the efficiency norms of large-scale enterprises. The routinization of staffing and personnel procedures in recruitment, wage-setting, hiring, and job placement were geared toward eliminating highly inefficient individual processing. But for older workers, undoubtedly moreso than for their juniors, optimum assignments often required custom-tailoring the job to the worker and giving personal attention to how such workers could be made to fit in. In an economic system characterized by small firm size and an intimate working environment, such personal attention was axiomatic, for employees of any age. But in large enterprises, notes Rosow, "sheer bureaucratic pride in 'running a taut ship' militate[d] against individual treatment."[71]

The Extent of Discrimination
Against Older Workers

By the turn of the century, there began to be an association of peak earning power with relative youth, which Catlin argues generated "a positive prejudice against taking on or even retaining older or middle-aged men and women."[72] Age discrimination was particularly severe for working women, reflecting also a sex bias. In 1910 the Labor Bureau undertook an in-depth study of female and child wage-workers, revealling that the earning power of women peaked at age 24. Except for the very small numaber who had been promoted to supervisory positions or who managed to acquire a unique skill, there was a

---

71 Rosow, "And Then We Were Old," p. 47.

72 Catlin, The Labor Problem, p. 161.

level of mediocrity." In about half the industries studied, older women earned less on average than did younger women.[73]

By the late 1920s, this bias against age would be extreme, as women as young as 30 were found to have difficulty in finding jobs or even retaining those they had.[74] In domestic work, where seasoned judgment and experience might be thought to be in demand, some employment agencies reported that the employers they served preferred women under 34. [75] In the clerical and mercantile occupations, the preference for youth and beauty was most pronounced of all.[76]

The upper age limit at which men could find or retain employment was higher than for women, but falling quickly at the turn of the century. The workforces of newer establishments had a lower average age than did those of older establishments, and the firms of growing industries employed younger men than those of industries that had stabilized or were declining.[77] As a rule, the average age of men was lower in manufacturing plants proper than in the less centralized trades.[78]

A study by Magnus Alexander, published in 1912, revealed that the average age of 40,000 males employed in 12 metal-working firms was 31.5, and in a typical steel plant employees older than 40 constituted only 23 percent of the workforce.[79] In an automobile plant employing 30,000 men, more than 80 percent were under 40, nearly half under 30. In all of these growing, concentrated industries the average age of employees was between 30 and 31.[80] Studies conducted in the 1920s confirmed a connection between plant size and the existence of age-discriminatory hiring policies: 45.5 percent of firms employing fewer than 25 persons maintained age hiring limits, but more than 95 percent of firms with at least 1000 employees had such policies.[81] Thus the common headline and catchword of the times, "too old at forty," is amply borne out by the scattered evidence available.

---

73 U.S. Commissioner of Labor, Woman and Child Wage-Earners, 18:26.

74 U.S. Secretary of Labor, Annual Report, by Mary Anderson, Head of the Women's Bureau of the U.S. Bureau of Labor (Washington, D.C.: Government Printing Office, 1930), pp. 123-24.

75 New York Times, 13 July 1930, p. 22; 13 March, 1932, sec. 9, p. 5, cited by Catlin, The Labor Problem, p. 162.

76 Ibid.

77 This is a pattern that continues to be evident, according to such scholars of the economics of age as Harold Sheppard, Robert Butler, James Schultz, and Juanita Kreps.

78 See U.S. Congress, Senate, Report by the U.S. Commissioner of Labor on Labor Conditions in the Iron and Steel Industry, S. Doc. 110, 62nd Cong., 1st sess., 1911, vol. 3.

79 Ibid.

80 Florence, Economics of Fatigue and Unrest, p. 315.

81 Barkin, The Older Worker, p. 222.

Discrimination apparently did not, however, affect all skill classes equally. Although no data exist before 1920 on employability by age and skill level, a 1930 study uncovered the following pattern: The bias against hiring unskilled workers set in at about age 40; skilled workers began on average to encounter difficulties at 45; and semi-skilled workers experienced significant discrimination after age 35, earlier than the unskilled.[82] This anomaly can perhaps be explained by considering the average length (stability) of employment for the various skill groups.

Because unskilled labor frequently was hired for temporary or seasonal work, older workers had less difficulty being accepted on such terms than if applying for semi-skilled positions which were generally of a more permanent nature. For females, the age of hiring handicap in skilled positions was found to be about 40, while for semi-skilled and unskilled positions it was closer to 30. Where older persons applied for jobs requiring great skill, they were more likely to meet with success than if applying for semi-skilled operative positions.[83]

Employers' Justification for Age Discrimination in Employment

On what grounds, and how legitimately, did employers base the practice of hiring and retaining only workers below a certain age? Why were men after age 35-40 and women as young as 30 considered by corporate capitalism to be obsolete? A practice so apparently common might be thought to have had strong if not impregnable justification.

There appear to have been three basic reasons for age discrimination in hiring: (1) firms' need to look out for their own aging workers, which made them unwilling to take on additional such individuals; (2) older people's remoteness from the training/educational establishment, which was gaining in importance relative to church and home as a disseminator of cultural values; and (3) older workers' unfitness for the demands of modern industry. These will be dealt with in turn.

(1) The most common reason given by employers when questioned as to why they did not generally take on middle-aged and older workers--and arguably the most defensible reason for such a policy--was that employers wished to maximize their scope for retaining and rewarding employees with many years of service, employees who would themselves face discrimination in seeking new employment.[84] In such cases, the hiring rule was not also a firing rule, and an attempt was made by management to promote workers to executive positions or shift them into duties consonant with their changing abilities. Employer loyalty had the advantage of reducing labor force turnover, thereby maintaining morale and efficiency.

---

82 Murray Webb Latimer, Relation of Maximum Hiring Ages to the Age Distribution of Employees (New York: American Management Association, Personnel Series No. 3, 1930), pp. 4-6.

83 Barkin, The Older Worker, p. 230.

84 Catlin, The Labor Problem, pp. 163-64.

Humane impulses might or might not enter into the picture, but it is clear that an enterprise committed to the welfare of its aging workers would be loath to increase its burden by taking on yet more older employees. Some corporations (primarily the railroads and the steel industry) had by the turn of the century adopted formal group insurance systems and/or retirement plans for their skilled employees, the costs of which varied with the average age of their workforces. As these sorts of schemes became more widespread, the cost of hiring older workers rose in a growing number of establishments, because more was now involved than merely amortizing employee training and adjustment costs.

Yet such corporate welfare plans remained relatively rare before the 1920s, and at any rate their existence made conditions more secure for those on the inside only while making them more difficult for outsiders. With the growth of private pension plans in the 15-20 years leading up to World War I, maximum hiring ages became more prevalent. A hard-heartedness of employers toward older applicants was not necessarily evidence of a low evaluation of their abilities but was required by the actuarial facts.

Invariably, however, the charge would arise against corporations that provided pensions that their managers saw fit to take advantage of a business slump by eliminating older employees who would soon reach the age or years-of-service criterion for pension eligibility.[85] Such charges were notoriously difficult either to substantiate or to refute. And certainly the practice of many concerns (usually owing to union pressure) was to lay off the newest workers when economic conditions deteriorated, and to show rehiring preference for those with longest service, who were typically the older workers.

But when the cause of unemployment was not business cycle fluctuations but technological or structural change, or illness, or the need to relocate for family or health reasons, then older workers would find themselves in long-term employment difficulty following severance from a job. Recessions surely aggravated such difficulties but they did not create them.

(2) A second reason employers had for preferring younger workers--especially those who were fresh from school and willing to make temporary sacrifices to be able to gain entrance to a trade or industry--was that they could be paid less than men and women with greater experience and family responsibilities. Workers without dependents could afford to wait for their earnings to rise with job tenure. The cheapness of such labor might be illusory, however, since an established worker embodied not just the skills of the trade, but also workaday habits of thought and behavior which might not be automatic in younger workers.

Indeed, young people's proximity to the latest instructions of the educational establishment could make for unrealistic expectations as to the nature of industrial employment,[86] and they might be more easily taken in by questionable management practices. The charge was frequently made that the shoe and leather industries of New England, for example, offered "fake" apprenticeships rotating among various tasks, ostensibly

---

85 Ibid., p. 164.

86 The late nineteenth century, and especially the first years of the twentieth, were steeped in the Horatio Alger maxim of virtually unlimited success being attainable by those who could prove their mettle (Alger died in 1899). Such myths were a mainstay of the educational curriculum, as any McGuffey's Reader from those years attests.

to allow new entrants to learn several aspects of the trade (while being paid little if at all); but the real goal may have been to keep the wages bill down while minimizing worker attachment to a specific trade and preventing the establishment of "institutional memory" among the workers.[87]

(3) Employers might eschew middle-aged and older workers on the grounds of their relative unfitness for the requirements of modern industry. This was the motive most often ascribed to managers by the champions of older workers, but it was rarely admitted. The nostalgia for the "old days"--when elders were admired, beloved, and vitally important-- may have been particularly powerful in a period when a substantial portion of the population was experiencing stress from rapid socioeconomic change.

Under the right work conditions, training and the ability to learn might be preserved indefinitely, but such conditions--in particular a scale of enterprise allowing for workers to be treated as individuals rather than as interchangeable inputs--were precisely what were disappearing from the range of occupational choice. In addition, there was the issue of older individuals' physical health under conditions of industrial capitalism. As has been noted, death rates for industrial wage-earners over the age of 40 were increasing in the U.S.[88], and so the prospects were not sanguine for the continued vigor of older workers. An individual suffering from a degenerative disease is likely to be a slower, less efficient employee, even if not acutely ill.

Clearly no enterprise should be condemned for wishing to limit the number of sub-par workers on the payroll. But one is again confronted with the inability of large organizations to make the necessary fine distinctions among employees, so the factor of the average health characteristics of the wage-earning population could be turned into a general edict that all applicants above a certain age should be rejected. Given the high rates of unemployment, this was less costly than administering medical examinations and performance tests; so the healthy older applicant was turned away with the ill and feeble.

Early Studies of Occupation and
Employment by Age

The practice of refusing to hire workers above a certain age, and to a lesser extent that of laying off workers when they reached a particular birthday, appears to have been widespread and growing at the beginning of the twentieth century. Aging workers' special difficulties in finding work once they became unemployed had begun to receive the attention of various states' labor bureaus by this time, articulated particularly in governmental reports issued by the eastern and midwestern states that had experienced the greatest degree of industrialization. But the problem almost invariably was presented as

---

87 Catlin, The Labor Problem, p. 165. "Institutional memory" refers to the entrenchment of a cadre of workers who might resist changes in work practices or rules. Frequent rotations of workers among various departments limited individual workers' sense of identification with a particular skill or task, as well as their identification with each other.

88 In addition, among industrial workers as a group, in the 1920s the death rate was significantly higher above the age of 25 than it was for other segments of the population. Catlin, The Labor Problem, p. 166.

a function of the declining productive powers of the individual; seldom was it expressed as a social or structural problem that might legitimately be addressed either by private sector initiatives or by public policy.

There continued to be a scarcity of hard data on the subject of the average age of workers displaced from different occupations up until the 1940s and 1950s, and therefore it is necessary to get at this question indirectly. Such studies as exist focusing on age-related declines in productivity in different occupations suggest a rather consistent pattern. Three early studies will be examined in the order in which they were undertaken; the second and third of these take us slightly beyond the period being examined, but are included for illustrative purposes and because of the dearth of even rudimentary studies prior to 1920.

The New Jersey Seven-Industry Study. The New Jersey Bureau of Statistics of Labor undertook an early study (in 1887 and in 1892) examining the ages at which wage-earners' productivity had begun to decline in seven industries, irrespective of job skill levels. The Labor Bureau report does not provide us with information on the methodology that was used. We are not told, for example, whether all New Jersey firms in the selected industries were covered, or merely those of a certain size or other characteristic. Nor is it made clear what criteria were used for measuring productivity, or even whether the workers knew they were being studied.

This information gap reflects the lax standards of social science research during the period. It is possible that, as in the contemporaneous measures of unemployment, the data are mere collations of employers' best guesses. Hence the results may be taken as merely suggestive, if not of an actual decline in productivity with age, then--equally important for the present thesis--of perceptions of older workers' productivity. All workers above the age of 20 were included in the study, but Table 10 provides the relevant information only for workers 40 or older.

TABLE 10

PERCENT OF EMPLOYEES WHOSE PRODUCTIVITY HAD BEGUN TO DECLINE, SELECTED INDUSTRIES, 1887-1892

Age	Hat making	Glass-working	Pot-tery	Print-ing	Bak-ing	Cigar-making	Build-ing
40-45	34.2	35.2	18.1	19.0	23.2	12.0	13.3
45-50	48.4	57.6	67.3	41.0	22.2	36.6	12.9
50-60	49.2	75.0	77.4	7.1	31.2	60.0	43.0
over 60	49.0	88.9	57.1	50.0	58.3	58.0	52.7
Total, age 20+	14.7	24.1	8.6	9.7	9.0	9.8	7.6

SOURCE: New Jersey Bureau of Statistics of Labor, Annual Report, 12:74-96; 14:193-94; 15:189-92; 385-86; 17:101-08, cited by Barkin, The Older Worker, p. 283.

Anomalous results are evident in pottery (ages 50-60 versus over 60) and printing (ages 45-50 versus 50-60), and the age categories are confusingly overlapped. What is clear, though, is that a considerable proportion of wage earners aged 40 and above were perceived to have experienced some decline in productivity and were vulnerable to displacement from their accustomed pursuits. If one omits the anomalous figure for the 50-60 age group in the printing profession (7.1 percent) and substitutes instead the next lower percentage for that age group (31.2 percent in baking), the study shows a clear trend in both lower and upper limits for declining productivity across industries with advancing age beyond 40.

The focus of the study was the incidence of apparent diminished economic usefulnes with age, yet there is no record as to what actually became of workers in the industries surveyed, that is, were they displaced or were they kept on despite their waning productiveness? Furthermore, the seven industries included in the study do not, with the possible exception of construction and glassworking, include some of the most rigorous or exhausting occupations, where survival of the fittest was most the rule. Had steelmaking, mining, or petroleum production been sampled, the incidence of productivity decline would doubtless have accelerated even before age 40.[89]

The Insurance Study. A 1924 investigation, the results of which appeared in the Monthly Labor Review, compared the occupations of industrial policyholders, at the time their policies were issued, with their occupations at the time of death.[90] The study found that in the insured interval, 41.5 percent of the workers had remained at the same occupation and 57.3 percent stayed within the same industry.[91] It was noted that the greater an employee's skill, the more probable was his continuation at the same job. Furthermore, the report noted, "a large proportion of the shifting of occupations...is due to the weakened conditions of the men brought about by the arduous labor, exposure to dusts, to fumes, to poisons, etc."[92]

Thus industrial superannuation as a cause for occupational displacement was established, but the survey did not provide information on the average age for the occupational shifts, the percentage of workers in each age group forced to leave their customary occupations, or the length of time that may have elapsed between an involuntary separation from last employment and death. No clear distinction was even made between voluntary and involuntary separations, and, as in the New Jersey study some 35 years earlier, there was no follow-up on the whereabouts of displaced employees.

The New York Study of Comparative Rates of Decline by Occupational Group. A quite detailed study was undertaken by Solomon Barkin in 1930 of the relative occupational longevity associated with groups of wage earners in New York State, broken down according

---

89 See Fitch, The Steel Workers, p. 183.

90 Louis I. Dublin and Robert J. Vane, Jr., "Shifting of Occupations among Wage-Earners as Determined by Occupational Histories of Industrial Policyholders," Monthly Labor Review 18 (April 1, 1924):732-40.

91 The use of very broad industry and job classifications no doubt caused the extent of occupational shifting to be understated.

92 Dublin and Vane, "Shifting of Occupations," p. 735.

to the categories used for the 1930 U.S. Census of Occupations.[93] Like the two earlier studies, this one also focused on the variable of declining productivity with age, but it had the advantage of trying to focus explicitly on the comparative superannuation of workers in well-defined occupational groupings.

Barkin surveyed manufacturing concerns employing 364,073 wage earners,[94] requesting that they provide the ages of persons on, added to, and separated from their payrolls for a three-month period beginning anywhere between June 15 and December 1, 1930. Although this puts the investigation a decade beyond the time frame being examined here, the data provide valuable corroboration of much that has been suggested earlier. The study is significant for being the first ever undertaken to count not only people being hired but also those leaving occupations, categorized according to age. Voluntary quits were distinguished from temporary lay-offs, discharges for cause, and retirements with pensions (although within the "discharge for cause" category the cause was not specified; it could have been illness, poor performance, injury, superannuation, or age prejudice). Despite the greater thoroughness of this study than its predecessors, there was no attempt to follow up on the displaced employees to determine their subsequent occupations, if any.[95]

Recall from earlier chapters that the "tolerant occupations" for older workers--agriculture, fishing and forestry, domestic and personal service--were those which helped to slow the growth of old-age dependency which accompanied American industrialization. Such pursuits might be contrasted with those occupations which regularly showed a greater-than-average decline in employment with advancing age. In Barkin's study the age-intolerant occupational categories were the transportation/communication industries, clerical and trade jobs, and to a lesser extent professional service jobs.[96]

For workers in the two other broad occupational groupings--manufacturing and mechanical industries and mineral extraction--the picture is mixed. Workers between 45 and 54 years of age showed a more gradual decline in their representation than for all occupations taken together, but workers 55 and over had a larger-than-average drop-off rate. Apparently the fatigue and strain of such pursuits began to take a significant toll on workers only at about age 55.

Not surprisingly, the group labelled "Workers on own account" had by far the greatest success in retaining employment in all age categories; there was, in particular, scarcely any difference in the rate of decline of workers in these occupations between ages 55-64 and 65-over. It is likely that such pursuits might even have absorbed workers displaced from other occupations during the period of the study. Individuals who could no longer meet the demands of organized industry, or who wished to escape them, probably

---

93 See Barkin, The Older Worker, pp. 283-88.

94 This represented 33 percent of total New York employment in 1929.

95 Such follow-ups are not easily accomplished. Even today, it is only for a handful of carefully studied plant closings that very good information exists on where workers go when their jobs disappear.

96 In Chapter 5, it was noted that by 1900 older workers were markedly underrepresented in transportation and trade.

tried to take refuge in independent establishments which they ran on their own behalf. The number who would be likely to have done so successfully, however, particularly after many years of working for others, must have been small. Barkin's study revealed little on this score.[97]

Within the manufacturing and mechanical groups,[98] the following results were obtained: In the building industry occupations, rates of displacement were very rapid above the age of 55, except for the unskilled.[99] The skilled and semi-skilled workers in these trades were being displaced more quickly than the average rate for all professions. For the semi-skilled, the rate of drop-off beyond age 45 was the highest of any manufacturing pursuit. Since in the unskilled jobs in the building trades the rate of decline for ages 55-64 was far slower than average, it is possible that many of the formerly skilled and semi-skilled workers had to settle for unskilled work in order to remain in the building trades as they aged. However, Barkin concluded that "the larger proportion of the upper strata of the working population in the building industries had to resort to employment in other industries, possibly as repairmen and in other similar pursuits."[100]

Another group evidencing a greater-than-average rate of decline in the number of practitioners over age 55 comprised manufacturers, contractors, managers, and officials. Barkin merely surmised, "Apparently, these persons took up other tasks requiring less constant applications."[101] The implication, as for the skilled and semi-skilled building trades employees, is that such individuals experienced downward occupational mobility upon the loss of their traditional employment.

---

97 It is perhaps inaccurate to imply, as some social scientists have, that there exists any necessary correlation between self-employment and occupational longevity. Such a notion is a generalization based primarily upon notable individual cases of professionals or craftsmen for whom productive autonomy has coincided with a very aged employment.

Self-employment has, nonetheless, provided older workers with greater freedom and control over their labor force participation rates. This may not have translated very precisely into economic security. Growing corporate size has made ownership and management of private businesses a precarious endeavor in many fields because of dramatic changes in the institution of property. Yet at all times in U.S. history, there has been considerable movement into and out of self-employment. Studies of occupational mobility for the post-World War II period show this quite clearly. Because self-employment is notoriously risky, the failure rate is high. But it has allowed the opportunity for older workers so inclined to attempt to continue working, especially when they have possessed a unique skill or ability.

98 These were already "intolerant" occupations for older workers in 1900, as noted in Chapter 5.

99 Again, the older worker without skills was more likely to be hired on a temporary basis, which of course conveyed little employment security anyway.

100 Barkin, The Older Worker, p. 287.

101 Ibid., p. 286.

The results in the manufacturing and mechanical pursuits were highly speculative, because jobs classified as operative positions ranged from completely unskilled manual labor to highly skilled positions requiring long months of specialized training. Some attempt was made by the Census Bureau to separate out the extremes, but the classifications remained hazy. Nevertheless, it was in the skilled and unskilled categories that the number of over-55 workers declined more rapidly than the average for all occupations in the manufacturing/mechanical group. For the majority, who were the semi-skilled, the rate of decline was slower than the average.[102]

The New York study clearly illustrated a significant degree of occupational displacement for wage-earners as they aged. Shifts in employment were frequently made by older workers because of the detrimental effects of their primary employment, because of a general waning of productive powers, and--in an unknown number of cases--because of "the age prejudice which may prevail at the employment."[103]   The 1930 survey substantiated the severity of the "older worker problem" that had been growing for several decades. The age barrier to continued employment or reemployment applied to all classes of workers, including the elite of engineers and professional people, but it applied in particular to those who had the least amount of control over their work, the industrial wage-earning classes.

Rapid Labor Turnover and the Employment
of Older Workers

So strong was the anti-age bias in hiring that it prevailed even during times of enormous labor turnover, which was in some trades so pervasive as to baffle workers' attempts at permanent organization.   Early in the twentieth century it was not uncommon for establishments in some industries--notably slaughtering and meatpacking, sawmills, automobiles, and furniture--to be faced with a labor turnover of several hundred percent per year (including quits, lay-offs, and discharges).[104]   The Ford Motor Company once hired 54,000 men in one year to be able to keep an average work force of 13,000.[105] Fifty-seven industrial plants in Detroit reported a turnover in 1917 of 250 percent or

---

102 Ibid., p. 287.

103 Ibid.

104 Paul F. Brissenden and Emil Frankel, Labor Turnover in Industry: A Statistical Analysis (New York: Macmillan Co, 1922), chapter 4.

105 E.A. Rumely, "Ford's Plan to Share Profits," World's Work, 27 (1914):665, cited by Catlin, The Labor Problem, p. 6.

more.[106] Numerous industries showed a rate of turnover for the decade 1910-1919 equivalent to taking on a completely new workforce every year.[107]

Such data, reflecting as they do a rather extreme degree of labor force mobility, suggest that firms might have tried very hard to keep their more experienced workers. But it was precisely those conditions of work which contributed to superannuation that also accounted for workers' dissatisfaction with their jobs in the first place.[108] Labor's unreliability was at its peak between 1914 and 1920 when, for the first time in many years, the growth in demand for labor outpaced the supply. Not only was the economy experiencing a war boom, but the supply of immigrant labor had virtually ceased. Thus workers readily shifted jobs without much risk of involuntary unemployment. Older workers were among the beneficiaries of the tight labor market until 1920, when all the employment barriers that had faced them in the pre-war years would return in force.[109]

Coinciding with the war years there was a burst of interest in resolving the employment difficulties of workers of middle age and beyond. In Chicago, the Employers Associations in 1917 helped to establish an employment office specifically for the placement of older men. Over a period of 20 months, some 18,200 men were placed, owing largely to the efforts of Victor T. G. Gannon.[110] Gannon pronounced in 1918: "The war, damnable as it is, is surely a cleansing fire. It has made junk of old ideas and has proved that the old men...have come back to stay back."[111] The movement received such wide attention that the Federal government began to subsidize the effort and finally authorized the establishment of a handicap section in the United States Employment Service which would include

---

106 Boyd Fisher, "Methods of Reducing Labor Turnover," Annals of the American Academy 65 (1916):144, cited by ibid.

107 Brissenden and Frankel, Labor Turnover, chapter 4.

108 H.L.R. Frain, "Do Workers Gain by Labor Turnover?", Monthly Labor Review 28 (June 1929):1298-1300.

109 As noted earlier, in the twenties the plight of the aged was particularly pronounced. The decade saw the steady advance of corporate concentration (primarily through vertical mergers) and the entrenchment of managerialism, while agriculture experienced a long and deep depression. By the 1920s, occupational transfer or adjustment for older workers was greatly limited by the diminished significance of such earlier cushions for displacement as agriculture and the trades. Older urban workers without any farming experience or rural ties were unlikely to pursue such work; and the commercialization of the trades had greatly restricted access to such occupations, which had been widely used as an escape route in earlier decades. Barkin, The Older Worker, p. 288.

110 Barkin, The Older Worker, p. 69.

111 Department of Labor, Bureau of Labor Statistics, Utilization of Men Past the Prime of Life, by Victor T. G. Gannon, Bulletin No. 247 (Washington, D.C.: Government Printing Office, 1919), pp. 197-99.

special placement activities for men over 44 who appeared to be barred from employment on account of age.[112]

The proponents of the hiring of middle-aged workers hoped to end the "riot of young blood" by converting employers to the view that "Applicants should be studied and judged as individuals, and jobs should be assigned to them according to their qualifications and aptitudes and not their age."[113] Special employment services targeted at the age-handicapped would be the backbone of a concerted effort to erase a blot on the record of industrial capitalism.

However, the gains from the movement were short-lived. The early death of its leader, Gannon, along with the disappearance of the favorable employment circumstances created by the war, effectively put an end to the interest and the programs that had developed during the war. Where older workers were concerned, Barkin noted, the ensuing labor surplus "erased the progress made during a period of labor shortage."[114]

Conclusion

Whether owing to long hours, increasing intensity of the work process, or age-based hiring rules, workers were being prematurely "worn out," or were so treated, as surely as if they had been machines. Like obsolete capital equipment, middle-aged and older workers were an undesirable element to be replaced as soon as possible. In trades not represented by strong unions--which is to say, in most occupations prior to 1920--such workers were subject to dismissal in downturns of the business cycle, but had progressively greater difficulty finding new employment.

Male wage-earners above 40 or 45 years of age were increasingly likely to be found in the following, possibly overlapping groups: (1) unskilled positions, in all industries, which did not require great physical strength--hence, working at low rates of pay, albeit more or less continuously; (2) working as casual labor at occupations most vulnerable to seasonal and cyclical fluctuations; industries most susceptible to fluctuations, such as construction, evidenced a greater proportion of older employees than industries in more stable markets, such as steel or textiles;[115] (3) chronically unemployed, for reasons of illness, disability, or discouragement, or involuntarily retired after displacement from their customary occupations.

The years after World War I were characterized by increasing unionization as labor sought to maintain and build upon the gains that had been made in the labor-scarce war years. Yet increasing worker organization was having paradoxical consequences for older

---

112 Gannon, "The 'Handicap Bureau' of the United States Employment Service: A Large Scale Test of a New Industrial Idea," Munsey's Magazine 66 (April 1919):56.

113 E. H. Fish, "Principles of Employing Labor," Industrial Management 57 (June 1919):481-82. See also William F. Kemble, Choosing Employees by Mental and Physical Tests (New York: Engineering Magazine Co., 1917), pp. 97-98.

114 Barkin, The Older Worker, p. 70.

115 Ibid., p. 303.

workers. On the one hand, their security in the jobs they currently held was enhanced through the codification of seniority rules that gave primary importance to workers' job tenure. Yet such worker protection mechanisms predisposed unions toward younger people who would not occupy senior positions with "bumping rights" for many years, if ever; in addition to which those in less senior positions were typically given the least desirable tasks and working hours, making them too arduous for older workers.

Thus unions reinforced employers' tendency to hire the young, who both cost less initially in wages and would likely not stay long enough to collect any pension. These subjects will be discussed in Chapter 7 in the context of the general public indifference or outright hostility to the idea that government should or could provide a safety net for displaced older workers.

CHAPTER 7

PUBLIC AND PRIVATE SECTOR RESPONSES TO
THE PLIGHT OF OLDER WORKERS

Introduction

This chapter examines the growing economic dependency of older Americans in the context of the political/philosophical climate of turn-of-the-century America. In particular it focuses on the enormous staying power, in the face of sweeping economic and institutional change, of the ideals of self-sufficiency and a minimal state. The inadequacy of wage earners' savings as a cushion for old age is examined against this background, and the effects of early public and private sector pension plans on workers' economic security is assessed.

With the exception of the meager efforts of a few of the individual states to assist those being left behind by industrialization,[1] prior to the New Deal there was no major departure from free-market principles with regard to the dependent elderly. Although what is known as the social insurance movement was launched in the U.S. in the second decade of the twentieth century, it was at the time limited to the establishment of workmen's compensation for work-related disability.[2] It was not until the 1920s that the aged became a key issue in social politics.[3]

---

1 Massachusetts was the first to study the problem officially, in 1907, but without action. Arizona was the first state to pass an old age pension law, in 1915, which was immediately declared unconstitutional. Except for the passage in 1920 of the United States Civil Service retirement law in 1920, nothing more happened until 1923, when Montana, Nevada, and Pennsylvania enacted old age pension laws that were optional by county. Nevada's law was entirely inoperative, Montana's was adopted by only a few counties, and Pennsylvania's was declared unconstitutional. John R. Commons, et al., History of Labor in the United States, vol. 3: Labor Legislation, by Elizabeth Brandeis, pp. 611-13.

2 The era of rapid enactment of state compensation legislation began in 1909 when Minnesota, Wisconsin, and New York passed their laws. By 1913, 21 states had enacted compensation legislation, and 43 had done so by 1920. Advocates of social insurance in the pre-war years were hopeful that the speed with which compensation laws were being adopted was a sign that other compulsory programs would soon follow. However, rather than being an entering wedge, workmen's compensation "solidified the opposition of private interests to any further extension of social insurance." Compensation was merely "accepted as an expedient by voluntary interest groups," but it reflected no newly emerging consensus on the need for secondary systems of income distribution under capitalism. (Lubove, Struggle for Social Security, pp. 53-54, 45.)

3 This was largely owing to organizations such as the American Association for Labor Legislation, the American Association for Old Age Security, and the Fraternal Order of Eagles; and to the efforts of individuals such as Isaac Rubinow, John B. Andrews, Abraham Epstein, Paul Douglas, and Eveline Burns.

Until then, older Americans' growing incidence of unemployment, poverty, and isolation from the mainstream of American life appears to have been viewed as unexceptional, the result of circumstances which had always threatened the elderly: Old-age dependency occurred because of physical or mental deterioration, the death of a spouse, loss of property, childlessness or inattentive offspring, bad luck, character flaws, and so forth. Dependency was not generally seen as having a connection to the country's rapidly changing economic structure.[4]

Charitable organizations and voluntary associations provided the majority of the care for the indigent, and their records did not indicate large numbers of the aged seeking aid in American cities, even though this was becoming common in the cities of Europe. However, many European nations had enacted systems of old-age relief near the turn of the century and subsequently discovered that the extent of the problem far exceeded initial estimates.

In Denmark, the first nation to institute a tax-supported national old-age pension system in 1891, [5] it was found that fully 35 percent of the 70-and-over population were entitled to a pension because their incomes were less than $26 per year. In the prosperous Australasian colonies (New Zealand, Victoria, New South Wales), the passage of old-age pension legislation between 1898 and 1901 almost instantly revealed in each instance large numbers of old people in poverty, from 25 to 50 percent of those over 65. [6]

The French experience was also revealing, since France was and is noted for its inhabitants' strong propensity to save and invest, and its low birthrate and stable population (actually declining early in the twentieth century). In 1907, pensions of two-to-four dollars per month were granted to aged persons with incomes of less than $6 monthly. More than half a million individuals, or about 50 percent of the elderly, were able to qualify.[7]

Great Britain did not act until 1908, when legislation was passed which granted a small weekly pension to anyone over 70 whose annual income was less than $105. When the law was made, the expectation was that 386,000 persons would be eligible, yet in just its first year the act generated 667,000 applicants, and the number rose during the prewar

---

4 A distinguished student of social reform announced in 1897, "In the United States the old-age problem is not yet so serious." (William Dwight Porter Bliss, "Old Age Pensions," The Encyclopedia of Social Reform [New York: Funk and Wagnalls, 1897], p. 954.) See also Frank A. Vanderlip, Insurance From an Employer's Perspective (Philadelphia: National Conference of Charities and Correction Proceedings, 1896); F. Spencer Baldwin, "Old Age Pension Schemes: A Criticism and a Program," Quarterly Journal of Economics 24 (August 1910):713-42.

5 Rubinow, Social Insurance, p. 310. Germany was the first nation to address old-age dependency through social insurance, in 1899, but it chose compulsory, contributory old age insurance rather than a pension scheme for the aged. (Lubove, Struggle for Social Security, p. 28.)

6 Rubinow, Social Insurance, p. 309; Lubove, Struggle for Social Security, p. 120.

7 Rubinow, Social Insurance, p. 309.

period to 1.08 million. The total number of Britons age 70 or older was approximately 1.25 million in the mid-teens, and 86 percent of them needed relief.[8]

In the United States, no one knew with any certainty the extent of elderly dependency. Official estimates continued up until the Great Depression to be modest relative to those made by academics, social workers, and journalists.[9] There is no indication that the dramatic errors in the Europeans' pre-legislation estimates stimulated much discussion in this country; it appears primarily to have given ammunition to those who warned of the "moral hazard of insurance," that is, the view that the availability of relief merely weakens personal responsibility and encourages people's willingness to let others support them. Apparently, few experts believed that the extent of the problem could be seriously understated. The European "experiments" continued to be repudiated as desperation measures applicable only to backward-looking societies, while the exhortations to thriftiness and personal responsibility grew ever more voluble.[10]

Although by the mid-1890s muckrakers and scholars had begun advocating reforms directed at the institutional causes of poverty, it was not until 1912 that the first full-length American monograph on the economic plight of the elderly was published, Lee Squier's Old Age Dependency in the United States. Squier based his calculations of the extent of old-age dependency on a study carried out in 1908-1909 by the Massachusetts Commission on Old Age Pensions, Annuities and Insurance. He estimated that approximately 1.25 million of the fewer than 4 million persons 65 years of age and over in the U.S. were dependent upon public and private charity.[11]

No other systematic attempt was made before 1920 to ascertain how many of the aged were dependent or were likely to become so. Guesses varied from virtually none, beyond those relatively few actually living in almshouses, to a majority. But by 1919, a widely circulated estimate of the odds facing older Americans was that:

---

8 Ibid.

9 The depression itself disrupted most of the existing pension programs and greatly worsened the problem of old-age dependency. (Achenbaum, Old Age, p. 129; Lescohier, Working Conditions, p. 396; Fischer, Growing Old, p. 176.) Yet the numbers of those acknowledged to be in need had been rising rapidly, particularly in the 1920s when most of the states enacted old-age pension legislation (virtually all of it defective, inoperative, or declared unconstitutional). (Lubove, Struggle for Social Security, p. 136.)

10 An apparent xenophobia, particularly toward Germany, underlay Americans' repudiation of the European social insurance models. (Rubinow, Quest for Security, p. 82.) Rubinow himself was among those whose views were rejected in the early years of the twentieth century. The leaders in the movement for old-age pensions were typically immigrants or the children of immigrants, disproportionately eastern European in origin, urban in residence, Jewish in religion, socialist in politics, and denounced by their enemies as "un-American." (Fischer, Growing Old, p. 172.)

11 Lee W. Squier, Old Age Dependency in the United States: A Complete Survey of the Pension Movement (New York: Macmillan Co., 1912), p. 3.

...out of one hundred average healthy men of 25, at 65
54 will be dependent upon relatives, friends or charity;
36 will be dead;
5 will be earning their daily bread;
4 will be wealthy;
1 will be rich.[12]

Nine years later, a special agent of the United States Census Bureau estimated that the proportion of dependent aged males was "somewhere between a minimum of 17.9 per cent and a maximum of 40 per cent, with strong probabilities that the actual proportion approaches 40 per cent."[13] Such assessments suggest a discouraging answer to the rhetorical question posed by Rubinow the year before passage of the Social Security Act:

> How many folks at sixty-five are in a position to retire on their savings?...How much of our wealth is in possession of the man who had been saving, after a long life full of mishaps, vicissitudes, and various obligations? The very insurance companies which sing a Pollyana song of the economic glories of this country still feel justified in drawing a very pessimistic picture as to the ability of the average man who draws a wage to provide a competence for his old age.[14]

The Inadequacy of Wage-Earners'
Savings for Old Age

The champions of a regularized system of aid to the needy old argued in vain against the prevailing wisdom that thrift and careful living were the best preventives against old-age dependency. The real conditions of the wage-earner's existence made a mockery of the supposition that most workingmen could save enough to provide for old age.[15] For the

---

12 Personnel: The Employment Managers' Bulletin 1 (July 1919):5. These statistics were a favorite selling device of the banks and insurance companies.

13 See National Civic Federation, Industrial Welfare Department, Extent of Old Age Dependency (New York: National Civic Federation, 1928), p. 154. This was a moderate estimate; others for the 1920s ranged as high as two-thirds of the older population in need of supplemental suport. See "Old Age Pensions and Relief," Monthly Labor Review 26 (June 1928):93-94; Rubinow, Quest for Security, pp. 242-46; Epstein, Insecurity, p. 500.

14 Rubinow, Quest for Security, pp. 232-33.

15 Social worker Mabel Nassau undertook one of the few investigations of old-age dependency prior to 1920, in Greenwich Village before the war, where she surveyed 100 aged individuals. Nassau discovered a pervasive "economic fear" of illness, institutionaliza-tion, or reliance on charity. Most of the elders worked or had worked as long as they could and tried to avoid burdening their families, the majority of which were already struggling and could ill afford to have their living standards further lowered. Individual saving for old

typical worker, saving for old age, wrote Rubinow, "would only be possible through a persistent, systematic, and obstinate disregard of the needs of the workingman's family, which would make the preaching of such special savings a decidedly immoral force."[16] Yet for the majority of Americans, "that...children or relatives [were] forced to give help is a fact too well known to be disputed."[17]

Even where it was possible, protection for old age through voluntary thrift was less practical than for other types of risk. Aging differed from accidents or illness in that it was not an abnormal occurrence but a normal life stage. In contrast to other areas where preventive measures lessened risk, Rubinow observed, "improvement in hygiene seem[ed] to aggravate it rather than relieve it." Since medical advances intensified the problem, and since old age could be a long-term rather than a transitory condition, there was no way to plan for the amount of saving required, even if it were attainable. Because aging was "the final emergency" and was "preceded by all the other emergencies of a workingman's existence," any savings had probably already been depleted before old age actually arrived.[18]

In most years between 1890 and 1920 workers' real wages were falling, so for the great majority, any saving for the emergencies of life was unlikely. In fact, most workers never even managed to attain the minimum standard of earnings deemed adequate by economists and governmental authorities for the day-to-day support of a family of five.[19] Even in the 1914-1920 period--when the U.S. was engaged in intensive industrial activity, when immigration was almost completely suspended, when great numbers of workers were drawn into military service, and when the industrial labor supply could not meet the explosion in demand--there was little improvement in wages in relation to the cost of living.[20]

---

age, she concluded, was beyond the means of a large proportion of working-class families. (Mabel Louise Nassau, Old Age Poverty in Greenwich Village: A Neighborhood Study [New York: Greenwich House Series No. 6, 1915], pp. 17, 35, 60.)

16 Rubinow, Social Insurance, p. 313.

17 Ibid.

18 Ibid., pp.3.

19 Basil M. Manly, Are Wages Too High? (Washington, D.C.: People's Legislative Service, 1922), pp. 3-6.

20 Ibid. During the war years the cost of living increased so rapidly that improvements in the standard of living were impossible for most workers. However, family incomes had the potential to increase with wartime inflation if additional family members could be employed or if overtime were available. In such instances, and particularly given the improved steadiness of work, family incomes, not wage rates, might rise rapidly in those industries the government listed as essential to the war effort. (Lescohier, Working Conditions, pp. 74-75.)

A study of real wages and living costs conducted in 1922 concluded that:

> With the exception of a few isolated occupations that were miserably under-paid in 1900, no class or group of workers has succeeded in maintaining unimpaired the real value of their wages as measured by the buying power which they possessed in 1900.
>
> With the exception of a few isolated and exceptionally skilled trades, the wages of American workers are insufficient, without supplement from other sources, to provide for the subsistence of a family consisting of husband, wife and three minor children, much less maintain them in that condition of "health and reasonable comfort" which every humane consideration demands.[21]

Wages were inadequate to allow for any sizable savings, both because earnings were low and because employment was for many so sporadic. According to the 1900 census, almost 6.5 million out of a total of 29 million gainfully employed persons--more than 22 percent--were unemployed at some time during the year. Over 2.5 million of these were out of work anywhere from four to six months, and approximately 736,000 were idle for seven months or more.[22] In 1901, 49.8 percent of the heads of families investigated by the U.S. Bureau of Labor were unemployed for some part of the year,[23] and 1901 was not a year of economic recession.

The problem of joblessness continued to be treated as a frictional phenomenon not meriting state intervention. Indeed, economic and political tracts at the turn of the century hinted strongly that the majority of unemployment was the workers' fault, or that it was a beneficial prod to wiser living, or both. The establishment view seemed to be that people were at all times as lazy as circumstances allowed; if they could count on public support when their earnings were reduced for any reason, they would have little incentive to provide for the future; while simultaneously, aggregate production would suffer. So long as "an unwise charity" did not "offer a bonus to incompetence," the working classes would be willing to provide for themselves" and their families.[24]

Workers seeking to lessen their potential dependency did give thought to earning a "competence," that is, saving to provide for bouts of unemployment and for eventual

---

21 Ibid., p. 4.

22 Epstein, Insecurity, p. 191.

23 U.S. Bureau of Labor, Eighteenth Annual Report of the Commissioner of Labor (Washington, D.C.: Government Printing Office, 1903), p. 42.

24 See Mary Willcox Brown, The Development of Thrift (New York: Macmillan Co., 1900), p. 9; Hadley, Economics, Chapter 2 ("Economic Responsibility"), pp. 26-63; Edward S. Cowdrick, Pensions: A Problem of Management (New York: American Management Association, Series No. 75, 1928), p. 11.

retirement. But testimony by workers indicated that even skilled craftsmen were hard-pressed to save any substantial amount of money. Many regularly fell into debt.[25]

Although some did acquire savings, and there was much hypothesizing as to the true extent of workers' bank deposits, the evidence suggests that these deposits, although large in the aggregate, were small per capita within the working class.[26] Earning a competence, a thoroughly middle-class goal, was considered an important measure of success, conveying status and respect. Yet few workers were able to save much money. With occupational and geographic mobility constrained by prevailing trends in firm size and economic concentration, most had to be content with pursuing the more attainable mark of achievement, home ownership.[27]

Property could, however, be lost overnight as a result of industrial accident or work-related illness. In the aggregate, industrial accidents caused a permanent lowering of living standards for scores of thousands of workers every year--at least 100,000 per year by one estimate.[28] When the Massachusetts Commission on Old Age Pensions made its 1910 report, it found that close to 38 percent of the state's 15,000 aged poor had at some time in their lives had property valued above debts, but for 46 percent of them the property's value had been under $1,000.

Of the 15,000 surveyed individuals (all of whom were receiving state aid), 56.1 percent had lost their property, for the following reasons: 60.1 percent because of extra expenses resulting from sickness or emergencies; 25.4 percent because of business failures and bad investments; 6.2 percent because of "intemperance or extravagance"; 5.1 percent owing to fraud; and 3.2 percent owing to fire.[29]

A substantial amount of elderly poverty, then, was clearly owing to illnesses or accidents earlier in life. Among industrial wage-earners, the prevalence of disease and sporadic sickness was higher, and the average length of life less, than among other population groups. As a result, death at "normal age" was rare, and therefore many urged the

---

25 For examples of early budget studies based upon current retail prices and the subsistence needs of a typical family of five, see Louise B. More, Wage Earners' Budgets (New York: Henry Holt Co., 1907); Robert C. Chapin, The Standard of Life in New York City (New York: Russell Sage Foundation, 1909); John A. Ryan, A Living Wage (New York: Macmillan Co., 1910).

26 Rubinow, Social Insurance, p. 44. Per capita saving in 1915 was $90. (Epstein, Insecurity, pp. 113-15.)

27 Yellowitz, Position of the Worker, p. 27; Idem, Industrialization, pp. 42-43.

28 Rubinow, Social Insurance, p. 16.

29 Massachusetts, Report of the Commission on Old Age Pensions, Annuities and Insurance, House Doc. 1400 (Boston: 1910), pp. 73, 74, 57-58, cited by Squier, Old Age Dependency, pp. 24-25.

establishment of pensions at least for surviving spouses and dependent children.[30] Leaving aside infant mortality and considering only deaths of occupied males, 73 percent died before age 65; 55 percent before 55; and a striking 39 percent of male workers in 1908 died before reaching the age of 45. Allowing for the relatively small number of wholly unattached individuals, the extent of economic distress was striking.[31]

Early American Responses to Elderly Poverty

The challenge of dependency in old age has always existed, as discussed in Chapter 2. And definitions of what constitutes dependency, and methods of dealing with it, have at all times arisen out of a particular socioeconomic matrix and cultural value system. Approaches to old-age dependency in the U.S. were remarkably stable until after the Civil War, as might be expected in a nation predominantly agricultural in production, rural in demographics, and "pre-industrial" in mode of thought. A nation established on the revolutionary principles of freedom, individualism, and independence long remained traditional in its ways of coping with economic need.

The Poorhouse

For the economic failures, the public asylum or poorhouse was always a much-feared possibility. Over time, an increasing number of alternatives to the poorhouse appeared, particularly through the auspices of philanthropists who since colonial times had recognized the desirability of private homes for the destitute aged. But up until the Civil War, charitable agencies did not provide relief to many elderly Americans. One estimate put the proportion of people aged 60 and over in the average public almshouse prior to the Civil War at between 16 and 25 percent, of whom an unknown but possibly substantial percentage had entered because of handicaps while still young.[32] Before 1860, many more agencies were set up to care for the blind or deaf, the mentally ill, or for orphans, than for direct assistance to the aged.[33]

---

30 If one were to take all deaths of persons under 65 to be premature, then in 1908, 77 percent of deaths in the U.S. were premature. (U.S. Department of Commerce, Bureau of the Census, Mortality Statistics [Washington, D.C.: Government Printing Office, 1908], p. 19, cited by Rubinow, Social Insurance, p. 414.)

31 Premature deaths among wage-earners were higher than for the professional classes. Deaths under the age of 45 constituted less than 50 percent of all deaths among the professional classes; of those in personal service it was 60 percent; in manufacturing and mechanical industries, 55 percent; and among laborers and servants, 68 percent. (Rubinow, Social Insurance, p. 414.)

32 Achenbaum, Old Age, p. 80.

33 See, for example, Michael Zimmerman, "Old-Age Poverty in Pre-Industrial New York City," in Growing Old in America, ed. by Beth B. Hess (New Brunswick, N.J.: Transactions Press, 1976), pp. 81-104; Gary B. Nash, "Poverty and Poor Relief in Pre-Revolutionary

After the Civil War, the number and variety of private benevolent societies for the elderly increased dramatically. Of the 1200 old-age homes in existence in 1939, nearly two-thirds had been established between 1875 and 1919. [34] Institutions catering to elderly members of particular nationalities and religions proliferated in the decades following the Civil War, and old-age asylums began to systematize admission standards and procedures to accommodate the growing dependent elderly population.[35]

Yet there continued to be significant proportions of the aged in traditional alms-houses, and their representation increased with the growth of economic superannuation in the late nineteenth and early twentieth centuries. In 1880, 25.6 percent of the national almshouse population was at least 65. Commerce Department data show that the percentage rose sharply and steadily after that, to 31.8 percent in 1890, 40.6 percent in 1904, and 42.7 percent in 1910. By 1923 the elderly accounted for 53.8 percent of those in poorhouses.[36] Various state commissions looking into the problem also found high percentages of the aged in almshouses. In particular, the Massachusetts Commission on Pensions and Annuities found in 1910 that 92 percent of that state's almshouse residents had been 60 or older on entering, and 23 percent of the state's over-65 population were dependent on some form of institutional support.[37] No account was made of the numbers who had to rely on informal charity from family, friends, or community.

Evidently, a large number of the elderly population were officially paupers, and a large proportion of institutionalized paupers were elderly. Massachusetts had the highest percentage of the over-65 aged in almshouses by 1910 (92 percent), followed by Wisconsin with 87 percent and Pennsylvania with 62 percent.[38] The Ohio Health and Old Age Insurance Commission reported a few years later, in 1919, that 60 percent of the state's

---

Philadelphia," in <u>Colonial America</u>, ed. by Stanley N. Katz, 2nd ed. (Boston: Little, Brown Co., 1976), pp. 375-401.

34 Achenbaum, <u>Old Age</u>, p. 80.

35 U.S. Department of Labor, Bureau of Labor Statistics, <u>Care of Aged Persons in the United States</u>, Bulletin No. 489 (Washington, D.C.: Government Printing Office, 1929), pp. 131, 176, 193.

36 U.S. Department of Commerce, <u>Paupers in Almshouses, 1923</u> (Washington, D.C.: Government Printing Office, 1925), p. 10, cited by Epstein, <u>Insecurity</u>, p. 501.

37 <u>Report of the Massachusetts Commission on Old Age Pensions</u>, p. 27; Squier, <u>Old Age Dependency</u>, p. 6.

38 In Wisconsin, in contrast with Massachusetts and Pennsylvania, industrialization was more of an indirect cause of elderly poverty. Predominantly a farming state, Wisconsin's population was becoming older because of the exodus of the young people to urban industrial areas; older residents of Wisconsin were not generally veterans of industry. (Epstein, <u>Facing Old Age</u>, p. 30.)

permanent infirmary inmates were over 60 years of age.[39] In the 1920s, the New York Commission on Old Age Security conducted a special study of five almshouses considered representative and reported that 74.1 percent of the inmates had passed their 60th birthday, 66.4 percent were 65 or older, and 50.6 percent were at least 70. [40]

Although the almshouse clientele changed in the late nineteenth and early twentieth centuries,[41] the institution itself did not. It continued to be a last-resort repository for unfortunate, feeble, aged individuals, a place they could go to die. It continued also to be perceived by some as the well-deserved lot of the economically inadequate and morally degenerate. The steward of a county almshouse in a Quaker district in Pennsylvania reported to the Pennsylvania Commission on Old Age Pensions in 1919:

> The dependents in almshouses are of such a character that inquiry as to their past life seems to me a waste of time. Most of them were nothing but parasites in society all their days, not one worthy of an old age pension, if it could be had. They are mentally and morally degenerates; most of them foreign born, and half of them never naturalized. Tramps in summer and here in winter. The only record that could be had would be unreliable, for there is no way to obtain it but from them. Hence, we go into few details when they are admitted. The average life of an inmate has been a failure largely due to the fact that they never realize what a successful life is.[42]

---

39 Report of the Ohio Health and Old Age Insurance Commission, 1919, p. 242, cited by ibid., p. 501.

40 Report of the New York State Commission on Old Age Security, 1930, p. 409, cited by ibid. By 1930, although elderly women slightly outnumbered elderly men, there were about twice as many men as women in the nation's poorhouses (ibid.). This is because older women had not been as directly affected as men by the growth in retirement and its accompanying poverty. So few women were in the labor force in the nineteenth century that the proportion of gainfully employed older females changed very little in the three-quarters of a century after 1870 (Fischer, Growing Old, p. 144). Furthermore, American women had always been "dependent," and so their greater need for support in old age was more readily accommodated by family, church, and informal community arrangements.

41 Almshouse populations over time became less "mainstream" in two ways: (1) they became more heavily "foreign," that is, peopled by the less fortunate aged of earlier generations of (perhaps unassimilated) immigrants; and (2) they became more conspicuously the refuge of an underclass, as growing numbers of Americans were unable to find acceptance within large-scale capitalist institutions. See, for example, "Old People's Homes Maintained by Nationality Groups," Monthly Labor Review 28 (April 1929): 691-94.

42 Cited by Epstein, Facing Old Age, p. 135.

The Family

Despite the growing importance of the almshouse for the dependent aged's subsistence, in keeping with custom, their primary source of support until well into the twentieth century was the family unit. Individually the colonies had passed statutes regulating family duties, modeled on the 1601 Elizabethan Poor Law in England. The Massachusetts Bay Colony had been the first to pass an act, in 1692, stipulating that family members were legally and morally responsible for their infirm and poor members, including their old. Similar legislation was adopted by other colonies and states until, by 1860, 18 of the 33 states had enacted laws specifying the family's responsibilities toward its dependent members of all ages. By 1915, 32 of the 48 states had such laws.[43]

However, there were no unique provisions for the aged until the courts and legislatures were pressured by litigation into defining the precise duties of adult children toward their aging parents. With the spread of such litigation by the 1920s, differences among states as to family members' responsibilities became obvious and probably helped serve as a spur to federal action.[44] There is no way of ascertaining whether children obeyed the legislative dictates to help their aged parents, but a significant percentage were unquestionably unable to do so, however willing they might have been. Yet objections to a federal system of old age assistance continued to be based primarily on the argument that the economic conditions of the working classes were such as to enable families to meet their needs without governmental assistance.

The strongest possible emphasis upon the family as the remedy for old-age destitution was made by the Massachusetts Commission, and in particular by the Commission's secretary, economics professor F. Spencer Baldwin, who became famous for his argument.[45] Baldwin's logic, promulgated through numerous lectures and articles, was used as one of the primary bases for establishing the nondesirability of public support for the dependent elderly, in the state of Massachusetts and elsewhere:

> The disintegrating effect on the family. A non-contributory system would take away...the filial obligation for the support of aged parents which is a main bond of family solidarity. It would strike at one of the forces that have created the self-supporting, self-respecting American family. The impairment of family solidarity is one of the most serious consequences to be apprehended.[46]

The tireless activist and leading American theoretician of social insurance, Isaac M. Rubinow, responded:

---

43 Achenbaum, Old Age, pp. 75-76.

44 Ibid., pp. 76, 121.

45 See, for example, F. Spencer Baldwin, "Old Age Pension Schemes: A Criticism and a Program," Quarterly Journal of Economics 24 (August 1910):713-42.

46 Report of the Massachusetts Commission on Old Age Pensions, p. 301; emphasis in the original.

There is a good, old-fashioned, atavistic nobility of sentiment about this argument which will greatly please all good men and women except those who have to be supported by their children, and those who have to support their parents and also their own families on a wage-earner's budget. Scientifically the argument is certainly original, because it assumes the basis of the family to be the support of the older generation by the younger, while it has always been fairly well agreed upon by all students of society that the shoe was on the other foot, and that care of the children by the parents was the proper function of family. It further seems to assume that we love our burdens, and that when parents cease being burdens the children cease loving them. It assumes that the standing of a superannuated parent in a family is in an inverse proportion to the amount he is able to contribute to the family budget. It is an appeal to an ideal of a patriarchal family which has been dead for a century in every industrial country,...Of course, its inapplicability to the aged single man or the aged spinster aunt will be evident.[47]

Another student of old-age dependency, Lee Squier, argued that the American family had never really conformed to the assumptions being made about it by those wishing to enforce its role in ameliorating economic hardships:

We Americans have not that conception of the family as the unit of society, and that reverence for old age, which is engrafted upon the heart of the Oriental....In this country no such esteem for the aged ones prevails, except...in agricultural communities. In our manufacturing centers...the helpless, destitute grandfather or grandmother is regarded as a distinct burden to the household, the carrying of which oftentimes forces children out of school and into the streets, factories, or shops, in order to provide for the added increment to the household expenses which the taking on of an aged relative entails.[48]

The vital distinction in the question of family support for aged relatives was that between the status of the family in the agricultural and industrial stages of economic development. In the context of industrial capitalism, said Rubinow, "There is nothing for the old-age pension to destroy."[49]

---

47 Rubinow, Social Insurance, p. 314.

48 Squier, Old Age Dependency, p. 312.

49 Rubinow, Social Insurance, p. 382. Furthermore, with increasing residential concentration, a rising standard of living, and a growing array of available consumption goods, a demonstration effect doubtless weakened the will to save even where it might have been accomplished.

Impediments to Social Insurance

The Gospel of Thrift and Voluntarism

It is understandable that in a Protestant nation, in which the impulse to save ran deep, the most popular remedies proposed for avoiding pauperism were variations on the theme of thrift. When savings were inadequate to escape poverty, recourse was to be had in the wide array of voluntary and charitable associations that had sprung up to cope with the problems of the old, the disabled, the alcoholic. The idealization of voluntary institutions was peculiarly American. As early as the 1830s de Tocqueville had been struck by the number of "intellectual and moral associations" in the United States, and hypothesized that the attraction to voluntary associations was closely related to the principle of equality. For de Tocqueville, it was not so much Americans' individualism which caused them to rely on voluntarism, but rather a strong streak of antistatism which seemed a natural outgrowth of the society's most prominent features: mobility, egalitarianism, and heterogeneity, coupled with the lack of any well-defined social classes or rigid institutional structures.

America's singular aversion to using the state to ameliorate social problems merits some elaboration, for the U.S. was the last of the industrialized nations to adopt programs of social insurance, although it had the greatest resources for doing so. These programs were ultimately an acknowledgement that the ideal of self-reliance had become irrelevant to the welfare of millions of individuals. In particular, this nation's very lack of a feudal past and aristocratic heritage was a primary determinant of its anachronistic reliance on voluntarism (by which is meant organized action by nonstatutory institutions) throughout the late nineteenth and early twentieth centuries.

The pre-capitalist, pre-industrial tradition of the feudal aristocratic state was one that elsewhere had provided for quite clearly-defined community responsibilities. Societies organized on estate lines, with explicit class divisions, were societies in which the dominant classes had duties to those under them. When capitalism developed in the feudal nations of Europe, it engendered a liberal, bourgeois ideology. This ideology repudiated the policies of the monarchical feudal state, policies such as mercantilism that had entailed responsibility for the entire community. The rising capitalist class sought policies that allowed business to operate in greater freedom, but this implied as well that nobody had duties to anybody else. Thus the essence of the new capitalist value system was individualism and competitiveness, and the weakening and overthrow of non-market bonds of mutual aid and reciprocity.[50]

The United States from colonial times was peopled with individuals who had to some extent internalized this new ethic of self-responsibility. Thus there were few of the lingering restraints on commercial relations that had had to be overcome in the nations of Western Europe. Because noblesse oblige was not a significant part of the American value system, the business classes (that is, the nineteenth-century-style liberals, today's conservatives) felt little or no responsibility for poor people and for those they employed. If business

---

50 Seymour Martin Lipset, "American Exceptionalism," in Capitalism and Socialism: A Theological Inquiry, ed. by Michael Novak (Washington, D.C.: American Enterprise Institute for Public Policy Research, 1979), pp. 34-42.

conditions soured, people were fired; if employees became ill, they were cast upon their own resources. Becoming old or economically redundant was an individual matter, and not a proper area for state action.

So the nineteenth-century conservatives stood for class hierarchy and a highly unequal division of the national product, but they also stood for social responsibility, welfare goals, and broad state involvement in the economy and in social life. The liberals, the rising business classes, were opposed to most such interventions. In this sense, the United States developed as a "liberal" capitalist society.

However, the elements of mobility, egalitariansim, and heterogeneity, in combination with the absence of well-defined classes or institutions, created obvious tensions and strains, particularly during downturns in the business cycle. Because individual roles and statuses were far more ambiguous than in the more rigid, post-feudal economies, there arose the peculiarly American institution of voluntary associations to intermediate between the individual and mass society. These associations were closely allied in American thought with a cluster of economic, social, and political principles: individual liberty, limited government, self-support, and a system of economic incentives which distributed rewards on the basis of merit in competitive markets; and hence they served a strategic socioeconomic and political function. Even voluntary associations and charity were considered suspect by some, because they represented "systems of secondary income distribution" that allocated goods and services on the basis of need rather than by participation in production.[51] Any such form of guaranteed income had the potential to harm incentives and work discipline.

Nevertheless, by the late nineteenth century, these institutions were firmly entrenched in the U.S. political economy, and their existence was widely accepted as proof that there was no need for a national system of old age, unemployment, or disability insurance. The extremeness of the dominant individualistic philosophy affected even the most concerned students of the social ills of poverty and unemployment. For example, Edward T. Devine, a champion of the dependent aged, argued in his 1909 book, Misery and Its Causes, that:

> Prevalence of ill health is due, in large part, of course, to ignorance and the continuous neglect of the elementary rules of personal hygiene....people--reckless in all classes--are slow to act upon these counsels, and they destroy foolishly and recklessly their most valuable personal asset next to good character; viz., their health. Economic necessity excuses some, but only a very little of the improvidence.[52]

Such blaming of the victim contrasts with the spirit in which the above-cited work began:

> The question which I raise is whether the wretched poor, the poor who suffer in their poverty, are poor because they are shiftless, because they are undisciplined, because they drink, because they steal, because they have superfluous children, because of personal depravity, personal inclination, and natural preference; or

---

51 Lubove, Struggle for Social Security, pp. 3-4.

52 Devine, Misery and Its Causes, p. 74. Yet Devine's central message was that prevailing economic arrangements created the greatest misfortune, dependency in old age.

whether they are shiftless and undisciplined...because our social institutions and economic arrangements are at fault. I hold that personal depravity is as foreign to any sound theory of the hardships of our modern poor as witchcraft or demoniacal possession; that these hardships are economic, social, transitional, measurable, manageable. Misery, as we say of tuberculosis, is communicable, curable, and preventable.[53]

As noted in this chapter's introduction, by the turn of the century several European nations had begun systems of compulsory insurance. The idea remained repugnant to Americans, although it was by no means new in the U.S. Thomas Paine had proposed a national pension plan in his 1796 pamphlet, Agrarian Justice, suggesting that a "national fund" be raised from ground rent on the land under cultivation. On reaching the age of 50 everyone would receive a yearly pension of 10 pounds, to be paid as "a right and not a charity" to "every person, rich or poor...to prevent invidious distinctions."[54]

But a century later, notes Fischer, the "national hostility to a compulsory pension plan" continued to be "rooted in the deepest political and moral principles of the Republic."[55]   Voluntarism, implying the right of citizens to define and pursue goals in freely-chosen association, was thought to lead to maximum liberty and a corresponding minimum of government intrusion. Voluntarism thus was, for all practical purposes, synonymous with democracy.

By the early 1900s, however, the once-clear distinction between what was voluntary and what was compulsory had become blurred. With the modernization of society, many structural similarities had developed between public and private institutions. Voluntary meant any type of free, nongovernmental association or enterprise, but defined so broadly it had begun to lose any meaningful connection with early twentieth-century reality. Encompassing as it did virtually all types of private institutions, the scope of voluntarism ranged from community burial societies to giant insurance companies writing millions of policies. As Lubove, author of several volumes on social insurance, has written, the ideology of voluntarism lagged behind evolving institutional arrangements; and

> ...many institutions defended as expressions of American voluntarism were more comprehensible as large-scale bureaucratic systems with their charactertistic features of great size, specialization, hierarchy, and routinization.   The nature of private, voluntary institutions in an industrial-urban society had changed, giving rise to an essentially bureaucratic phenomenon....[voluntarism] viewed public institutions as

---

53 Ibid., pp. 11-12.

54 Moncure D. Conway, ed., The Writings of Thomas Paine, 4 vols. (New York: AMS Press, 1967), 3:322-44. See also Alexander Everett, New Ideas on Population (Boston: Oliver Everett, 1823) for another early proposal for nationally-funded pensions to lessen indigency among the aged.

55 Fischer, Growing Old, p. 168.

generically different from private; the latter, presumably, were neither bureaucratic nor coercive.[56]

Yet private bureaucratic institutions <u>did</u> possess coercive power in the context of a concentrated economy based on wage labor. For the wage-earner, such organizations were the source of all that counted--earnings, status, property ownership, and mobility--and they were capable of imposing wide-ranging sanctions.

The dominance of the profit motive provided a powerful barrier to private insurance plans, which constituted a very real threat to established private interests. Managers of industrial establishment funds, commercial insurance companies, and trade union benefit funds, among others, viewed their prospects for survival in terms of preventing the government from getting into the insurance business.[57]

Finally, the ideology of voluntarism prevailed because there existed no cohesive, well-organized constituency on behalf of the dependent aged's need of a compulsory old-age pension system. Edward Everett Hale, clergyman and noted writer on social ills, had repeatedly urged until his death in 1909 that the Massachusetts legislature enact at least a limited old age pension bill, whereby citizens of the state over 65 who had paid a poll tax for 25 years, and who had not been convicted of any crime punishable by imprisonment, would receive $2 per week. Noting a similar system had been adopted in Belgium, Denmark, France, Austria, Norway, Sweden, Switzerland, Russia and Australia, Hale proposed setting aside a part of the poll tax for this purpose, which he argued would be more than compensated by the savings for the state's poorhouses.[58]

Yet in 1910 the special commission to study the pension question in Massachusetts regarded compulsory pensions as antithetical to the American way of life. The commission argued, "If such a scheme be defensible or excusable, then the whole economic and social system is a failure. The adoption of such a policy would be a confession of its breakdown."[59] Compulsory old-age pensions were denounced by the clergy as being corruptive of morality, by most economists as destructive of thrift and effort, by capitalists as incipient socialism, and by labor leaders as being merely a form of deferred wages which were unlikely ever to be received (an objection to be dealt with later in this chapter). Even the industrial workers with the most to gain from such insurance adhered to an "I'm all right, Jack" philosophy and apparently preferred to take their chances of being able to achieve old-age security through independent means or through their unions' wage negotiations with employers.

---

56 Lubove, <u>Struggle for Social Security,</u> p. 8.

57 Ibid., pp. 8-9.

58 See Harriet E. Paine, <u>Old People</u> (Boston: Houghton Mifflin Co., 1910), pp. 131-32.

59 <u>Report of the Massachusetts Commission on Old Age Pensions,</u> cited by Fischer, <u>Growing Old,</u> p. 168.

Social Darwinism

The national value system was heavily influenced by the survival-of-the-fittest notions put forth by Charles Darwin and popularized by such Social Darwinists such as Herbert Spencer and William Graham Sumner. Spencer had probably the greatest influence of any Victorian thinker on both American and European thought. From him Sumner derived many of his ideas, in particular his idealization of the solid middle-class citizen--the "Forgotten Man"--who was perfectly capable of supporting himself in old age. Between them, Sumner and Spencer bore primary responsibility for spreading the view that the individual, not the group, was the basic component of society, that only the fittest individuals should survive in the struggle against both nature and other people, and that the state should refrain from becoming involved in that struggle.

The Social Darwinists' monistic premise that the same laws governed nature and society fed the familiar late-nineteenth century conservative opposition to collective behavior on behalf of society's unfortunates. Darwinian ideas of natural selection thus served the accustomed conservative purposes of justifying the status quo and opposing rapid social change. Such views were particularly likely to be popular with those who stood to benefit most from the growth of privately purchased annuities. For example, Prudential Life Insurance Company President Frederick L. Hoffman agreed with Sumner that "sympathy with hard struggling" was needed but not merely "sympathy with suffering"; for unfortunately, the "kindly thought of the world" was too readily "wasted upon those who least deserve it." The independent, self-reliant citizen would be the loser if the state were to become the provider of pensions; his tax burden would increase, and his self-reliance would be undermined, to his further economic loss. Dependency and poverty would not disappear with state aid, but rather such aid would only debase a segment of the population previously "outside the scope of poor law administration or private charitable aid."[60]

Darwin himself took a gloomy view of the future, in light of humanity's increasing ability to manipulate the environment to protect the unfit. Among economists, Alfred Marshall had grave apprehensions concerning the survival of the feeble who owed their existence to improved sanitation, medical discoveries, and the humanitarianism of others. Richard Ely provided the following assessment of the view that progress was leading to the increasing survival of the unfit:

> The great advances in medicine are in the region of preventive medicine,...which aims by general sanitary measures and correct mode of life to prevent disease, or at any rate to reduce it to its lowest terms. But if this is leading to an increasing number of an increasingly feeble population, should it not be checked? Man's increased power in the production of wealth means that it is easier than heretofore to furnish to all the necessities and even the comforts of life. The struggle for bare existence declines. If the view to which reference has been made is sound, should not efforts be put forth to hold back the wheels of industrial progress? May there

---

60 Frederick L. Hoffman, "The Problem of Poverty and Pensions in Old Age," American Journal of Sociology 14 (September 1908); idem, "State Pensions and Annuities in Old Age," American Statistical Association Quarterly Publications 11 (March 1909), cited by Lubove, Struggle for Social Security, pp. 116-17.

not have been, then, a higher wisdom than has ever been supposed in the efforts of riotous workingmen in England, early in the last century, to smash machines?[61]

Ely was to conclude that the problem lay not so much in the "strenuous atmosphere" of the competitive system, but in the fact of the "existence of these feeble persons." Although he felt that the economically obsolescent and socially rejected had to be cared for and given "as happy an existence as possible," this was only on condition that such provision did "not encourage the increase of those who belong to this sad human rubbish-heap.[62]

Although unprepared to accept Darwinian laws as a basis for state inaction in social affairs, Ely accepted the truth of the assertion that modern methods of human engineering were enabling greater numbers to live who in earlier times would have died young. Death was increasingly coming to be associated almost exclusively with age, rather than being something that could strike at any time. Whereas in the nation's infancy, surviving to old age was a mark of superiority and distinction, it now was within the reach of the unfit, as death rates fell continuously after the Civil War for all age groups under 50. Writers began to argue that with overcrowding, and with the cultural stagnation that could result from the world's being "overshadowed by too many hoary Methuselahs," the demise of the elderly should be seen as socially beneficial.[63]

The influence of the national ideology extended beyond simply an aversion to systematized social welfare programs. It was reflected in an apparent unwillingness even to collect the data which might bring into relief the plight of the nation's elderly, poor, and unemployed. Thus, as Rubinow wrote in 1913, "... our extreme individualistic philosophy has interfered not only with the elaboration of the necessary remedial measures, but even with a proper appreciation of the problems."[64] Two decades later, the indefatigable social reformer, Abraham Epstein, reiterated this point with respect to unemployment:

Nothing so well illustrates our devil-may-care attitude and our shameful indifference to social distress as the fact that, despite the gravity of our unemployment, we are the only industrial nation with so little accurate information regarding its extent. We are a most statistically minded country. We know the exact number of bushels of wheat, corn and oats which we produce annually. We know almost to the dozen the number of eggs laid, the number of hogs slaughtered; and we, of course, keep close records of the number of automobiles produced, the number of shares of stock sold,

---

61 Ely, Evolution of Industrial Society, p. 166.

62 Ibid., p. 163.

63 Newman Smyth, The Place of Death in Evolution (London: T. Fisher Unwin, 1897), pp. 173-74.

64 Rubinow, Social Insurance, p. 205.

177

and the number of shoes manufactured. But we do not know the number of unemployed.[65]

As summed up by Wesley Mitchell in 1929, "There are few branches of statistics in which the United States lags further behind the leaders than in statistics of unemployment."[66]

The debate over various types of social insurance generally (accident, sickness, and unemployment compensation), and with respect to the question of old-age pensions in particular, had an interesting effect on the relations between the various classes into which American society was being divided by powerful economic forces. Pensions were often advocated as a measure of social peace, yet for the same reason they were often vigorously attacked by opponents.

Those in favor, the "mild" social reformers, argued that pensions would serve to advance the gospel of the unity of interests of capital and labor; the business classes and mainstream economists opposed it for its debilitating effects upon working people's motivation to produce; while the radical fringes of the labor movement attacked all forms of social insurance as an insidious means of sapping the forces of an inevitable social revolution.[67]

As far as the general population's views were concerned, the situation was unclear at any given moment. Social insurance was a good thing because it was conducive to peace among economic classes. It was bad because it weakened motivation; or because it devitalized the movement toward revolution. Where some form of social insurance had been put in place, it had succeeded in accomplishing the desired results, and it had dismally failed. If it failed, then both the reactionary and revolutionary views were justified, but the moderate reformers were wrong. The American public must have been thoroughly confused by an issue that had both extremes of the political spectrum dissatisfied with the general effects of social insurance on the class relations of industry.[68]

The view that apparently prevailed--the dominant ethos--was that compulsory pensions encouraged improvidence, impaired morals, and undermined thrift. They were paternalistic at best, or tantamount to socialism or communism, and in any case decidedly un-American. Industrial leaders apparently viewed most proposed actions on behalf of wage-earners in this light, and yet they saw no violation of the principles of rugged individualism in government's interference on behalf of business. While free education and public health programs were decried as socialistic, franchises and subsidies to the railroads, shipping, and public utilities were not seen as being inconsistent with the tenets of private enterprise.

Worker compensation for industrial accidents, or job-induced illness, was an unwarranted intrusion in firms' internal affairs, but tariff protection of both infant and mature

---

65 Epstein, Insecurity, p. 189.

66 Wesley Claire Mitchell, Recent Economic Changes (New York: Macmillan Co., for the National Bureau of Economic Research), 2:877.

67 Rubinow, Social Insurance, p. 498.

68 Ibid., pp. 498-99.

industries was incessantly lobbied for and won by appeal to considerations of national security and prestige. Pensions for the aged, for widows and orphans, were paternalistic and fostered profligacy, but guaranteed returns on railroad investments were a proper object of federal largesse.

At another level, there existed objections to pensions and other forms of socialized assistance on purely economic grounds, the primary one being that pensions in particular would do little other than have a depressing effect on wages. The 1910 Report of the Massachusetts Commission on Old Age Pensions cited three such economic considerations:

(1) The establishment of pensions would have the unfavorable effect, said the Report, of attracting foreign sources of labor into greater competition with U.S. wage-earners. Such an objection had a superficial appeal, and yet a glance at the immigration figures suggests that at no time in the period between 1860 and 1920 was immigration apparently favored by those over 50. [69] As to younger immigrant workers, it would be far-fetched to think that their relocation would be based on considerations of what they could anticipate at age 60 or 65, rather than on more immediate prospects.

(2) A puzzling objection by the Commission was the effects of possible competition from the pensioners themselves. The Report apparently assumed a pension that granted the old person a minimal guarantee against starvation (this was thought to be all that any state pension scheme could afford or should attempt) must increase his/her power as a competitor in the labor market. Of course, such an argument could also have been used, but was not, against privately-purchased annuities, support by relatives, or reliance on a small savings account. At any rate, a person of 60 or 65 at the time of receiving a pension, if still physically able to perform useful work, would be far less dangerous as an employment competitor than an individual without such means of support. Noted Rubinow, "Any labor leader knows what a professional economist may sometimes disregard, that a competitor in the labor market is never as dangerous as when he is starving."[70]

(3) The third argument cited in the Report was the one most commonly put forth by labor leaders, that the prospect of a pension in future old age would tempt and enable workers to offer their labor for lower wages in the present. Such a view presumed a theory of wages which included saving for old-age as the normal behavior of industrial workers, but the theory was not supported by workers' actual behavior.[71]

Government policy in general both supported and mirrored this negative attitude toward state intervention up until the legislation of the New Deal. Shortly before the U.S. government began loaning billions of dollars to bail out private banks and insurance companies in the Great Depression, the Secretary of Agriculture opposed granting food relief to drought-stricken farmers (although seeds, animal feed, and fertilizer were legitimate aid categories). The reason given was that if public loans were granted for the direct purchase

---

69 See, for example, Brennan, Taft, and Schupack, The Economics of Age, p. 13.

70 Rubinow, Social Insurance, p. 383.

71 Ibid.

of food for people, it would be an "approach perilously near the dole system and would be a move in the wrong direction."[72]

Pension Plans, Public and Private

Despite the Federal government's generosity toward a select subgroup of the aged, military veterans (discussed in the next section), it continued to resist the idea of old-age pensions for all. Even following Great Britain's enactment of a pension program in 1908, following some 30 years of political debate in that country, Congress rejected bills put forth in 1909, 1911, and 1913. Because military pensions had become acceptable, the 1911 bill was couched in military terms, stating that "the work of the soldiers of industry is infinitely more necessary than the bloody work of the soldier....The aged working men and women have therefore a claim on society that is even better than the claims of the soldier."[73]

A small minority of industrial workers were covered by company pension plans prior to World War I, but these plans were viewed by industry more as a favor than as a right. Yet, however poor the coverage of workers in private enterprise, it was government's own employees, outside of the military, who were least protected against the insecurities of old age. The Federal government had no regular retirement or pension system for its employees until after the war. Those in the Civil Service merely worked as long as they were physically and mentally able, and frequently longer. Superannuated employees had become a serious problem in the Federal bureaucracy by 1910, and although Congress considered a retirement bill in almost every session after 1900, no action was taken until 1920 [74] because the issue was political dynamite for the majority of congressmen. The U.S. Government was kinder to its four-legged workforce; animals belonging to the government retired on full rations, to the dismay of human civil servants.[75]

Also, few state or municipal workers received pensions. As of 1910 only nine of the 56 largest American cities had pension coverage for teachers, police, and firemen.[76] Overall, government workers (today among the most fortunate of pension recipients) were probably worse off even than the mass of industrial workers. The problems of superannuation were a national disgrace, and yet the dominant ideology continued to be self-sufficiency and pursuit of the success ethic of years past. The McGuffey Readers, through which most Americans were first exposed to the success ethic as schoolchildren,[77]

---

72 From New York Times, 9 December 1930, cited by Epstein, Insecurity, p. 68.

73 U.S. Congress, House, 62nd Cong., 1st sess., 1911, Congressional Record 47:3699, cited by Achenbaum, Old Age, pp. 84-85.

74 In 1920 the United States Civil Service retirement law was enacted.

75 Fischer, Growing Old, p. 167.

76 Report of the Massachusetts Commission on Old Age Pensions, p. 272.

77 Sixty million copies of these readers were sold between 1870 and 1900. (Yellowitz, Position of the Worker, p. 7.)

constantly stressed the message of the free-market economy designed and sanctioned by God. The sermons of clergymen were laced with references to laissez-faire economic precepts; the clergy glorified the struggle for material success as being in the national interest, and intimated strongly that dissatisfaction with American conditions was equivalent to repudiation of the Lord.[78]

Even after the appearance in the 1880s of the work of Richard Ely, Edward James, and other so-called New Economists, the vast majority of the economics profession continued to stress the absolute validity of orthodox economic laws. Textbooks, learned journals, and lecture halls were dominated by the laissez-faire doctrines of Amasa Walker, Arthur Perry, and Lyman Atwater.[79] The minority who opposed these views, especially Ely and John R. Commons, had less access to the public for their argument that the success ethic distorted reality in numerous ways, and that social idealism should be allowed to intervene in the economic order and, where necessary, rearrange the outcomes of impersonal market forces.

Hadley's widely-used textbook on economics at the turn of the century argued that if the American public were to "countenance a system of morals or laws which justifies the individual in looking to the community rather than to himself for support in age or infirmity," the fear of dependency would be removed as a spur to enterprise.[80] It was this fear which was a "chief discipline in the interest of wholesome living."[81] In particular, the

---

78 "It is a religious duty to work for the good of this country, and it is not easy to imagine that any one can love God or man and hate America," wrote one J.L. Spalding in "Are We in Danger of Revolution?", The Forum 1 (July 1886), p. 415, cited by Yellowitz, Position of the Worker, p. 8. The Reverend Francis Wayland, later professor of moral philosophy and president of Brown University, published The Elements of Political Economy in 1837, whose various editions were in use into the 1880s. Wayland wrote, "The results which our Creator has attached to idleness are all to be considered as punishements [sic]....And, on the other hand, God has assigned to industry rich and abundant rewards." (Cited by Hacker, Course of American Economic Growth, p. 194.) The Reverend Francis Bowen, Harvard professor of natural religion and moral philosophy, was equally sure that God was on the side of free-market capitalism, in his American Political Economy of 1870:

> "Society is a complex and delicate machine, the real Author and Governor of which is divine....Men cannot interfere with His work without marring it. The attempts of legislators to turn the industry of society in one direction or another, out of its natural and self-chosen channels...are almost invariably productive of harm. Laissez-faire; "these things regulate themselves," is the common phrase, which means, of course, that God regulates them by his general laws, which means in the long run, work to good." (Cited by Hacker, Course of American Economic Growth, p. 195).

79 Yellowitz, Position of the Worker, p. 7.

80 Hadley, Economics, p. 63.

81 James H. Hamilton, Savings and Saving Institutions (New York: Macmillan Co., 1902), p. 128.

frightening prospect of dependency in old age was the "most powerful incentive which makes for character and growth in a democracy." If this possibility were to disappear it would be a death blow to the "root of national life and character." Although the vast majority of citizens were "thrifty and industrious," progress was threatened because the population's "capacity for suffering, self-sacrifice, and self-denial" was already being weakened, and compulsory pensions could only speed the deterioration.[82]

The Anomaly of Military Pensions

Paradoxically, while the debate about mandatory pensions was heating up, the U.S. government was funding what may have been the costliest pension system in the world, in the form of military pensions. Disability pensions had begun to be provided in 1789 for veterans of the Revolutionary War. Up to the Civil War, the government continued to pay pensions and benefits to incapacitated and/or impoverished veterans, but these were considered gratuities for military service only. Poor, helpless veterans received assistance because they had given military service, not because they were old and impoverished.

As time passed, the veterans program grew enormously, reflecting additional wars and the introduction of systematized military retirement policies for selected career officers and enlisted men. The number of pensioners increased from 126,772 in 1886 to nearly one million in 1902; and the direct costs rose from $21 million in 1867 to $153 million in 1912. The cost of all military pensions in fiscal year 1913 was $174.2 million, a figure representing 18 percent of that year's total Federal expenditures. Between the Civil War and World War I, the Federal government paid out more than $5 billion in veterans' benefits, a huge sum in a period when the average budget was only about $300 million per year ($300 million was the total of government expenditures in 1890). [83]

By the turn of the century, most of the veterans of the Civil War were in their sixties and seventies, and thus military pensions had become a de facto system of old age assistance, yet not in name. Perhaps as many as two-thirds of America's elderly benefited from them,[84] yet the old who most needed them might be least likely to qualify for them. Many blacks, immigrants, and paupers who had served in the Union army were unable to establish eligibility. Although the war pensions system undoubtedly helped hundreds of thousands of the aged, it was, according to Rubinow, "honeycombed with dishonesty and absurdity" because it was "not based upon any constructive social principle."[85]

Ostensibly it was meant to be a reward for service, but such service was measured quixotically. For example, in 1890 Congress liberalized the act to grant benefits to anyone over 62 who had served at least 90 days in the Union army. The necessary evidence of

---

82 Hoffman, "State Pensions and Annuities in Old Age," pp. 368, 367, 389, cited by Lubove, Struggle for Social Security, p. 117.

83 Fischer, Growing Old, p. 169; Achenbaum, Old Age, p. 84; Lubove, Struggle for Social Security, p. 125.

84 Tishler, Self-Reliance, p. 89.

85 Rubinow, Quest for Security, p. 237.

disability was so poorly monitored that it was not unusual for veterans classified as gravely or totally disabled to be found employed in Federal or state government service. Least of all was the system based upon demonstration of need. Rubinow pointed out that for the most part, it benefited the native white population "least in need of old-age pensions."[86] It was "haphazard, inequitable, wasteful, and above all demoralizing" because it existed "not so much in consideration of the problem of old age as by brazen log-rolling and wire pulling."[87]

To outsiders and to social reformers, Americans' insistence on defending military pensions as necessary for maintaining the honor of the nation, while eschewing old-age pensions as corruptive and socialistic, was baffling. Advocates found it "difficult, if not impossible," notes Lubove, "to disprove the argument that voluntary institutions could expand and provide universal economic security."[88] But "to true believers," writes Fischer,

> the line between military and old age pensions was...clear....When the pension problem was wrapped in Old Glory, the veterans' bread and wine was miraculously changed into the flesh and blood of patriot soldiers. But when it came in other forms the sacred change did not take place.[89]

Recognition of this increasingly arbitrary distinction underlay the first bill for a national pension plan, which was introduced in Congress in 1909. Representative William B. Wilson, a coalminer and union leader who was to become President Wilson's labor secretary, proposed an "Old Age Home Guard of the United States Army." All Americans of 65 or over were invited to "enlist" as privates if they had property of less than $1500 or a monthly income of less than $20. Their "army duty" was to make an annual report to the War Department on the state of military and patriotic sentiment in their communities, for which they would be paid $120 per year (although no privates were to be discharged or disciplined for failure to file reports). The bill was never reported out of the House Committee on Military Affairs.[90]

Long after payment of military pensions had become a sacrosanct tradition, attempts to broaden pension coverage were greeted with hostility or silence. A popular system of old-age pensions continued to be seen as a radical departure from American tradition, even though the nation's pension rolls numbered several hundred thousand more names than that of Great Britain with its universal coverage.[91]

---

86 Rubinow, Social Insurance, p. 408.

87 Rubinow, Quest for Security, p. 237.

88 Lubove, Struggle for Social Security, p. 24.

89 Fischer, Growing Old, p. 171.

90 Ibid.

91 Rubinow, Social Insurance, p. 404.

Impact of Early Private Sector
Retirement Plans

The practice of retirement was only beginning to be formalized in the late nineteenth century;[92] much of the idleness of older Americans continued to be a form of disguised, long-term unemployment and underemployment. The elderly increasingly existed "on the margin of society,"[93] while society increasingly questioned whether the aged were capable of making meaningful contributions.[94] Formal retirement plans could be a cost-effective way of dealing with the undesirable consequences of an aging work force. As economics professor Baldwin of Boston University argued in 1908,

---

92 Early in the nineteenth century, according to the linguistic evidence provided by Achenbaum, to "retire" merely meant to withdraw temporarily from public notice, something that could occur at any age. By late century it had a different meaning, its modern one, in Webster's American Dictionary (1880): "to cause to retire; specifically to designate as no longer qualified for active service." (Achenbaum, Old Age, p. 50.)

93 Fischer, Growing Old, p. 122.

94 Among the more extreme statements of this position is Sir William Osler's farewell address to John Hopkins University in 1905:

> "I have two fixed ideas well known to my friends....The first is the comparative uselessness of men above forty years of age....the world's history bears out the statement. Take the sum of human achievement in action, in science, in art, in literature--subtract the work of men above forty, and...we should practically be where we are today. It is difficult to name a great and far-reaching conquest of the mind which has not been given to the world by a man on whose back the sun was still shining. The effective, moving, vitalizing work of the world is done between the ages of twenty-five and forty years--these fifteen golden years of plenty, the anabolic or constructive period, in which there is always a balance in the mental bank and the credit is still good....
> My second fixed idea is the uselessness of men above sixty years of age, and the incalculable benefit would be in commercial, political and professional life, if, as a matter of course, men stopped work at this age." (Sir William Osler, in Scientific American 92 [1905], p. 243, cited by Fischer, Growing Old, pp. 140-41.)

Osler's extreme views on the comparative intellectual worthlessness of the elderly and middle-aged were widely published in the first three decades of this century. Osler-ism--based upon a liberal interpretation of Sir William's remarks--came to represent by the 1920s a credo of employment managers and efficiency experts, who assumed that youth was more efficient than age and who thus pursued policies which condemned older workers "to walk the plank wherever they made their appearance." (W.S. Hiatt, "Worth of Men Past Forty," New York Times, 2 October 1927; S.C. Martin, "Men Over 50," American Machinist 71 [September 1928]:404, cited by Barkin, The Older Worker, p. 87. See also N.E. Hildreth, "A Reaction Against Oslerism," American Machinist 47 [September 1917]:407-08.)

It is well understood nowadays that the practice of retaining on the pay-roll aged workers who can no longer render a fair equivalent for their wages is wasteful and demoralizing. The loss is twofold. In the first place, payment of full wages to workers who are no longer reasonably efficient, and in the second place, there is the direct loss entailed by the slow pace by the presence of worn-out veterans, and the consequent general demoralization of the service.[95]

Retirement plans for old or disabled workers had begun to be introduced in the late nineteenth century (the first industrial old-age pension plan in the U.S. was established by the American Express Company in 1875),[96] ostensibly out of recognition that the old, irregular methods of handling individual cases of superannuation had serious shortcomings, and the adoption of a formal system would be more practical and efficient.[97] Thus rationalization in getting rid of superannuated workers followed--uncertainly and with a lag--the rationalization of production and work roles which had to some extent created the superannuation problem in the first place.

The spread of industrial pension plans was frequently offered as proof that voluntary institutions were adequate to the task of providing for superannuated workers. In keeping with the ethos of voluntarism, early pensions were predominantly of the "formal-discretionary" variety, implying a moral rather than a legal obligation on the employer's part.[98] Industrial pensions were most importantly a mechanism of labor control. It was generally acknowledged by employers that such plans were expected to pay for themselves in the increased loyalty, stability, and efficiency they would engender in the workforce.[99]

It was hoped the existence of pensions would facilitate the removal of workers whose efficiency had begun to decline because of age or disability, and that younger employees would react favorably to this painless removal of obsolescent workers. Pensions seemed

---

95 F. Spencer Baldwin, "Retirement Systems for Municipal Employees," Annals of the American Academy of Political and Social Science 38 (1911):6. Although Baldwin favored mandatory retirement, recall his objection to pensions (in the Massachusetts Commission's report) on the grounds that they would weaken family structure.

96 Lescohier, Working Conditions, p. 386.

97 Catlin, The Labor Problem, pp. 186-87. The word "superannuation" also was undergoing a change of meaning. Whereas before the Civil War it had had reference to a person's being old relative to a station in life (such as a superannuated student at age 25), by late century the word had a clear connection with the elderly. Superannuate meant "to give pension to, on account of old age, or other infirmity; to make, declare, or prove obsolete or out of date; to become antiquated." (Achenbaum, Old Age, p. 50.)

98 Lubove, Struggle for Social Security, p. 128.

99 Ibid., pp. 129, 130; Robert W. Dunn, Company Unions, Employers' "Industrial Democracy" (New York: Vanguard Press, 1927), p. 4; Leo Wolman, "The Frontiers of Social Control," American Labor Legislation Review 17 (September 1927):239.

to promise young workers that they would be looked after in their later years if they would stick with the company and perform adequately. Also, pensioning off the old had the advantage of improving opportunities for promotion within the ranks. The prospect of a pension not only served to keep labor in the company's service, but gave workers "an incentive to good conduct" and would "decrease the liability to strike."[100]

A further inducement to the development of industrial pensions undoubtedly was the possibility that government would step in if voluntary institutions did not make an attempt to cope with the need. To American businessmen, the choice between private and public paternalism was no choice at all. Private institutions were efficient and maximized welfare; state pensions would "place a premium upon inefficiency and improvidence" and lead in the direction of socialism.[101]

However satisfactory pension schemes were perceived to be by employers, there were sound reasons why, particularly in their earliest form, they were universally condemned by labor organizations as not being in the best interests of the average wage-earner. Yet, one of the clearest statements of why they might be objectionable to workers came from a manager of the American Telephone and Telegraph Company when, in 1912, the firm was considering the combined pension and insurance scheme it ultimately adopted:

> Old-age pensions have always appeared to me to be something to talk about rather than an actually realized benefit....By many companies the hope is held out to the faithful employee that sometime in the dim future, if he is very faithful and escapes discharge for a long period of years, he may receive as a solace to his declining years an annuity representing a portion only of his yearly wage while actually employed. This promise to care for the indigent worker after his usefulness is past is not always realized, for frequently the usefulness of the man is found to have passed before the time set by the system for retirement. In this case he is discharged and nothing is done to make his old age free from hardship.[102]

With the exception of certain industries requiring specialized skills and possessing a permanent labor force, such as the railroads, most industrial workers had neither the job tenure nor the length of working lives to benefit from such pension schemes. The man who was already industrially old--superannuated--at 45 could hope for little comfort from a pension that might await him if he could hang on until 60 or 65 years of age.

Quite aside from the questionable likelihood that a pension would be forthcoming, or if received that it could meet subsistence needs, there were two ways in which retirement plans were actually harmful to older workers. First, there was the very serious effect such

---

100 Vanderlip, Insurance from an Employer's Perspective, pp. 462-64; Squier, Old Age Dependency, pp. 71 et seq., 120 et seq.

101 National Industrial Conference Board, Industrial Pensions in the United States (New York: National Industrial Conference Board, 1925), p. 2; Wolman, "Frontiers of Social Control," p. 239.

102 Theodore N. Vail of AT&T Company, in Literary Digest, August 31, 1912, p. 350, cited by Catlin, The Labor Problem, pp. 190-91.

plans had upon the independence and bargaining power of the workers. That which was a boon to employers--that pension systems presumably would promote good conduct and reduce workers' propensity to strike--was a loss to the workers of what little leverage they possessed. Unions recognized that the prospect of a pension could rob workers of their greatest bargaining chip, their mobility. And part of retirement plans' reason for being was that they discouraged collective bargaining to improve the pay and working conditions of all employees.[103]

Pension schemes served to divide the workforce into various segments so that workers' experiences and perceptions differed, in this case along age lines. This undermined the basis for labor's solidarity in furthering their class interests in opposition to employers. An older employee nearing pensionable age was unlikely to risk discharge by becoming involved in labor disputes. It was not uncommon for the worker's contract to state explicitly that should he leave work under strike orders, he would forfeit all claims to his pension. Some even stipulated that pensioners might be expected, if asked by the company, to lend their knowledge and experience in instances of labor unrest. The use of pensioners as strike-breakers was seriously considered at the time of the threatened railroad tie-up in 1916, and was actually attempted during the "outlaw" strike of railway workers early in 1920 and again by the Western Maryland Railroad in 1926. [104]

A second way in which the existence of pension plans harmed older workers relates to the mobility issue. Pension plans protected, at least nominally, those already on a company's payroll, but they created a heavy emphasis on considering only young employees when it came to filling vacancies. Not only could the employer benefit from the remoteness of the pension to the young worker, but the younger the new hire was, the greater the probability he would not still be with the company upon reaching pensionable age.[105] At the same time, the prospect of a pension to cover his old age effectively lowered the new worker's asking wage, because he felt somewhat relieved of the necessity to provide for the future. Pensions could, in effect, be considered nothing more than deferred wages the employee frequently never received.

---

103 The stringent continuous-service requirements for drawing a pension--in some cases as much as 30 years or more--if complied with, prevented wage earners from changing jobs to better themselves. (Lescohier, Working Conditions, p. 389.) Workers referred to the employer-managed welfare plans as "company unions" because they had little or no relationship to labor organizations and were designed to produce results profitable to the company. (Dunn, Company Unions, pp. 2-4.)

104 Catlin, The Labor Problem, pp. 191-92; Epstein, Facing Old Age, pp. 150-51.

105 Some pension plans did not specify a definite period of service to qualify for a pension, but all of these established definite retirement ages, and length of service was controlled by the employment offices, which simply refrained from hiring persons beyond a certain age. Usually this was 40 years and often as low as 30. Thus "private pension plans led almost inevitably to employment 'dead-lines,'" and it was questionable "whether the pensions were worth enough to the few who drew them to balance the denial of employment opportunity to the many who had passed the 'dead-line.'" (Lescohier, Working Conditions, p. 389.)

This was, in fact, how they were viewed by organized labor. The deferred wage theory was that pensions represented a foregone increase in wages workers would have received in the absence of a pension program. Unions stressed that since employees had no contractual rights in the pension fund, pensions represented only conditional wages; it was "deferred" only if stringent (and company-set) terms were fulfilled.[106] Furthermore, besides weakening the efforts of workers' organizations,[107] most discretionary industrial pension funds were established with a shocking disregard for actuarial considerations,[108] they carried the "stigma of charity,"[109] and they limited workers' economic mobility.

Above all, industrial pensions did little to improve the economic security of superannuated workers. As late as 1932, only 15 percent of American workers were covered, and these were concentrated in only a few industries.[110] Pension benefits were far too meager to prevent dependency, averaging a fraction of workers' final pay.[111]

So long as pensions were an expression of voluntarism, they could be reduced or withdrawn, or made more difficult to qualify for, at the employer's discretion. Finally, industrial pensions appear not even to have accomplished managerial objectives of increased worker loyalty and efficiency, stable workforces, and industrial harmony. Unions were apathetic if not hostile to industrial pensions, and workers resented the autocratic and

---

106 Albert deRoode, "Pensions as Wages," American Economic Review 3 (June 1913):287. See also Luther Conant, Jr., A Critical Analysis of Industrial Pension Systems (New York: Macmillan Co., 1922), p. 91.

107 Abraham Epstein, The Problem of Old Age Pensions in Industry: An Up-to-Date Summary of the Facts and Figures Developed in the Further Study of Old Age Pensions (Harrisburg: Pennsylvania Old Age Pension Commission, 1926), p. 33; Merchants Association of New York, Industrial Pensions: Report of the Special Committee on Industrial Pensions and Report of a Survey of Industrial Pension Systems by the Industrial Bureau (New York: Merchants Association of New York, 1920), p. 14.

108 Epstein, ibid., p. 43; National Industrial Conference Board, Industrial Pensions in the United States (New York: National Industrial Conference Board, 1925), p. 101.

109 Epstein, ibid., p. 22.

110 The vast majority, almost 80 percent, were in railroads, public utilities, and the metal industries. (Lubove, Struggle for Social Security, pp. 128-29.) As late as 1929, over 82 percent of beneficiaries of public and private pension plans were receiving war-related survivor and disability pensions, accounting for 80 percent of all money distributed. (U.S. Bureau of Labor Statistics, Care of Aged Persons in the United States, pp. 2-3.)

111 Murray Webb Latimer, Industrial Pensions in the United States and Canada (New York: Industrial Relations Counselors, Inc., 1932), p. 895.

paternalistic way they were managed.[112] Industrial pensions exemplified the futility of attempting to alter market outcomes via exclusive reliance on the welfare goals and programs of capitalist institutions.

Conclusion

It has been shown that in the 1860-1920 period the problem of economic super-annuation and old-age dependency was becoming a significant social and political problem. There was growing evidence that older individuals were being separated by revolutionary institutional change from meaningful economic roles, and that industrial wage-earners as a group were unable to provide for an indefinite and unknowable period of nonproductive life. The rising incidence of elderly poverty and dependency was a mute challenge to the contention that the United States had the highest and most rapidly rising standard of living in world history. The conditions of industrial capitalism were incompatible with an exclusive reliance on voluntary institutions, yet Americans clung stubbornly to the ethic of individual responsibility and self-sufficiency and to the view that the family and charitable institutions should be the mainstay of the elderly, poor, and disabled.

Social Darwinism in particular had tremendous appeal in a laissez-faire economic system which so clearly was producing an underclass. In the U.S. there existed neither a feudal tradition of noblesse oblige nor an organized and empowered constituency to atten-uate the distress of those who could not meet the pace and benefit from the opportunities for enrichment. Older Americans were a rising proportion of the victims of industrial progress throughout the decades between 1860 and 1920; and although, by the turn of the century, commissions were coming into being to study the problem of old-age dependency, their findings largely endorsed the status quo or fell on deaf ears.

Industrial pensions were a typically American response to the superannuated worker issue, but they were inadequate. Unilateral, voluntary, underfunded, and poorly admin-istered, they were essentially a technique of labor-cost control rather than a serious attempt to provide economic security in retirement. Perhaps the most important contribution of the industrial pension movement was the implicit testimony it gave to the need for collective action to address old-age dependency. Even so, no meaningful start was made in this direction until 1935, when the economy's poor performance was threatening the well-being of everyone; and no substantial inroads would be made against elderly poverty until the 1960s.

---

112 Edward S. Cowdrick, Pensions: A Problem of Management (New York: American Management Association, 1928), pp. 16-17; Conant, Critical Analysis of Industrial Pension Systems, p. 18.

CHAPTER 8

CONCLUSION

I have lived some thirty years on this planet, and I have yet
to hear the first syllable of valuable or even earnest advice
from my seniors. They have told me nothing and probably
cannot teach me anything.

- Henry David Thoreau

Nature abhors the old, and old age is the only disease;
all others run into this one. We call it many names--
fever, intemperence, insanity, stupidity and crime;
they are all forms of old age; they are rest, conser-
vatism, appropriation, inertia; not newness, not the
way onward....

- Ralph Waldo Emerson

The period between 1860 and 1920 was one of far-reaching changes in the status
of older Americans, arising from a revolution in how people made their livings. This study
has examined several interrelated aspects of American industrial development in these years
that had especially profound effects on the socioeconomic circumstances of middle-aged
and older workers. The primary cause of the declining labor force participation of older
Americans in this period was grounded in the maturation of capitalism and the very rapid
pace of technological change generated by firms' desire to minimize the use of costly labor
skills.

This dynamism both mirrored and reinforced several other aspects of American life
during this period that also contributed to diminished socioeconomic circumstances for older
people. Capitalist technology revolutionized labor requirements in farming, transportation
and communication patterns, methods of production, skill requirements for industrial labor,
living patterns, average firm size, and the managerial and administrative practices of capitalist enterprises.

It has been demonstrated that institutional barriers to the employment of older
workers began to surface in the United states from about the time of the Civil War, as the
economy entered its industrial phase. The nature of the industrial transformation gave rise
to a new phenomenon, age discrimination directed against the old and near-old. In contrast
with the situation in colonial America and the early nationhood period, when older Americans had been looked to for economic and political leadership; and when any discrimination
on age grounds was directed against younger generations; advancing years became a negative in the years bracketing the Civil War and World War One. Age began to join race,
sex, and class as an identifier of people's prospects for labor force participation and economic success.

These decades saw the rise to prominence of the corporate form of capitalist enterprise, as well as the separation of ownership from control within the nation's largest, most technologically-dynamic firms. Furthermore, the Civil War itself precipitated some of the transformations that enabled industrialization to occur in the manner it did. The war effort called forth a new scale of organization, as personnel and supplies were required to be moved about rapidly and in large numbers. The lessons learned out of harsh necessity were subsequently put to profitable peacetime use; many of the earliest giant corporations were outgrowths of Civil War government contracts.

The war reinforced the priority of a transcontinental rail system, with important ramifications for the rate at which national markets, and hence national businesses, were able to develop. Before 1860, the U.S. was essentially agrarian in its economic base, rural in its living patterns, primarily reliant on self-employment and small-scale production, relatively technologically static, and oriented toward the family as the provider for those in their nonproducing years. Older individuals were likely to possess valued experience and skills requiring long gestastion. Ownership of land, particularly farm land, was the basis of power, prestige, and economic security; and it was disproportionately in the hands of people of middle age and beyond. The defeat of the South in the Civil War, and the effective ending of the plantation system conveyed the lesson that the nation's economy could not remain rooted in agricultural production and agrarian values. The future lay with the maturing capitalist industry of the north east and midwest.

By 1920, the nation had become predominantly industrial and urban, and its labor force, having been separated from ownership of the means of production, was preponderantly engaged in wage-work in the service of others, frequently absentee owners of corporations. The impacts of technology and labor specialization had greatly reduced the skill level in most production jobs. Although the family remained the most important safety net for the unemployed and the unemployable, the family's fortunes were increasingly beyond the immediate control of individual members, as wage-labor in large establishments supplanted self-employment and small-scale production for the majority of working Americans.

The growing severity of the problem of elderly dependency is revealed by the fact that two-thirds of the states by 1920 had enacted legislation requiring families to be the source of support for their aged dependents, disregarding the evidence that most were financially unable to fulfill this role except at great sacrifice by the younger generations. The growth of industry and cities, the decline in agriculture's importance, and the spread of the corporate form of business organization had all contributed to a new concept of property, one bearing little relation to the earlier land-based valuation of property which had favored the status of older Americans.

Among the background forces which paved the way for the economy's industrialization were several developments whose impact upon older Americans was more profound than for the rest of the population. The first of these was the relative decline in the importance of agriculture to the nation's economic vitality, and the replacement of family farms and small firms by manufacturing, finance, transportation, and commerce as the sources of economic growth and prosperity. A system of family agriculture and petty capitalist firms had maximized the productive contribution people could continue to make as they grew older. In these endeavors, retirement from the world of work could proceed gradually, in accordance with individual strength and abilities. With work largely carried out in the home or adjacent shop, the older generation could gradually turn duties over to the younger ones, who benefited from the proximity to the time-tested experience of their seniors. If the older individual was not the firm/farm owner, he was likely to be treated more as family than employee, and accommodations could readily be made for any diminished capacities with age.

Westward migration, which contributed to an oversupply of agricultural labor, was facilitated by the establishment of the transcontinental railroad and by improved communications, both of which were outgrowths of the Civil War. As transportation became more reliable and rapid, the relevant marketplace for goods, services, and labor was vastly expanded; regional market characteristics thus became less distinctive as more uniform supply and demand characteristics began to predominate for productive inputs and finished goods. Government policies such as the Homestead Act further encouraged the movement of population, but the primary beneficiaries were not individuals and families but rather the railroad interests, speculators, and well-placed entrepreneurs.

Both the declining importance of agriculture (hastened by the agricultural overproduction encouraged by homesteading) and the improvements in transportation reinforced Americans' historically unique degree of geographical mobility. The demographic counterpart of a rising share of industrial production in the national product was the move to cities. In 1860, fewer than one American in five lived in a town or city larger than 2,500 population; by 1920, more than half lived in cities.

The rise of industry and increasing urbanization had the greatest effects upon the old and near-old. Once people ceased being able to control the terms of their labor, they were forced to confront the employment opportunites afforded by increasingly impersonal capitalist enterprises. Corporate concerns were not geared to the needs or the capabilities of individuals; they were established with the interests of investors and the perpetuity of the enterprise foremost in mind. In the cities, living quarters were smaller, causing the fragmentation of the extended family unit. The cost of living rose, leading to smaller families and a greater concern for the life chances of the young. And family tensions undoubtedly increased as the career paths of the younger generations diverged from the experiences of their elders.

Widespread immigration was encouraged by governments at all levels, to overcome the nation's historic labor scarcity. Immigration not only hastened the trend to urbanization (because most immigrants located in cities, chosen by friends and family who had migrated earlier), but it reinforced the deskilling of labor to accommodate diverse ethnic and linguistic backgrounds. By the end of the nineteenth century, the source of the majority of immigrants was southern and eastern Europe, where industrial skill levels were below those of earlier Americans. As a result, skill-levelling became an important determinant of the success of large capitalist firms seeking to make use of this diverse new labor pool.

Thus, two major interrelated changes in economic life created the circumstances that enabled the rapid technological changes leading to the reduced security of employment for all workers, and to the devaluation of older workers in particular. The first was the spread of market relationships, an outgrowth of technology propelled by Civil War exigencies and reinforced by the requirement of reducing production costs by minimizing the contribution made by costly labor. This led to the growing importance of regional and national markets at the expense of locally-oriented economic activity.

The second was the conversion of artisans, craftsmen, and independent producers to wage-labor status, and their attendant loss of control over the hours and the terms of work. These twin phenomena, a rapidly changing industrial structure and a labor force increasingly

192

dependent upon a wage contract for its means of subsistence, were the keys to the diminished economic circumstances of older Americans between 1860 and 1920.

The economy's industrialization entailed a significant growth in the average size of business establishments, a trend which had primarily a technological imperative. The high cost of scarce capital and its rapid obsolescence required efficient use of capital. This in turn made a large volume of output necessary to achieve scale economies, particularly since rapid technological change meant that capital had to be scrapped well before it had physically worn out. In addition, technological dynamism generated the imperative for keeping plant and equipment operating as fast and as long as possible. This pace put many production tasks beyond the abilities of workers whose stamina and strength might be waning, and it made many old before their time.

Another aspect of the ongoing revolution in technology was the need to establish new organizational principles within the capitalist firm. This organizational imperative for growth in firm size was more subtle than the directly technological motive, but it was no less vital. As management became more important as a separate factor of production, its assumption of the decision-making responsibilities that had once resided with the individual producers (the "head-work" or thinking roles) caused increased reliance upon all-purpose rules of thumb in establishing work procedures, as well as in filling and vacating jobs. The goal was to separate thought from action, and a natural consequence was a diminished importance given to the experience and time-tested judgment that older, more established workers could contribute to production. The scientific management movement began to be important in the early years of the twentieth century as a result of the business community's interest in clarifying and coordinating procedures to minimize administrative errors, duplication, and conflicting production goals.

Because the skill content of most jobs was being redefined by trends in technological innovation and the division of labor, capitalist firms increasingly determined the value of various labor force characteristics. Rapid changes in production technologies meant that individual forms of acquired skill were of dwindling importance to the overall success of a productive enterprise. Training became an internal firm function with the growing homogeneity of productive inputs, and the returns to skills with a long gestation period were accordingly reduced.

The growing size of firms, mandated by the need to make use of expensive technology and by cutthroat competition, resulted in a premium being given to workers' ability to follow orders and demonstrate physical strength. Industry in the United States became noted for its productive rigor, its rapid pace and long hours of work. Consequently, one of the most desirable traits of a prospective laborer was his relative youthfulness--both for physical reasons of general health and stamina, and because younger workers were more apt to be amenable to new methods and could be paid lower wages. Rapid technological change created the conditions for these criteria of employment, and strenuously competitive conditions encouraged their renewed application. Hence, age discrimination in employment began to be introduced into the economic system through the management practices of the largest firms in the nation's most centralized and fastest-growing industries.

Although older people's representation in the population was rising, their labor force participation rates were falling as they were forced out of jobs. The emphasis in production on quickness, alertness, and willingness to follow instructions without question led inexorably to a preference by employers for younger workers. By the early 1900s, men found it difficult to secure employment at ages as low as 35 or 40; for women it was younger still. Middle-aged and older workers were increasingly found in occupations that had been relatively unaffected by the trends in technology, division of labor, and deskilling. These tended to be jobs of increasingly marginal relevance to the economy, in the shrinking industries of the time.

Because experience no longer counted for as much in the labor market, and with the nation's labor scarcity largely overcome by immigration, older workers were becoming expendable, a factor of production to be scrapped, much as capital equipment was--not because it wasn't functional, but because it wasn't adequately profitable. Thus, older Americans in the years between 1860 and 1920 became another instance of an irrationality of capitalism, wasting resources that are, by definition, scarce.

Unfortunately for those who confronted ageist employment practices in this period, few options were available. Families often could not or would not provide support despite legal requirements to do so. Poorhouses were a last-resort refuge increasingly occupied by elderly inhabitants. Private sector pensions were uncommon, underfunded, and capriciously administered. Yet the power of laissez-faire doctrine prevailed in the face of compelling evidence of older Americans' rising unemployment, poverty, and dependency. The gospel of the Social Darwinists--the myth of the self-made man, pursuit of the success ethic, and the belief that public pensions would undermine the average individual's capacity for hard work and thrift--proved more powerful than the argument of the "New Economists" and social reformers who insisted that modification of market outcomes could be compatible with capitalist enterprise.

Some Contemporary Concerns

The effects are still with us of the economic and social transformations that replaced a family-centered rural society with an organization-centered urban society, for the fundamental problem of today's older workers is little different than when industrialization got underway, and that is, occupational obsolescence. Obsolescence of skills, training, and education is the cost of economic progress. A century ago the shift from an agriculturally-based to a manufacturing-based economy created a disjuncture between skills supplied and skills demanded.

At any given moment older workers were less equipped than younger ones to cope with changing job requirements, because older workers embodied the patterns of training, education, and socialization of a generation or two earlier. Today the shift is well underway from manufacturing to an information/services economy, and among those being most seriously affected are middle-aged and older workers. Because their skills are often industry-specific and not readily transferrable, these individuals face the prospect of permanent unemployment or underemployment, or early retirement.

This sort of massive realignment of industries and occupations was unknown prior to the mid-nineteenth century, when the idea of continuous economic growth fueled by mechanization and the division of labor began to be widely accepted. A relative devaluation of older workers' skills and experience in most jobs is more readily accepted today (though no more acceptable), but there is implicit in this assessment a devaluation of the aged and near-aged as human beings. U.S. society is characterized by instrumentalism and is still dominated by the Protestant work ethic, so that to be retired or nearing retirement (whether it is desired or not) is to be relegated to society's margins.

194

It is expected that people reaching the age of 65, or much younger in many instances, will move out of established, recognized positions into roles that are poorly-defined, conditional, and generally lacking in prestige. A rapidly growing number of people are surviving middle age to face the prospect of living for many years in a society that has few meaningful roles for its older citizens. Although financial arrangements for retirement or widowhood have enabled many older people to live far better than would have been possible 50 years ago, because they are not engaged in remunerative work they remain socially isolated, ghettoized, and often ignored.

The productivity-based valuation of human worth not only dictates the division of national income among productive factors but it also strongly influences how people are treated at each stage of the life cycle. Age has become as significant as race, sex, or class in identifying and rewarding members of U.S. society. As a result of ageism and age stratification, the elderly have acquired many of the characteristics of a minority group; on the free labor market, outside of the largest firms offering their employees substantial job security, older workers are in the traditionally marginal position of blacks, a secondary labor force. They are the last hired and first fired, and whether and when they work is primarily dependent on the overall scarcity or abundance of labor.

Until very recently, American business has been almost exclusively concerned with catering to the needs and desires of the young, both in terms of the markets to which it targets its products and in its employment practices. Fears of joblessness on the part of older workers have been attenuated, to be sure, by the spread of private pensions and improved adequacy of Social Security benefits on the one hand, and by anti-discrimination legislation and the existence of seniority rules in the unionized trades on the other. But age discrimination practices can be notoriously subtle, and laws against them are difficult to enforce because they fly in the face of a durable popular value that youth is superior to age. And seniority is no longer a guarantee for older workers that their jobs are secure. Older workers were one of the groups most vulnerable to dismissal in the prolonged stagflation of the Western economies in the 1980s. Although seniority may offer protection to older workers when an individual firm undergoes contraction, it is of little value when entire industries are undergoing substantial restructuring, as in recent years.

The discouraged worker syndrome seems to be prevalent among older job-losers. A relatively high rate of nonparticipation in the labor force begins to appear at about 45 years of age. Older workers who lose their jobs remain unemployed longer than younger unemployed persons, and they frequently drop out of the labor force rather than continue to face rejection. It is difficult to assess how much of the growth of early retirement is due to discouragement or poor health, and how much to the general improvement in financial support for retirement. Although a large proportion of retirees cite failing health as the reason they stopped working (including those compulsorily retired), some analysts suggest this may be a face-saving device; that being turned out to pasture is experienced by the individual as shameful, despite the practice having become institutionalized, and it is easier to embrace the sick role than to admit that one is simply superfluous.

As to the adequacy of retirement income as an inducement to early retirement, studies suggest many early retirees lack pension coverage beyond Social Security, and most involuntary early retirees (job-losers and those in poor health) experience a dramatic cut in income. Many who retire find themselves financially strapped (even those with private pensions, which are in only rare instances adjusted for inflation) and subsequently seek to re-enter the labor force. They then may discover their retirement status has added to their undesirable labor market characteristics so that finding a job commensurate with their experience is nearly impossible.

Some manpower experts anticipate little near-term improvement for older workers in an economic climate characterized by mass displacements of entire workforces. The rapid pace of technological change and shifting market trends--a changing demography and composition of demand, the rise of Third World manufacturing, capital hypermobility and the globalization of production, growing U.S. dependence on trade, and competition from Western Europe and Japan--promise to be with us for some time. In such circumstances, employment will depend more than ever on the level and relevance of a worker's formal training rather than on experience. In the context of today's knowledge explosion, the information gap can be great even between the young and the early middle-aged This suggests periodic lifelong training may be necessary to prevent a growing convergence of age and class stratification as education increasingly becomes a distinguishing attribute of socioeconomic status.

Yet most firms are reluctant to invest in training older workers, viewing training for the young as having a greater pay-off. This situation may change as employers confront the coming labor shortage, and as they become persuaded this is irrational by observing older workers' job performance. Older workers stay on the job longer, have fewer workplace accidents, and take less time off than do younger workers--factors that affect productivity and the corporate bottom line.

In the public policy realm, younger groups who hold the power have tended to tie help for the aged to need and to political weight, rather than to what is ethical. In a period of slow or no growth, the funds allocated to the elderly are more clearly perceived as reducing the monies available for other programs, and this can give rise to intergenerational tensions and reinforce ageist biases. This has led some analysts to suggest that a backlash against the elderly may be developing as they command an increasing share of resources in an era of constrained growth, and as the working population comes to appreciate the real cost of supporting a growing proportion of dependent older persons.

Ironically--and this has been equally true of attempts to improve the economic, social, and political prospects of blacks, women, hispanics, and other groups that suffer discrimination--the legislative process itself and the movements that precede and accompany it call attention to those with minority status. When these groups are singled out for special treatment, majorities come to view them as requiring unique assistance to make it in the world, and the result can be an increase in stereotyping, prejudice, and discrimination.

Nowhere are the ambiguities of age relations and the precariousness of the elderly's economic situation more noticeable than in the area of Social Security. Economic theory cannot answer the question of appropriate levels of income maintenance for those past their producing years, but the role played by economic ideology cannot be overlooked. Those who decry the long-term unsoundness of Social Security point out that it was not intended to be the comprehensive retirement insurance program it has become; that it was enacted to provide partial relief to a segment of the population suffering most acutely from the Great Depression. On the other side are those who point to the impressive reductions in elderly poverty with rising benefit levels, as evidence of how an American social insurance scheme can succeed.

The entire debate, however, is misleading in its premise and myopic in its focus. Social Security payments are the sole source of income for a substantial minority of beneficiaries, and for the majority they mean the difference between economic sufficiency and poverty. Additionally, they reduce the burden on younger generations for support of their elders. The overwhelming importance of Social Security in the lives of nearly 39 million citizens--one in seven--makes it essential that policies be consistent, that they not be subject to the forces of political expediency, and that changes in the methods of finan-cing the system and distributing its benefits not result in sudden and dramatic changes of direction. Resort to short-run formula-tinkering as a means of easing a budget crunch is akin to shooting ones own troops because supplies are running low.

It is regrettable that so much of aging policy rests on this kind of myopic and short-term perspective, because it can lead to results that are worse than doing nothing. Given what is today known with certainty about our demographic future, short-term fixes for age-related economic problems are inappropriate in the extreme. It is in the nature of a society whose average age is rapidly increasing to be continually faced with the dilemma of providing for its senescent members. Continued population aging in the future will surely increase the need for an understanding of the myths and realities of the economics of aging at the individual and societal level.

Difficult decisions will have to be made about age-related living standards, employ-ment and training policies, and lifetime allocations of work and leisure. These decisions will demand great foresight and planning within our major economic, political, and social institutions. Foresight cannot be grounded only in the present; it must also be informed by a sense of the past. This book has sought to trace the origins of older Americans' labor market difficulties from the time when these began to have serious, widespread implications for their ability to support themselves and to participate in what is still the most cherished American value, remunerative work. Through understanding the historic interplay between the functioning of economic institutions and the expression of social/ political values, it is possible to distinguish between what might be unique about the present circumstances of the elderly, and what is fundamentally a reflection of trends that are rooted in the nation's emergence as an industrial power.

The modern American economy has tended to exclude older people from meaningful productive roles. Whether this continues depends upon many factors--the pace of occupa-tional change, rates of economic growth, activism by and on behalf of the elderly, immi-gration policy, falling birth and death rates that raise the elderly dependency ratio, and so forth. But it also depends upon political will and a clear understanding of the stake all Americans have in the treatment of their future selves. It is hoped that awareness of the economic history of old age will contribute to such understanding.

BIBLIOGRAPHY

Achenbaum, W. Andrew. "The Obsolesence of Old Age in America." Journal of Social History 8 (Fall 1974):48-62.

Achenbaum, W. Andrew. Old Age in the New Land: The American Experience Since 1790. Baltimore: Johns Hopkins University Press, 1978.

Achenbaum, W. Andrew, and Peter N. Stearns. "Old Age and Modernization." The Gerontologist 18 (June 1978):307-12.

Anderson, Barbara, and Margaret Clark. Culture and Aging. Springfield, Ill.: Charles C. Thomas, 1967.

Atkinson, Edward. "Common Sense Applied to the Tariff Question." Popular Science Monthly 37 (September 1890):593-96.

Averitt, Robert T. The Dual Economy: The Dynamics of American Industry Structure. New York: W.W. Norton, 1968.

Bailey, L.H., ed. Cyclopedia of American Agriculture. New York: Macmillan Co., 1907-1909.

Baker, Elizabeth F. Displacement of Men by Machines: Effects of Technological Change in Commercial Printing. New York: Columbia University Press, 1933.

Baldwin, F. Spencer. "Old Age Pension Schemes: A Criticism and a Program." Quarterly Journal of Economics 24 (August 1910):713-42.

Baldwin, F. Spencer. "Old Age Insurance." American Labor Legislation Review 3 (June 1913):202-212.

Barkin, Solomon. The Older Worker in Industry: A Study of New York State Manufacturing Industries. Albany: J.B. Lyon for the New York State Commission on Old Age Security, 1933.

Barron, Milton. The Aging American: An Introduction to Social Gerontology and Geriatrics. New York: Thomas Y. Crowell Co., 1962.

Beard, George M. Legal Responsibility in Old Age, Based on Researches into the Relationship of Age to Work. New York: Russells', 1874.

Bennett, Ruth, and Judith Eckman. "Attitudes Toward Aging: A Critical Examination of Recent Literature and Implications for Future Research." The Psychology of Adult Development and Aging. Edited by Carl Eisdorfer and M. Powell Lawton. Washington, D.C.: American Psychological Association, 1973.

Berg, Ivar. Education and Jobs: The Great Training Robbery. New York: Praeger, 1970.

Beveridge, William H. Unemployment: A Problem of Industry. London: Longmans, Green and Co., 1909.

Binstock, Robert H. "Aging and the Future of American Politics." The Annals of the American Academy of Political and Social Science (1974):199-212.

Binstock, Robert H., and Ethel Shanas, eds. Handbook of Aging and the Social Sciences. New York: Van Nostrand Reinhold, 1977.

Blau, Zena Smith. Old Age in a Changing Society. New York: New Viewpoints, 1973.

Bliss, William Dwight Porter. "Old Age Pensions." The Encyclopedia of Social Reform. Edited by William D.P. Bliss. New York: Funk and Wagnalls, Co., 1897.

Bolen, George L. Getting a Living: The Problem of Wealth and Poverty--Of Profits, Wages and Trade Unionism. New York: Macmillan Co., 1903.

Bowles, Samuel. "The Integration of Higher Education into the Wage Labor System." The Review of Radical Political Economics 6 (Spring 1974):100-33.

Brady, Dorothy S., ed. Output, Employment and Productivity in the U.S. After 1800. New York: National Bureau of Economic Research, 1966.

Brandeis, Elizabeth. Labor Legislation. Vol. III of History of Labor in the United States, 1896-1932. Edited by John R. Commons et al. New York: Macmillan Co., 1935.

Braverman, Harry. Labor and Monopoly Capital: The Degradation of Work in the Twentieth Century. New York: Monthly Review Press, 1974.

Brennan, Michael, Philip Taft, and Mark P. Schupack. The Economics of Age. New York: W.W. Norton and Co., 1967.

Bridenbaugh, Carl. Cities in the Wilderness. New York: Alfred A. Knopf, 1938.

Brissenden, Paul F., and Emil Frankel. Labor Turnover in Industry. New York: Macmillan Co., 1922.

Brown, Mary Willcox. The Development of Thrift. New York: Macmillan Co., 1900.

Brown, Richard D. Modernization, The Transformation of American Life. New York: Hill and Wang, 1976.

Bullock, Charles J. Selected Readings in Public Finance. Boston: Ginn and Co., 1906.

Burgess, Ernest W., ed. Aging in Western Societies. Chicago: University of Chicago Press, 1960.

Burkhauser, Richard V., and G.S. Tolley. "Older Americans and Market Work." The Gerontologist 18 (October 1978):449-53.

Burns, Arthur. Production Trends in the United States Since 1870. New York: National Bureau of Economic Research, 1934.

Butler, Elizabeth B. Women and the Trades: Pittsburgh, 1907-1908. New York: Russell Sage Foundation, 1911.

Butler, Robert N. Why Survive? Being Old in America. New York: Harper and Row, 1975.

Carp, Frances M., ed. Retirement. New York: Human Sciences Press, 1972.

Catlin, Warren B. The Labor Problem in the United States and Great Britain. Revised ed. New York: Harper and Bros., 1935.

Chandler, Alfred D. Jr. Strategy and Structure: Chapters in the History of the Industrial Enterprise. Cambridge: Harvard University Press, 1962.

Chandler, Alfred D. Jr., Stuart Bruchey, and Louis Galambos, eds. The Changing Economic Order: Readings in American Business and Economic History. New York: Harcourt, Brace and World, 1968.

Chapin, Robert C. The Standard of Life in New York City. New York: Russell Sage Foundation, 1909.

Chenery, William L. Industry and Human Welfare. New York: Macmillan Co., 1922.

Chicago, Mayor's Commission on Unemployment. Report. Chicago: Cameron, Amberg Co., March 1914.

Clague, Ewan, Walter J. Couper, and E. Wight Backke. After the Shutdown. New Haven: Yale University Institute of Human Relations, 1934.

Clague, Ewan, Balraj Palli, and Leo Kramer. The Aging Worker and the Union: Employment and Retirement of Middle-Aged and Older Workers. New York: Praeger, 1971.

Clark, Margaret. Culture and Aging: An Anthropological Study of Older Americans. California: Langley Porter Neuropsychiatric Institute, 1967.

Clark, Robert, Juanita Kreps, and Joseph Spengler. "Economics of Aging: A Survey." Journal of Economic Literature 16 (September 1978):919-62.

Clark, Victor S. History of Manufactures in the United States. 3 vols. Reprint ed. New York: Peter Smith, 1948. Vo. 2: 1860-1893, and Vol. 3: 1893-1928.

Cochran, Thomas C., and Thomas B. Brewer, eds. Views of American Economic Growth, 2 vols. New York: McGraw-Hill Book Co., 1966. Vol. 2: The Industrial Era.

Cohen, Stephen Z., and Bruce Michael Gans. The Other Generation Gap: The Middle-Aged and Their Aging Parents. Chicago: Follett, 1978.

Commager, Henry Steele. The American Mind. An Interpretation of American Thought and Character Since the 1880s. New Haven: Yale University Press, 1952.

Commons, John R., David L. Saposs, Helen L. Sumner, E.B. Mittelman, H.E. Hoagland, John B. Andrews, and Selig Perlman, eds. History of Labor in the United States, 1896-1932, 4 vols. New York: Macmillan Co., 1935. Vol. 3: Working Conditions, by Don D. Lescohier, and Labor Legislation, by Elizabeth Brandeis.

Commons, John R. "Labor Conditions in Meatpacking and the Recent Strike." Quarterly Journal of Economics 19 (November 1904):1-32.

Commons, John R. Race and Immigrants in America. New York: Macmillan Co., 1907.

Commons, John R. "The Right to Work." Arena 21 (February 1899):131-42.

Commons, John R. Trade Unionism and Labor Problems. New York: Ginn and Co., 1905.

Conant, Luther Jr. A Critical Analysis of Industrial Pension Systems. New York: Macmillan Co., 1922.

Conway, Moncure D., ed. The Writings of Thomas Paine. 4 vols. New York: AMS Press, Inc., 1967.

Copley, F.B. Frederick W. Taylor, Father of Scientific Management. New York: Harper and Bros, 1923.

Corson, John J., and John W. McConnell. Economic Needs of Older People. New York: Twentieth Century Fund, 1956.

Cottrell, Fred. "The Technological and Societal Basis of Aging." Handbook of Social Gerontology. Edited by Clark Tibbits. Chicago: University of Chicago Press, 1960.

Cowdrick, Edward S. Pensions: A Problem of Management. New York: American Management Association, 1928.

Cowgill, Donald O., and Lowell D. Holmes, eds. Aging and Modernization. New York: Appleton-Century-Crofts, 1972.

Cumming, Elaine, and William E. Henry. Growing Old, The Process of Disengagement. New York: Basic Books, 1961.

Curtin, Sharon. "Aging in the Land of the Young." Atlantic Monthly 230 (July 1972):68-78.

Cutler, Neil. "Population Dynamics and the Graying of America." Urban and Social Change Review 10 (Summer 1977):2-5.

Davis, Lance E., and John Legler. "The Government in the American Economy, 1815-1902: A Quantitative Study." Journal of Economic History 26 (December 1966):514-52.

Derber, Milton. The Aged in Society. New York: Industrial Relations Research Association, 1950.

De Roode, Albert. "Pensions as Wages." American Economic Review 3 (June 1913):287-95.

Devine, Edward T. Misery and Its Causes. New York: Macmillan and Co., 1909.

Dewey, Davis R. "Irregularity of Employment." Publications of the American Economic Association, no. 9 (1894), pp. 53-67.

DiBacco, Thomas B. "Viewpoint." American Magazine (July/August 1979):19-20.

Dorfman, Joseph. The Economic Mind in American Civilization. 3 vols. New York: The Viking Press, 1949. Vol. 3: 1865-1918.

Dorr, Caroline J., and Marian G. Spenser, eds. Understanding Aging: A Multidisciplinary Approach. New York: Appleton-Century-Crofts, 1975.

Douglas, Paul H. Real Wages in the United States, 1890-1926. Boston: Houghton-Mifflin, 1930.

Douglas, Paul H., and Aaron Director. The Problem of Unemployment. New York: Macmillan Co., 1931.

Downey, Sheridan. Pensions or Penury? New York: Harper and Bros., 1939.

Dublin, Louis I., and Robert J. Vane, Jr. "Shifting of Occupations among Wage Earners as Determined by Occupational Histories of Industrial Policyholders." Monthly Labor Review 18 (April 1924):732-40.

Duckles, Margaret, Robert Duckles, and Michael Maccoby. "The Process of Change at Bolivar." Journal of Applied Behavioral Sciences 13 (Summer 1977):387-99.

Ducoff, Louis J., and Margaret Jarman Hagood. Labor Force Definition and Measurement. New York: Social Science Research Council, 1947.

Dunn, Robert W. Company Unions, Employers' "Industrial Democracy". New York: Vanguard Press, 1927.

Durand, John D. The Labor Force in the United States, 1890-1960. New York: Social Science Research Council, 1948.

Eckler, A. Ross. "A Measure of the Severity of Depressions, 1873-1932." Review of Economic Statistics 15 (May 1933):75-81.

Edwards, Richard C. Contested Terrain: The Transformation of the Workplace in the Twentieth Century. New York: Basic Books, 1979.

Ellis, David M. "Comments on 'The Railroad Land Grant Legend in American History Texts.'" Mississippi Valley Historical Review 32 (March 1946):557-63.

Ely, Richard T. Evolution of Industrial Society. New York: Macmillan Co., 1903.

Ely, Richard T. The Labor Movement in America. New York: Thomas Y. Crowell and Co., 1886.

Emerick, C.F. "An Analysis of Agricultural Discontent in the United States. I." Political Science Quarterly 11 (September 1896):601-39.

Engels, Friedrich. The Housing Question (1872) in Marx-Engels Selected Works. 5th ed. 2 vols. Moscow: Foreign Language Press, 1962.

Epstein, Abraham. The Challenge of the Aged. New York: Vanguard Press, 1928.

Epstein, Abraham. Facing Old Age: A Study of Old Age Dependency in the U.S. and Old Age Pensions. New York: Alfred A. Knopf, 1922.

Epstein, Abraham. Insecurity: A Challenge to America. 2nd revised ed. New York: Random House, 1938.

Epstein, Abraham. The Problem of Old Age Pensions in Industry: An Up-to-Date Summary of the Facts and Figures Developed in the Further Study of Old Age Pensions. Harrisburg: Pennsylvania Old Age Pensions Commission, 1926.

Erickson, Charlotte. American Industry and the European Immigrant, 1860-1880. Cambridge: Harvard UniversityPress, 1957.

Espenshade, Thomas J., and William J. Serow. The Economic Consequences of Slowing Population Growth. New York: Academic Press, 1978.

Everett, Alexander. New Ideas on Population. Boston: Oliver Everett, 1923.

Faulkner, Harold U. The Decline of Laissez Faire, 1897-1917. New York: Holt, Rinehart and Winston, 1951.

Fei, John C.H., and Gustav Ranis. Development of the Labor Surplus Economy: Theory and Practice. Homewood, Ill.: Richard D. Irwin, 1964.

Fels, Rendigs. American Business Cycles, 1865-1897. Chapel Hill: University of North Carolina Press, 1959.

Field, Minna. The Aged, the Family, and the Community. New York: Columbia University Press, 1956.

Fine, Sidney. Laissez-Faire and the General-Welfare State: A Study of Conflict in American Thought, 1865-1900. Ann Arbor: University of Michigan Press, 1956.

Fischer, David H. Growing Old in America. New York: Oxford University Press, 1977.

Fishlow, Albert. American Railroads and the Transformation of the Ante-Bellum Economy. Cambridge: Harvard University Press, 1965.

Fitch, John A. The Steel Workers. New York: Charities Publication Committee, 1911.

Florence, Philip S. Economics of Fatigue and Unrest and the Efficiency of Labour in English and American Industry. New York: Henry Holt and Co., 1924.

Fogel, Rogert W. Railroads and American Economic Growth: Essays in Econometric History. Baltimore: Johns Hopkins University Press, 1964.

Foner, Anne. "Age Stratification and Age Conflict in Political Life." American Sociological Review 39 (April 1974):187-96.

Ford, Henry, and Samuel Crowther. My Life and Work. Garden City, N.Y.: Garden City Publishing Co., 1922.

Frain, H.L.R. "Do Workers Gain by Labor Turnover?" Monthly Labor Review 28 (June 1929):1298-1300.

Frankfurther, Felix, and Josephine C. Goldmark. The Case for the Shorter Work-Day. New York: National Consumers' League, 1916.

Galbraith, John Kenneth. Economics and the Public Purpose. New York: Houghton-Mifflin Co., 1973.

Garraty, John A., ed. Labor and Capital in the Gilded Age: Testimony of the Times, Selections from Congressional Hearings. Boston: Little, Brown and Co., 1968.

Gates, Paul W. "Discussion of Theodore Saloutos' paper, 'Land Policy and its Relation to Agricultural Production, 1862-1933.'" Journal of Economic History 22 (December 1962):473-76.

Gates, Paul W. "Frontier Estate Builders and Farm Laborers." Views of American Economic Growth: The Industrial Era. Edited by Thomas C. Cochran and Thomas B. Brewer. New York: McGraw-Hill Book Co., 1966, pp. 136-47.

Gates, Paul W. "Land Policy and Tenancy in the Prairie States." Journal of Economic History 1 (May 1941):60-82.

George, Henry. The Condition of Labor. New York: United States Book Co., 1891.

George, Henry. Social Problems. New York: Doubleday, 1883.

Gilbreth, Frank B., and Lillian M. Gilbreth. Fatigue Study. New York: Macmillan Co., 1919.

Gintis, Herb. "Education, Technology and the Characteristics of Worker Productivity." American Economic Review Papers and Proceedings 61 (May 1971):266-79.

Goldmark, Josephine. Fatique and Efficiency: A Study in Industry. New York: Russell Sage Foundation, 1912.

Gordon, David, Richard Edwards, and Michael Reich. Segmented Work, Divided Workers. Cambridge: Cambridge University Press, 1982.

Gordus, Jeanne Prial, Paul Jarley, and Louis A. Ferman. Plant Closings and Economic Dislocation. Kalamazoo, Mich.: W.E. Upjohn Institute for Employment Research, 1981.

Gunderson, Gerald. A New Economic History of America. New York: McGraw-Hill Book Co., 1976.

Gutman, Herbert. "Labor's Response to Modern Industrialism." Main Problems in American History. 2 vols. Edited by Howard Quint, Milton Cantor, and Dean Albertson. Homewood, Ill.: Dorsey Press, 1964, vol. 2, pp. 75-78.

Gutman, Herbert. "The Worker's Search for Power: Labor in the Gilded Age." The Gilded Age: A Reappraisal. Edited by Howard W. Morgan. Syracuse: Syracuse University Press, 1963.

Hacker, Louis M. The Course of American Economic Growth and Development. New York: John Wiley and Sons, 1970.

Hadley, Arthur T. Economics: An Account of the Relations Between Private Property and Public Welfare. New York: G.P. Putnam's Sons, 1896.

Hall, John P. "The Knights of St. Crispin in Massachusetts, 1869-1878." Journal of Economic History 18 (June 1958):161-75.

Hamilton, James H. Savings and Saving Institutions. New York: Macmillan Co., 1902.

Hansen, Alvin H. "Factors Affecting the Trend of Real Wages." American Economic Review 15 (March 1925):27-42.

Hareven, Tamara K. Family and Population in the Nineteenth Century. Princeton: Princeton University Press, 1978.

Hart, Hornell. Fluctuations in Employment in Cities of the United States, 1902 to 1917. Cincinnati: Helen S. Trounstine Foundation, 1918.

Hauser, Philip M. "Facing the Implications of an Aging Population." Social Service Review 27 (June 1953):162-76.

Hauser, Philip M. and Raul Vargas. "Population Structure and Trends." Aging in Western Societies. Edited by Ernest W. Burgess. Chicago: University of Chicago Press, 1960, pp. 29-53.

Havighurst, Robert J. "Life Beyond Family and Work." Aging in Western Societies. Edited by Ernest W. Burgess. Chicago: University of Chicago Press, 1960, pp. 299-353.

Havighurst, Robert J., and Ruth Albrecht. Older People. New York: Longmans, Green and Co., 1953.

Heisler, W.J., and John W. Houck. A Matter of Dignity: Inquiries into the Humanization of Work. Notre Dame: University of Notre Dame Press, 1977.

Hendrick, Burton J. "The Superannuated Man, Labor Pensions and the Carnegie Foundation." McClure's Magazine 32 (December 1908):115-27.

Hendricks, Jon, and C. Davis Hendricks. Aging in Mass Society. Cambridge, Mass.: Winthrop Publishing, 1977.

Herzog, Barbara Reiman, ed. Aging and Income: Programs and Prospects for the Elderly. New York: Human Sciences Press, 1978.

Hess, Beth B., ed. Growing Old in America. New Brunswick, N.J.: Transaction Press, 1976.

Hibbard, Benjamin Horace. A History of the Public Land Policies. New York: Macmillan Co., 1924.

Higgs, Robert. The Transformation of the American Economy, 1865-1914. New York: Wiley, 1971.

Hoffman, Charles. "The Depression of the Nineties." Journal of Economic History 16 (June 1956):137-64.

Hollingworth, Harry L. Mental Growth and Decline: A Survey of Develomental Psychology. New York: D. Appleton and Co., 1927.

Hourwich, Isaac A. "The Social-Economic Classes of the Population of the United States. I." Journal of Political Economy 19 (March 1911):188-215.

Hourwich, Isaac A. "The Social-Economic Classes of the Population of the United States. II." Journal of Political Economy 19 (April 1911):309-37.

Hoxie, Robert F. Scientific Management and Labor. New York: D. Appleton and Co., 1915.

Hudson, Robert B. "The 'Graying' of the Federal Budget and its Consequences for Old-Age Policy." The Gerontologist 18 (October 1978):428-40.

Hunter, Robert. Poverty. New York: Macmillan Co., 1904.

Institute of Gerontology. The Economics of Aging. Ann Arbor: Institute of Gerontology, 1976.

Institute of Gerontology. No Longer Young. Ann Arbor: Institute of Gerontology, 1975.

International Association of Gerontology. Old Age in the Modern World. Report of the Third Congress held at London. Edinburgh: E. & S. Livingstone, 1955.

Jarvik, Lissy F., ed. Aging into the 21st Century: Middle-Agers Today. New York: Gardner Press, 1978.

Jenks, Jeremiah W., and W. Jett Lauck. The Immigrant Problem. 6th ed. New York: Funk and Wagnalls, 1926.

Jenks, Jeremiah W., and Walter E. Clark. The Trust Problem. 5th ed. New York: Doubleday Page and Co., 1920.

Jenks, Leland H. "The Railroads as an Economic Force in American Development." Journal of Economic History 4 (May 1944):1-20.

Jerome, Chauncey. History of the American Clock Business for the Past 60 Years, and Life of Chauncey Jerome. New Haven: F.C. Dayton, Jr., 1860.

Jones, Rochelle. The Older Generation: The New Power of Older People. Englewood Cliffs, N.J.: Prentice-Hall, 1977.

Katz, Stanley N., ed. Colonial America. 2nd ed. Boston: Little, Brown, Co., 1976.

Kellor, Frances. Out of Work: A Study of Employment Agencies. New York: G.P. Putnam's Sons, 1904.

Kemble, William F. Choosing Employees by Mental and Physical Tests. New York: The Engineering Magazine Co., 1917.

Kendrick, John W. Productivity Trends in the United States. New York: Princeton Press, for the National Bureau of Economic Research, 1961.

Kennedy, M.C. "The Division of Labor and the Culture of Capitalism: A Critique." Unpublished Ph.D. dissertation, University of Michigan, 1968.

King, Willford I. Wealth and Income of the People of the United States. New York: The Macmillan Co., 1915.

204

Kirkland, Edward C. A History of American Economic Life. New York: Appleton Century-Crofts, 1969.

Kirkland, Edward C. Industry Comes of Age: Business, Labor, and Public Policy, 1860-1897. Chicago: Quadrangle Books, 1961.

Knowlton, Evelyn H. Pepperell's Progress, History of a Cotton Textile Company, 1844-1945. Cambridge: Harvard University Press, 1948.

Kolko, Gabriel. Wealth and Power in America: An Analysis of Social Class and Income Distribution. New York: Praeger, 1962.

Krooss, Herman E. American Economic Development: The Progress of a Business Civilization. 3rd ed. Englewood Cliffs, N.J.: Prentice-Hall, 1974.

Kuznets, Simon. Capital in the American Economy. Princeton: Princeton University Press, 1961.

Kuznets, Simon, and Ernest Rubin. Immigration and the Foreign Born. New York: National Bureau of Economic Research, 1954.

Latimer, Murray Webb. Industrial Pensions in the United States and Canada. New York: Industrial Relations Counselors, 1932.

Latimer, Murray Webb. Relation of Maximum Hiring Ages to the Age Distribution of Employees. New York: American Management Association, 1930.

Lebergott, Stanley. Manpower in Economic Growth: The American Record Since 1800. New York: McGraw-Hill Book Co., 1964.

Lescohier, Don D. Working Conditions. Vol. 3 of History of Labor in the United States, 1896-1932. Edited by John R. Commons et al. 4 vols. New York: Macmillan Co., 1935.

Lewis, W. Arthur. "Economic Development with Unlimited Supplies of Labour." The Manchester School of Economic and Social Studies 22 (May 1954):139-91.

Lewis, W. Arthur. Growth and Fluctuations, 1870-1913. London: George Allen and Unwin, 1978.

Lipset, Seymour Martin, and Reinhard Bendix. Social Mobility in Industrial Society. Berkeley: University of California Press, 1967.

Long, Clarence. Wages and Earnings in the United States, 1860-1890. Princeton: Princeton University Press, 1960.

Lubin, Isador. "Measuring the Labor Absorbing Power of American Industry." Proceedings of the American Statistical Association 24 (March 1929):27-32.

Lubove, Roy. The Struggle for Social Security, 1900-1935. Cambridge: Harvard University Press, 1968.

Maccoby, Michael. The Gamesman: Winning and Losing the Career Game. New York: Bantam Books, 1978.

Manley, Basil M. Are Wages Too High? Washington, D.C.: People's Legislative Service, 1922.

Manney, James D. Jr. Aging in American Society: An Examination of Concepts and Issues. Ann Arbor: University of Michigan-Wayne State University, 1975.

Marglin, Stephen A. "What Do Bosses Do? The Origins and Functions of Hierarchy in Capitalist Production." Review of Radical Political Economics 6 (Summer 1974):60-112.

Mark, Jerome A. "Comparative Job Performance by Age." Monthly Labor Review 80 (December 1957):1467-71.

Marshall, Alfred. Principles of Economics. 8th ed. London: Macmillan and Co., 1930.

Marx, Karl. Capital: A Critique of Political Economy. Translated by Enest Untermann. 3 vols. New York: Modern Library, 1906.

Massachusetts Board to Investigate the Subject of the Unemployed. Report. House Document No. 50. Boston: Wright and Potter, 1895.

McKelvey, Jean T. A.F.L. Attitudes Toward Production, 1900-1932. Ithaca, N.Y.: Cornell University Press, 1952.

McMaster, John B. A History of the People of the United States. 8 vols. New York: D. Appleton, 1915.

Mavor, James. "Labor Colonies and the Unemployed." Journal of Political Economy 2 (1893-1894):26-53.

Means, Gardiner C. "The Growth in the Relative Importance of the Large Corporation in American Economic Life." American Economic Review 21 (March 1931):10-42.

Merchants Association of New York. Industrial Pensions: Report of the Special Committee on Industrial Pensions and Report of a Survey of Industrial Pension Systems by the Industrial Bureau. New York: The Merchants Association of New York, 1920.

Mill, John Stuart. Principles of Political Economy. New York: Augustus M. Kelley, 1919.

Mitchell, John. The Wage Earner and His Problems. Washington, D.C.: P.S. Ridsdale, 1913.

Mitchell, Wesley C. Business Cycles--The Problem and Its Setting. New York: National Bureau of Economic Research, 1928.

Mitchell, Wesley C. Business Cycles and Unemployment. New York: National Bureau of Economic Research, 1923.

Moody, John. The Truth about the Trusts. New York: Moody Publishing Co., 1904.

More, Louise B. Wage Earners' Budgets. New York: Henry Holt, 1907.

Myers, Robert J. "Occupational Readjustment of Displaced Skilled Workmen." Journal of Political Economy 35 (August 1929):473-89.

Nassau, Mabel L. Old Age Poverty in Greenwich Village: A Neighborhood Study. New York: Fleming H. Revell Co., 1915.

National Civic Federation. Extent of Old Age Dependency. New York: National Civic Federation, 1928.

National Council on the Aging. The Myth and Reality of Aging in America. Washington, D.C.: National Council on the Aging, Inc., 1975.

National Industrial Conference Board. Industrial Pensions in the United States. New York: National Industrial Conference Board, 1925.

Nelson, Daniel. Managers and Workers: Origins of the New Factory System in the United States, 1880-1920. Madison: University of Wisconsin Press, 1975.

Neuberger, Richard L., and Kelley Loe. An Army of the Aged. Caldwell, Idaho: Caxton Printers, 1936.

New York, Bureau of Labor Statistics. Fourteenth Annual Report. Albany, 1897.

New York, Bureau of Labor Statistics. Seventeenth Annual Report. Albany, 1900.

Niemi, Albert W. Jr. U.S. Economic History: A Survey of the Major Issues. Chicago: Rand McNally College Publishing Co., 1975.

North, Douglass C. The Economic Growth of the United States, 1790-1860. New York: W.W. Norton, 1966.

North, Douglass C. Growth and Welfare in the American Past. 2nd ed. Englewood Cliffs, N.J.: Prentice-Hall, 1974.

Ohrbach, Harold, and Clark Tibbits, eds. Aging and the Economy. Ann Arbor: University of Michigan Press, 1963.

Oliver, Thomas, ed. Dangerous Trades: The Historical, Social and Legal Aspects of Industrial Occupations as Affecting Health. London: J. Murray Co., 1902.

Olson, Laura Katz. The Political Economy of Aging: The State, Private Power, and Social Welfare. New York: Columbia University Press, 1982.

Ozanne, Robert. A Century of Labor-Management Relations at McCormick and International Harvester. Madison: University of Wisconsin Press, 1967.

Paillat, Paul. "Bureaucratization of Old Age: Determinants of the Process, Possible Safeguards, and Reorientation." Family, Bureaucracy, and the Elderly. Edited by Ethel Shanas and Marvin B. Sussman. Durham, N.C.: Duke University Press, 1977, pp. 60-74.

Paine, Harriet. Old People. Boston: Houghton-Mifflin Co., 1910.

Palmore, Erdman B., and Kenneth Manton. "Modernization and the Status of the Aged: International Comparisons." Journal of Gerontology 29 (March 1974):205-10.

Parker, William N., and Judith L.V. Klein. "Productivity Growth in Grain Production in the U.S., 1840-1860 and 1900-1910." Output, Employment and Productivity in the U.S. After 1800. Edited by Dorothy S. Brady. New York: National Bureau of Economic Research, 1966, pp. 523-82.

Peterson, John M., and Ralph Gray. Economic Development of the United States. Homewood, Ill.: Richard D. Irwin, 1969.

Plowman, Edward G. The Pros and Cons of Hiring Age Limits. New York: American Management Association, 1930.

Puth, Robert C. American Economic History. New York: Dryden Press, 1982.

Quaintance, Hadley W. "The Influence of Machinery on the Economic and Social Conditions of the Agricultural People." Cyclopedia of American Agriculture. 4 vols. Edited by Liberty H. Bailey. New York: Macmillan Co., 1907-1909.

Ransom, Roger L., and Richard Sutch. "Two Strategies for a More Secure Old Age: The Case of Late Nineteenth-Century American Workers." Paper presented at the Washington, D.C. Area Economic History Seminar, University of Maryland, March 31, 1989.

Reder, Melvin. "Age and Income." American Economic Review 44 (May 1954):661-70.

Rees, Albert. Real Wages in Manufacturing, 1890-1914. Princeton: Princeton University Press, 1961.

Reich, Michael, David M. Gordon, and Richard C. Edwards. "Dual Labor Markets: A Theory of Labor Market Segmentation." American Economic Review Papers and Proceedings 63 (May 1973):359-65.

Reich, Robert. The Next American Frontier. New York: Time Books, 1983.

Rhine, Shirley. Older Workers and Retirement. New York: The Conference Board, 1978.

Riesman, David. The Lonely Crowd: A Study of the Changing American Character. New Haven: Yale University Press, 1950.

Riley, Matilda White, and Associates. Aging and Society. 3 vols. New York: Russell Sage Foundation, 1968-1972.

Ripley, William Z. Main Street and Wall Street. Boston: Little, Brown and Co., 1929.

Ripley, William Z. Trusts, Pools and Corporations. Revised ed. Boston: Ginn and Co., 1915.

Rosenberg, Nathan, ed. The American System of Manufactures. Edinburgh: University of Edinburgh Press, 1969.

Rosenberg, Nathan. Technology and American Economic Growth. New York: Harper and Row, 1972.

Rosow, Irving. "And Then We Were Old." Transaction/Society 2 (January-February 1965):20-26. Reprinted in Growing Old in America. Edited by Beth B. Hess. New Brunswick, N.J.: Transaction Press, 1976, pp. 41-54.

Rosow, Irving. "Old Age: One Moral Dilemma of an Affluent Society." The Gerontologist 2 (December 1962):182-91.

Rosow, Irving. Social Integration of the Aged. New York: Free Press, 1967.

Rostow, Walter W. The Stages of Economic Growth: A Non-Communist Manifesto. Cambridge: Cambridge University Press, 1960.

Rubinow, Isaac M. The Quest for Security. New York: Henry Holt and Co., 1934.

Rubinow, Isaac M. Social Insurance, With Special Reference to American Conditions. New York: Henry Holt and Co., 1913.

Ryan, John A. A Living Wage. New York: Macmillan Co., 1910.

Schloss, David F. Methods of Industrial Remuneration. New York: G.P. Putnam's Sons, 1892.

Schmidt, Louis B. "Internal Commerce and the Development of National Economy Before 1860." Journal of Political Economy 47 (December 1939):798-822.

Schulz, James H. The Economics of Aging. Belmont, Cal.: Wadsworth Publishing Co., 1976. 4th ed., Auburn House Publishing Co, Dover, Mass., 1988.

Schumpeter, Joseph A. Business Cycles: A Theoretical, Historical, and Statistical Analysis of the Capitalist Process. 2 vols. New York: McGraw-Hill Book Co., 1939.

Schumpeter, Joseph A. "The Instability of Capitalism." The Economic Journal 37 (September 1928):361-86.

Schumpeter, Joseph A. The Theory of Economic Development: An Inquiry into Profits, Capital, Credit, Interest, and the Business Cycle. Cambridge: Harvard University Press, 1934.

Seligman, Edwin R.A. Essays in Taxation. 8th ed. London: Macmillan and Co., 1913.

Shanas, Ethel, and Marvin B. Sussman, eds. Family, Bureaucracy, and the Elderly. Durham, N.C.: Duke University Press, 1977.

Shanas, Ethel. Financial Resources of the Aging. New York: Health Information Foundation, 1959.

Shanas, Ethel, Peter Townsend, Dorothy Wedderburn, Henning Friis, Paul Milhoej, and Jan Stenouwer. Old People in Three Industrial Societies. New York: Atherton Press, 1968.

Shannon, Fred A. The Farmer's Last Frontier: Agriculture, 1860-1897. New York: Farrar and Rinehart, 1945.

Sheldon, Henry D. The Older Population of the United States. New York: John Wiley and Sons, 1958.

Sheppard, Harold L., Louis Ferman, and Seymour Faber. Too Old to Work, Too Young to Retire. Report to the U.S. Senate Special Committee on Unemployment Problems (Washington, D.C.: Government Printing Office, 1960).

Sheppard, Harold. Toward an Industrial Gerontology. Cambridge, Mass.: Schenkman Publishing Company, 1970.

Simmons, Leo. The Role of the Aged in Primitive Societies. New Haven: Yale University Press, 1945.

Smith, Adam. An Inquiry into the Nature and Causes of the Wealth of Nations. New York: Modern Library, 1937.

Smith, Bert Kruger. Aging in America. Boston: Beacon Press, 1973.

Smith, Elliott D. What Are the Psychological Factors of Obsolescence of Workers in Middle Age? New York: American Management Association, 1930.

Smuts, Robert W. Women and Work in America. New York: Schocken, 1971.

Smyth, Newman. The Place of Death in Evolution. London: T. Fisher Unwin, 1897.

Sohn-Rethel, Alfred. Intellectual and Manual Labour: A Critique of Epistemology. Atlantic Highlands, N.J.: Humanities Press, 1978.

Soltow, Lee. Men and Wealth in the United States, 1850-1870. New Haven: Yale University Press, 1975.

Spahr, Charles B. An Essay on the Present Distribution of Wealth in the United States. 2nd ed. New York: Thomas Y. Crowell and Co., 1896.

Spencer, Marian G., and Caroline J. Dorr, eds. Understanding Aging: A Multidisciplinary Approach. New York: Appleton-Century-Crofts, 1975.

Squier, Lee Welling. Old Age Dependency in the United States: A Complete Survey of the Pension Movement. New York: Macmillan Co., 1912.

Steiner, Peter O., and Robert Dorfman. The Economic Status of the Aged. Berkeley: University of California Press, 1957.

Stewart, Bryce M. Unemployment Benefits in the United States. New York: Industrial Relations Counselors, 1930.

Stigler, George J. Trends in Output and Employment. New York: National Bureau of Economic Research, 1947.

Stone, Katherine. "The Origins of Job Structures in the Steel Industry." Review of Radical Political Economics 6 (Summer 1974):113-73.

Streib, Gordon F., and Clement J. Schneider. Retirement in American Society in Fact and Process. Ithaca: Cornell University Press, 1971.

Taylor, Frederick W. On the Art of Cutting Metals. New York: American Society of Mechanical Engineers, 1906.

Taylor, Frederick W. The Principles of Scientific Management, in Scientific Management. New York: Harper and Bros., 1911.

Taylor, Frederick W. Shop Management, in Scientific Management. New York: Harper and Bros., 1911.

Tebbel, John. Aging in America: Implications for the Mass Media. Monograph No. 2. Washington, D.C.: National Council on the Aging, Inc., 1976.

Tella, Alfred. "Labor Force Sensitivity to Employment by Age, Sex." Industrial Relations 4 (February 1965):69-83.

Telland, George A. Human Aging and Behavior. New York: Academic Press, 1968.

Temin, Peter. "Labor Scarcity and the Problem of American Industrial Efficiency in the 1850s." Journal of Economic History 26 (September 1966):277-98.

Temin, Peter. "Labor Scarcity in America." Journal of Interdisciplinary History 1 (Winter 1971):251-64.

Thorndike, Edward L., Elsie O. Bregman, J. Warren Tilton, and Ella Woodyard. Adult Learning. New York: Macmillan Co., 1928.

Thurow, Lester C. The Zero Sum Society: Distribution and the Possibilities for Economic Change. New York: Basic Books, 1980.

Tibbits, Clark, ed. Aging and Social Health in the United States and Europe. Ann Arbor: University of Michigan, 1959.

Tishler, Hace Sorel. Self-Reliance and Social Security, 1870-1917. Port Washington, N.Y.: Kennikat Press, 1971.

Tocqueville, Alexis de. Democracy in America. 2 vols. Translated by Henry Reeve. New York: Century Co., 1898.

U.S. Bureau of Labor. First Annual Report of the Commissioner of Labor. Washington, D.C.: Government Printing Office, 1886.

U.S. Congress. Senate. Report by the U.S. Commissioner of Labor on Labor Conditions in the Iron and Steel Industry. S. Doc. 110, 62nd Cong., 1st sess., 1911, vol. 3.

U.S. Department of Commerce. Bureau of the Census. Eighth Census of the United States, 1860, vol. 3

U.S. Department of Commerce. Bureau of the Census. Historical Statistics of the United States, Colonial Times to 1957. Washington, D.C.: Government Printing Office, 1960.

U.S. Department of Commerce. Bureau of the Census. Historical Statistics of the United States: From Colonial Times to 1970. 2 vols. Washington, D.C.: Government Printing Office, 1975.

U.S. Department of Commerce. Bureau of the Census. Immigrants and Their Children, by Niles Carpenter. Census Monograph No. 7. Washington, D.C.: Government Printing Office, 1927.

U.S. Department of Commerce. Bureau of the Census. The Integration of Industrial Operation, by Willard Thorp. Census Monograph No. 2. Washington, D.C.: Government Printing Office, 1924.

U.S. Department of Commerce. Bureau of the Census. Statistical Abstract of the United States. Washington, D.C.: Government Printing Office, 1904.

U.S. Department of Commerce. Bureau of the Census. Statistical Abstract of the United States. Washington, D.C.: Government Printing Office, 1919.

U.S. Department of Commerce. Bureau of the Census. The Statistical History of the United States from Colonial Times to the Present. Stamford, Conn.: Fairfield Publishers, Inc., 1934.

U.S. Department of Commerce. Bureau of the Census. Thirteenth Census of the United States, 1910, vol. 8.

U.S. Department of Labor. Bureau of Labor Statistics. Care of Aged Persons in the United States, by Florence E. Parker. Bulletin No. 489. Washington, D.C.: Government Printing Office, 1929.

U.S. Department of Labor. Bureau of Labor Statistics. "Hiring and Separation Methods in American Factories." Monthly Labor Review 35 (November 1932):1005-15.

U.S. Department of Labor. Bureau of Labor Statistics. "Old People's Homes Maintained by Nationality Groups." Monthly Labor Review 28 (April 1929):691-94.

U.S. Department of Labor. Bureau of Labor Statistics. Utilization of Men Past the Prime of Life, by Victor T.G. Gannon. Bulletin No. 247. Washington, D.C.: Government Printing Office, 1919.

U.S. Immigration Commission. Reports of the Immigration Commission. 42 vols. Vol. 1: Abstracts, with Conclusions and Recommendations and Views of the Minority. Washington, D.C.: Government Printing Office, 1911.

U.S. Industrial Commission. Report of the Industrial Commission. 19 vols. Washington, D.C.: Government Printing Office, 1900-1902.

Vanderlip, Frank A. Insurance from an Employer's Perspective. New York: National Conference of Charities and Proceedings, 1896.

Veblen, Thorstein. Absentee Ownership and Business Enterprise in Recent Times: The Case of America. New York: B.W. Huebsch, 1923.

Wachter, Michael L., and Susan M. Wachter, eds. Toward a New U.S. Industrial Policy? Philadelphia: University of Pennsylvania Press, 1981.

Walton, Gary M., and Ross M. Robertson. History of the American Economy. 5th ed. New York: Harcourt Brace Jovanovich, 1983.

Ware, Norman. The Industrial Worker, 1840-1860. Boston: Houghton-Mifflin Co., 1924.

Warne, Frank J. The Immigrant Invasion. New York: Dodd, Mead and Co., 1913.

Welford, Alan T. Skill and Age, An Experimental Approach. London: Oxford University Press, 1951.

Wells, David A. Recent Economic Changes. New York: D. Appleton and Co., 1889.

Whelpton, Pascal K. "Occupational Groups in the United States, 1820-1920." Journal of the American Statistical Association 21 (September 1926):335-43.

Willcox, Walter F. International Migrations. 2 parts. New York: National Bureau of Economic Research, 1929-1931.

Williams, Richard H. et al., eds. Processes of Aging. 2 vols. New York: Atherton Press, 1963.

Williamson, Jeffrey G., and Peter H. Lindert. American Inequality: A Macroeconomic History. New York: Academic Press, 1980.

Wilson, Arnold T., and G.S. Mackay. Old Age Pensions: An Historical and Critical Study. New York: Oxford University Press, 1941.

Wright, Carroll D. The Factory as an Element in Civilization. Boston: Little, Brown, Co., 1882.

Wright, Carroll D. History and Growth of the U.S. Census. Washington, D.C.: Government Printing Office, 1900.

Yellowitz, Irwin. Industrialization and the American Labor Movement, 1850-1900. Port Washington, N.Y.: Kennikat Press, 1977.

Yellowitz, Irwin. The Position of the Worker in American Society, 1865-1896. Englewood Cliffs, N.J.: Prentice-Hall, 1969.

Young, Allyn A. "Increasing Returns and Economic Progress." The Economic Journal 38 (December 1928):527-42.

Zimmerman, Michael. "Old Age Poverty in Preindustrial New York City." Growing Old in America. Edited by Beth B. Hess. New Brunswick, N.J.: Transaction Press, 1976.